450 Best Sales Letters
for Every Selling Situation

dedicated to
Paul, Judy, and Eric Gilleland
and
George, Kristin, and Lisa Coel

450 *Best* Sales Letters for *Every* Selling Situation

Karen Gilleland

Margaret Coel

PRENTICE HALL
Englewood Cliffs, New Jersey 07632

Prentice-Hall International (UK) Limited, *London*
Prentice-Hall of Australia Pty. Limited, *Sydney*
Prentice-Hall Canada Inc., *Toronto*
Prentice-Hall Hispanoamericana, S.A., *Mexico*
Prentice-Hall of India Private Limited, *New Delhi*
Prentice-Hall of Japan, Inc., *Tokyo*
Simon & Schuster Asia Pte. Ltd., *Singapore*
Editora Prentice-Hall do Brasil, Ltda., *Rio de Janeiro*

© 1991 *by*

PRENTICE HALL, INC.

Englewood Cliffs, N.J.

10 9 8 7 6 5 4 3 2 1

Library of Congress Cataloging-in-Publication Data

Gilleland, Karen.
    450 best sales letters for every selling situation / [compiled by]
Karen Gilleland & Margaret Coel.
       p. cm.
    ISBN 0-13-327370-9
    1. Sales letters. I. Coel, Margaret, 1937- . II. Title.
III. Title: Four hundred fifty best sales letters for every selling
situation.
HF5730.G55 1991   90-23634
658.8′1—dc20   CIP

ISBN 0-13-3273709

PRENTICE HALL
BUSINESS & PROFESSIONAL DIVISION
A division of Simon & Schuster
Englewood Cliffs, New Jersey 07632

Printed in the United States of America

Acknowledgments

We are indebted to our many friends and associates who contributed letters, advice and good ideas for this book. We thank them all.

In particular, Mary Cook, for suggesting the idea for this book and graciously encouraging us every step of the way;

John Speas, a 20-year manufacturer's representative in the clothing business, who read the manuscript and suggested many ways to make this book an easy-to-use tool for sales reps in the field;

Sales experts, Walter Bond, former executive vice-president of Tupperware International; Alan Caplan, former sales representative with WIOQ FM, Philadelphia; Mary Cook, president, Mary Cook & Associates; Julie Ann DeSa Lorenz, vice-president, marketing and communications, On-Line Instrument Systems, Inc.; and John Speas, manufacturers rep, Wrangler.

Most especially, we thank the sales representatives at the following companies for their generosity in allowing us to include their successful sales letters in this book:

ADS Associates, Inc.
Amdahl Corporation
American Seating Company
Bio-Medical Resources, Inc.
Boulder Toyota
Central Bank Chatfield
Century 21
China Coast
Circus Circus
Clarion Harvest House
Coldwell Banker
Colorado & West
Mary Cook & Associates
Coors Brewing Company
Denver Cable Interconnect
Digital Design Group, Inc.

Engineered Products Service
    Company
Free Spirit Travel, Inc.
Golden West Foods, Inc.
Hewlett-Packard Company
IBM Corporation
Initial Stitch, Inc.
Karsh & Hagan Advertising, Inc.
LIFECARE
Marc Interiors
Marketing Communications
Mary Kay Cosmetics
Meetings and Management
Moore and Company
Morgan County Prerelease Center, Inc.
Mutual of Omaha Insurance Company

NSA Water Filters

Ogden Allied Aviation Services

On-Line Instrument Systems, Inc.

Pepsi Cola Company

Pinkerton

Play Fair Toys

Alice Price & Associates

RELA, Inc.

Rocky Mountain News

Rosie's Bird Farm

Sanford Homes

Sarns 3M Health Care

Kevin Seitz

The Shapes Company

Thuro Steam Cleaners

Toyota U.S.A.

U S West Cellular

Universal Training

Valleylab, Inc.

Vistakon, Inc., a Johnson & Johnson Company

Western Freelance Services, Ltd.

WIOQ FM

Wrangler

How to Put These Letters to Work for You

The more time you spend with clients and prospects, the more revenue you generate—and the more commission you earn. Administrative tasks, such as letter writing, cut into face time. This model letter book gives you a professional tool to help you write effective letters—letters that get appointments, make special offers, close deals. You can write these letters effortlessly and in a fraction of the time you now spend writing letters.

Use *450 Best Sales Letters for Every Selling Situation* with confidence. More than 250 letters were written by sales representatives at 50 American companies, including such giants as IBM, Amdahl, Hewlett-Packard, U S West Cellular, Coors Brewing Company, Pepsi-Cola, Toyota U.S.A., Johnson & Johnson, and Mutual of Omaha.

We've also developed letters exclusively for this book. Like those written by sales reps, these letters employ effective writing techniques that grab the reader's attention, get the message across, and make the sale. They will show you how to connect with customers and build the strong relationships that lead to further sales.

Along with hard-hitting sales letters, you will find letters that deal with such mundane business issues as confirming orders and shipping dates, as well as such sensitive issues as asking for salary increases and protesting territory cuts.

You'll get help writing letters that deal with training classes and trade shows. You will also find a selection of public relations letters covering invitations, congratulations, condolences—the social exchange necessary to build client confidence and trust.

All the model letters combine the best techniques of writing and salesmanship. For those situations that sales people face frequently, we have included different choices of model letters. Some letters, such as those dealing with proposals, contain in-depth technical information so that you can see how to handle specific details about your products or service.

Since sales reps often must write lengthy proposals, we have included a chapter containing five successful proposals. They cover a variety of industries, situations and styles.

Every chapter contains suggestions to help you adapt the models to your business situations. You will find advice from sales experts on how to write effective letters and professional writing tips to sharpen your writing skills. Look for the "Bonus"—100 Power Words and Phrases.

450 Best Sales Letters for Every Selling Situation is easy to use. Letters are grouped by topic in 27 chapters. The different categories of letters found in each chapter are listed in the Contents. By scanning the Contents, you can quickly select the letter you need for the job at hand.

450 Best Sales Letters for Every Selling Situation is your competitive edge in the market-driven sales environment of the 1990s. Let these model letters do your letter writing for you. Spend your time prospecting new accounts and closing major orders.

Karen Gilleland

and

Margaret Coel

Contents

4 / Further Letters Regarding Appointments 43

5 / Announcements 53

6 / Follow-Ups 65

7 / **Special Offers**   87

22 / Trade Shows and Conventions   235

23 / **Accommodations** 247

24 / **Speaking Engagements** 253

25 / **Business-Social Invitations and Gifts** 261

27 / Five Model Sales Proposals   281

Chapter One

Introduction Letters

A letter of introduction should be like a first handshake—firm and congenial — signaling that you are happy to meet the person and confident your two companies will enjoy working together for many years.

Use the letter to introduce yourself and your company; to state how your products or services can benefit the prospect; and to suggest future contact, such as a telephone call or meeting. The following letters can be used for mass mailings or for single prospects. They send a message about your company, product or service without regard to industry, location, management position or other criteria. Catchy openings break the ice, and the letters try to motivate the reader to keep the dialogue going, either in writing, in person or by telephone.

1-1 General prospects

Dear _____:

- Are you nearing computer system capacity?
- Can you no longer depreciate your computer system?
- Would you like to move to IBM's latest technology without significantly increasing your business computing expense?

Consider these four factors:

1. IBM recently announced new models of our most popular mid-sized business computer, the AS/400.* These new models make it possible to substantially reduce the cost of moving to the AS/400 and require a fraction of the office space compared to previous models.
2. IBM Credit Corporation has a guaranteed buyout of your existing System/36. This is available for a limited time only, and may be an attractive alternative to retaining your current machine.
3. IBM offers more and better migration tools and assistance. We also have the continued assistance of our local business partners.
4. IBM can deliver TODAY exciting and new leading-edge technologies, such as image, voice and knowledge-based processing. These technologies allow customers like you to develop and maintain a COMPETITIVE ADVANTAGE in your business.

I would like to get together to discuss how these developments apply to your business situation. If you're interested, please give me a call at _____ or simply fill out the enclosed reply card. I look forward to speaking with you.

Sincerely,

IBM Corporation
Denver, Colorado
*AS/400 is a trademark of the IBM Corporation.

1-2 General prospects

Dear _____:

Hello from Boulder, Colorado...last best place for Rocky Mountain meetings!

Just 25 minutes from Stapleton International Airport, Boulder is located at the foot of the Flatiron Mountains of the Colorado Rockies.

The Clarion Harvest House Hotel is located on 16 acres of ground adjacent to the University of Colorado Campus. Fifteen tennis courts, volleyball courts, two swimming pools and a complete Nautilus workout facility highlight the leisure side of our property.

If you'd like further information, I'd love to talk with you.

Keep us in mind.

Sincerely,

P.J. Wright
Clarion Harvest House
Boulder, Colorado

1-3 General prospects

Dear _____:

"Almost half the people who turned on their television sets this summer selected non-network channels . . ." (Source: New York Times—August.)

"We can't be successful appealing only to the 70% watching network T.V.," says Robert J. Gillespie, president of Best Foods.

DDB Needham says it routinely recommends media plans that include 20% to 30% cable T.V. In some cases the recommendation could go as high as 50%. (Source: Advertising Age, May '89.)

The great news about cable television continues to come in! Enclosed are recent articles illustrating the many ways agencies and advertisers are successfully using cable. More articles will follow these in the near future.

Cable is making television better.

We look forward to a productive future with _____ and its many outstanding clients.

Sincerely,

Tim Kilbride
Denver Cable Interconnect
Denver, Colorado

1-4 General prospects

Dear _____:

We just received the enclosed from Nielsen that illustrates the incredible under-delivery of broadcast networks and independents in cable households.
Consider these eye-opening facts:

*   Denver's cable penetration is over 51%.
*   The decline in ratings in cable households for broadcast and independents issignificant:

(Example: Mon.— Fri., 6:30 p.m.—7:00 p.m.)

K___ (___)	-13%
K___ (___)	-34%
K___ (___)	-30%
K___ (INDY)	-20%
K___ (INDY)	-68%
K___ (INDY)	-16%

Conclusion: People buy cable television to watch cable networks. Hope you find this interesting.

Sincerely,

Doug Barrington
Denver Cable Interconnect
Denver, Colorado

1-5 General prospects

Dear _____:

It takes more than aggressive salesmanship and creative marketing to make a home sell. Necessary ingredients for selling are: price, location, exposure and condition.

If you are thinking of selling at this time or in the near future, please give me a call. I have the marketing skills to help you determine the top dollar for your home, and we at Century 21 Executive Realty can effectively market your home and sell it in the shortest possible time.

Let's get together soon and put a plan into action tailored specifically for you.

Jenny Moraitis
Century 21
Houston, Texas

1-6 General prospects

Creative letters get the prospect's attention. In this letter, the one looking for employment is a new computer system.

Dear _____:

I am interested in a full time position with your firm. My specialties include data evaluation, budget tracking, report generation and data security. I am willing to work 24 hours a day, 7 days a week, 365 days a year. My strong technical background, diverse capabilities and friendly personality make me an outstanding candidate.

I have enclosed a copy of my resume for your review. I believe I would be a valuable addition to your staff and would appreciate your considering my application.

Sincerely,

IBM Business Solution
IBM Corporation
Denver, Colorado

1-7 General prospects

Dear_____:

    If your company's new product development efforts are lagging — for whatever reasons — and you need help in beating the competition or meeting today's shortened market windows, you should investigate the ways RELA, Inc. could help you achieve your product.

    Briefly, RELA is a contract designer, developer, and manufacturer of electronic and electromechanical-based products and systems. RELA is capable of taking a client's product or system idea from the earliest concept stage through hardware and software design and development, mechanical and industrial design, printed circuit board design, prototype development and manufacturing. For the client that does not require the complete development package, RELA offers any portions thereof.

    RELA services clients of all sizes, ranging from members of the Fortune 500 to startup companies.

    Because we believe that RELA's expertise could make it a valuable outside resource for your organization, we would welcome an opportunity to make a presentation of these capabilities to you and interested associates.

    To talk about the possibility of this presentation, I plan to phone you in the days ahead.

Cordially yours,

RELA, Inc.
Boulder, Colorado

1-8 General prospects

Dear_____,

    I would like to take this opportunity to introduce you to RELA, Inc. A brochure describing RELA's capabilities and other relevant collaterals are enclosed for your review.

    RELA is a contract designer, developer, and manufacturer of electronic and electromechanical-based products and systems. RELA is capable of taking a client's product or system idea from the earliest concept stage through hardware and software design and development, mechanical and industrial design, printed circuit board design, prototype development and manufacturing. For the client that does not require the complete development package, RELA offers any portions thereof.

When your resources for new design, development, or manufacturing are overtaxed, RELA, Inc. can serve as your external resource. In the past eleven years RELA has served clients of all sizes, ranging from members of the Fortune 500 to startup companies, with invaluable experience in lowering the costs and risks normally associated with launching a new product or redesigning an existing one.

Because we believe that RELA's expertise could make it a valuable outside resource for your organization, we would welcome an opportunity to make a presentation of these capabilities to you and interested associates.

To talk about the possibility of this presentation, I plan to phone you in the days ahead.

Cordially yours,

RELA, Inc.
Boulder, Colorado

1-9 Prospects within targeted groups

Like letters to general prospects, these letters may be used for large mailings or for individual prospects. However, they zero in on particular kinds of businesses, management levels or other common factors.

Dear _____:

RE: Increase Gross Profit from 1–15%
Increase Sales Percent from 5-15%
Reduce Inventory from 1-15%

I am writing to introduce myself to you in the hope of getting the opportunity to know you and your business.

IBM has total system solutions for retail businesses like yours that will give you profitable results.

We need to hear from you!! IBM wants to better understand your company's automation needs and to provide you with up-to-date information about what is available, why it should be considered, its benefits and cost justifications.

One of our primary goals is to form business partnerships. Please take a moment to check the appropriate areas of interest and complete the information about your company on the postage-free reply card and return it. By receiving the information you provide, I can get to know your business better. I am committed to your success as your local IBM representative.

Due to the overwhelming attendance at previous seminars in Denver and interest levels expressed in automating business functions through our low-cost retail systems, we plan to conduct seminars in Colorado Springs in the next few months. With your help, we will structure and plan the seminars around your needs and at your convenience.

Thank you for taking the time to fill out the information card. I look forward to working with you in the future. Should you have any questions, please feel free to contact me at any time. It will be my pleasure to assist you in any way I can.

Sincerely,

IBM Corporation
Denver, Colorado

P.S. Mark your calendar for March 15 for a retail industry seminar. This seminar will be free of charge. More details to follow. Please call me if you would like to attend.

1-10 Prospects within targeted groups

Dear _____:

Would you like to know how to operate the desktop system your secretaries are so at home with?

Executives like yourself often tell us they would like to be able to sit down, punch a few keys and get a quick answer, whether it is a current balance, the latest stock quote, or maybe a business projection.

Like you, they've been too busy to learn how to operate the system. And besides, they pay people to do that. Nevertheless, there are times when it would be nice — and efficient — to pull answers out of the computer themselves.

Burlington Computer Systems specializes in teaching executives how to operate their office systems. Even if your system was specifically tailored to your business needs, one of our experts will know how to put it through its paces, and will be able to show you.

Sessions will be arranged at your convenience. Some executives prefer to have lessons outside of working hours — when the office staff is not around.

I will contact you next week to see whether Burlington Computer Systems can provide you with an additional edge — knowledge and control over your office systems.

Sincerely,

1-11 Prospects within targeted groups

Dear _____ :

If you have hesitated to implement a corporate pension plan or HR10 plan in your business because you would have had to include all of your employees ... consider this!

You may now offer selected employees the opportunity to have their own retirement plan under the Individual Retirement Annuity provision of the Tax Reform Act of 1986.

You can reward key personnel with a plan that provides a substantial annuity for their retirement years while deferring personal tax dollars every year. And, if you wish, you can do it without any cost to you.

Under the current tax law, you can not only choose selected employees to have a retirement plan, but you can set up different plans for each. And, you have the choice of contributing to the plan or allowing the employee to finance it.

Let's get together so I can highlight the advantages this law offers you and your employees. I'll be calling in a few days to set up an appointment.

Sincerely,

Clifford Schultz
Mutual of Omaha Insurance Company
Omaha, Nebraska

P.S. If you wish, I can show you how United of Omaha can help you set up this Individual Retirement Annuity for you alone.

1-12 Prospects within targeted groups

Dear _____:

TAX-FREE VS. TAXABLE INCOME
You Have a Choice

We don't want you to pay one penny more in taxes than you have to! When you invest in a Mutual of Omaha Tax-Free Income Fund, your dividend income is not subject to Federal Income Tax.* Since your dividends aren't taxed, you net more income than you would from a taxable savings account paying the same or even a higher rate of return. And, with a minimum investment of $1,000, the Tax-Free Fund is affordable, even if you're on a fixed income.

The professional money managers at the Mutual of Omaha Fund Management Company invest your money in a broad portfolio of high quality, tax-exempt municipal bonds with the highest possible yield, while considering the safety of your investment. And, you can easily convert your shares into cash at any time.

Wouldn't you enjoy your retirement more if you could stop sharing your investment income with the IRS? I'll call you in the next few days to arrange a convenient time for us to get together to discuss how you can earn a tax-free income by investing in the Mutual of Omaha Tax-Free Income Fund. I'll bring a prospectus with more information about the Fund, including charges and expenses, which you'll want to review before investing.

Sincerely,

Clifford Schultz
Mutual of Omaha Insurance Company
Omaha, Nebraska
*State and local taxes may apply.

1-13 Prospects within targeted groups

Dear _____:

If you're like most literary agents, when you receive a query from an author for a hot book idea, after the initial elation, you immediately start wondering whether the author can follow through on the writing end. Can the author put together a marketable book proposal or an organized, reader-accessible manuscript?

At Alice Price & Associates, we recognize that many authors with inspired book projects simply don't have the professional writing skills necessary to publish in today's market. While I was working as a literary agent, this author/writer dichotomy inspired me to form a writing service firm to specialize in book proposals, substantive manuscript editing and ghostwriting. Of the submitted proposals and manuscripts we've worked on in the past three years, over 85% have resulted in book sales to publishers, including sales to: (list of publishers).

Professional Writing Services handles such diverse nonfiction as pop psychology, environmental, business, how-to, inspirational and scholarly books. We even tidy up the occasional novel. And my associates and I know agenting, publishing and the book market from the inside.

As the leading book proposal and manuscript specialists in the country, we can provide your clients with the writing assistance they need to produce high-profile, salable books. Call me, 9 to 5 MST weekdays, to discuss our writing services and rates. I'll look forward to hearing from you.

Sincerely,

Alice I. Price
Alice Price & Associates
Boulder, Colorado

1-14 Prospects within targeted groups

Dear _____:

____ has unique qualities that set it apart in the home building industry.

Our clients say that Communication Design's innovative, cost-effective marketing, advertising and public relations programs bring in results.

Isn't it time we got together to see how our creative ideas can enhance your business?

I'll call next week to arrange an appointment.

Sincerely,

1-15 Prospects within targeted groups

Hi!

My name is JENNY MORAITIS. I'm a resident of Champion Forest and I live on Champion Drive. I am interested in values in Champion Forest not dwindling as they have in some neighborhoods.

I am a full-time agent for Century 21 Executive Realty. I would like to visit with you and give you a market analysis on your home. There is no charge and no obligation!

Additionally, I offer a reduced price for listing your home. In no way, however, a reduced service.

Should you have any questions, please call me at ____.

Thank you very much!!

Jenny Moraitis
Century 21
Houston, Texas
P.S. We just sold ____ Oxted and ____ Oxted.

1-16 Prospects within targeted groups

Dear _____:

Congratulations on your recent consolidation with ____. This growth is a tribute to you and your company.

The purpose of this letter is to discover if your company is like other companies in the need for training, especially when experiencing growth.

You may be considering product knowledge training for your employees associated with your new products. ____ asked us to produce training programs to educate their sales force, management, engineers and specialists on the metals and railroad industries. This educated employees who had contact with these industries so that they could improve their client relationships and the company's productivity.

Universal Training has been a leading national designer and developer of custom training for 20 years. We have developed more than 3,000 programs for more than 300 major companies, many of which are industry leaders. ____, _____, ____ are but a few of the corporations we have served.

Universal Training offers you full service. We have a program development staff providing research, writing and editing; a graphic arts staff; and an award-winning audiovisual production team (over 40 awards in the past 10 years).

Mr. ____, I hope you will review the enclosed information describing Universal Training. The credentials included in these materials are divided into service categories such as sales, customer service and management training. Perhaps as you review examples of projects we have designed for other clients, you'll see how our expertise can apply directly to your needs.

I will call you soon to discuss your upcoming training needs. We are eager to apply our training skills to assist your expanded company in achieving continued success.

Sincerely,

Doug Barrington
Universal Training
Northbrook, Illinois

1-17 Prospects within targeted groups

Dear _____:

Welcome to your new home in Boulder!

There are many wonderful things about living in Boulder, and one of them is the Meadows Club. The Meadows Club is a family-oriented swim and tennis club located off 55th street between Baseline and Arapahoe, easy to reach from all parts of town. That's just the beginning!

We play tennis year round on our eight outdoor courts. (Yes, on sun-filled winter days, members are out playing tennis.) With four lighted courts, we also play in the evenings.

There are tennis teams, clinics, lessons for mom, dad and kids. Something for everybody from the beginner to the Agassi look-alike. Ask any tennis player in town—the Meadows' pro, ____, is one of the best around.

Our swimming pool is Olympic sized, big enough for lap lanes, kiddie pool and diving area, with room for floating around and cooling off on hot summer days. Kids from 8 to 18 can swim on the Meadows summer league team, get some great coaching, compete at inter-club meets and have a good time. There are swim lessons, too, for all ages and abilities.

Every Thursday evening in the summer, we have family night: families bring picnics, swim, play tennis and volleyball, and relax on the grassy park-like area between the pool and fishing pond. And there are special events, such as our famous 4th of July celebration, tennis tournaments, cocktail parties and dinners by the pool.

Get the point? The best part about the Meadows Club is the people. They're the friendliest, nicest and most interesting people in town. Active, sports-loving and kid-supporting.

Come out and judge for yourself. We'd like to have you join us for a complimentary swim and tour of the club. Please call the Meadows office at ___ or call me at ___ to arrange a time convenient for you.

Treat yourself and your family to a great Boulder experience!

Sincerely,

George W. Coel
Meadows Club
Boulder, Colorado

1-18 Prospects within targeted groups

Dear_____:

The purpose of this letter is to acquaint you with RELA and its capabilities in the contract design, development and manufacture of electronic- and electromechanical-based medical devices. We can help your organization meet the needs of an increasingly more competitive marketplace with state-of-the-art devices.

RELA is a 12-year-old company with nearly 50% of its activities devoted to the medical field, including both the development of devices and disposables. Its clients range from Fortune 500 to startup companies.

RELA's staff includes many electrical, software and mechanical engineers with years of experience in the design and development of a broad variety of medical devices.

RELA's recent experience includes:

- Ventilators, Pacemakers, Electrosurgery Hardware and Disposables, Infusion Pumps, Fluid Pumping Mechanisms, Electro Physiology

- Software Design and Development, Software Verification and Validation

RELA Manufacturing Division is a Registered Device Manufacturer with the FDA and meets the agency's Good Manufacturing Practices requirements. The division offers quality turnkey contract manufacturing services to clients nationwide.

A brochure and other collaterals describing RELA's capabilities are enclosed for your review.

I plan to phone you in the days ahead to discuss the possibility of an appointment for a presentation of the RELA capabilities to you and your associates.

Cordially yours,

RELA, Inc.
Boulder, Colorado

1-19 Prospects by referral

"Joe suggested I contact you" letters top any list of most effective letters. Prospects pay attention to their friends and business associates. Letters introducing yourself based on referrals should open with two pieces of information: the name of the person referring you and the reason for writing. That done, you can deliver your credentials or provide information of particular interest to the reader.

Dear _____:

M____, with your Dallas office, asked me to send the enclosed materials to you.

The purpose of this letter is to introduce ourselves and our capabilities. We have worked with other information processing companies, including ____, for whom we have produced over 30 programs.

Universal Training has been a leading national designer and developer of custom training for 20 years. We have developed more than 3,000 programs for more than 300 major companies, many of which are industry leaders. ____, ____, ____ are but a few of the corporations we have served.

Universal Training offers full service. We have a program development staff providing research, writing and editing; a graphics arts staff; and an award-winning audiovisual production team (over 40 awards in the past 10 years).

Mr. ____, I hope you will review the enclosed information describing Universal Training. Our credentials are divided into service categories, such as sales, customer service and management training. Perhaps as you review examples of projects we have designed for other clients, you'll see how our expertise can apply directly to your needs.

I will call you soon to discuss your training needs. We are eager to apply our training skills to assist you in achieving continued success.

Sincerely,

Doug Barrington
Universal Training
Northbrook, Illinois.

1-20 Prospects by referral

Dear _____:

John _____ came up with another one of his good ideas last week — he suggested I contact you. Your store, he said, has a reputation for carrying excellent clothing at moderate prices. Since I represent Wrangler, which makes fine quality clothing that families can afford without floating a loan, it sounds as if we would make a good match.

You may be surprised to know that Wrangler clothing is not just for cowboys and cowgirls (although our western styles stay popular year round). We also manufacture sharp-looking casual wear for men, women and children — everything from jeans to shirts, blouses, jackets and skirts.

Fabrics and workmanship? They're the best, and that is not just a sales pitch. Last year we had a phenomenal increase in sales. And we have a loyal following of customers who depend on our quality.

I'd like to meet with you to discuss the possibility of your joining our family of Wrangler retailers and show you our current catalog and samples. They will let you see the variety and good looks of the Wrangler line. I'll call you next week to set up an appointment.

Sincerely,

John Speas
Wrangler
Portland, Oregon

P.S. John may have told you what a virtuoso I am at spotting the best restaurants in town. Hope to prove it to you when I visit.

1-21 **Prospects by referral**

Dear _____:

Jennifer P____ suggested that I contact you. I am the area representative for Wrangler, manufacturers of fine quality, moderately priced clothing for men and women. In talking with Jennifer, I learned that your store has a reputation for carrying quality products and providing excellent service. I believe you would benefit from being an authorized sales outlet for the Wrangler line.

Over the past few years, our line has expanded to include casual sports wear along with our traditional western styles. Enclosed is a catalog showing our year-round selection of Wrangler shirts, jeans and jackets.

I will be in your area Thursday, June 2, and would like to meet with you to discuss the possibility of your becoming a Wrangler retailer. I'll call you next week to arrange an appointment.

Sincerely,

John Speas
Wrangler
Portland, Oregon

1-22 **Prospects for specific offers**

You've spotted a need that your company can fill. A brief, friendly letter that tells how you can help the prospect shows you've already turned your attention to his/her problems and are ready with a solution. In the openings, these letters refer to what is important to the prospect.

Dear Coach:

I know your team is excited about the fast-approaching basketball season. Before that first tip-off, your players will no doubt want new court shoes.

Teamwear has supported Craven County athletes for years by offering players a special 20% discount on name-brand athletic shoes at the start of each season.

The Teamwear van is loaded with shoes of all styles and sizes and is ready to roll to your school. Students may order shoes and pay for them on delivery — usually within a week. I'll call you this week to arrange a time convenient for your team.

Good luck on your season!

1-23 Prospects for specific offers

Dear _____:

Welcome to White Mountain. I visited the condo complex you're completing at Ski Pass and was impressed with the craftsmanship and decor of the units.

I notice that 30 units will be rented furnished, complete with toasters, coffee makers and crock pots.

I represent White Mountain Appliances, and I believe we can make you the best deal on small appliances.

I'll stop by the complex next week to drop off some brochures. If you'll let me know what you need, I'll work up a special bid for you.

Sincerely,

1-24 Prospects for specific offers

Dear _____:

Would you like to pick your new neighbor?

Review the enclosed information. This property may be of interest to you or one of your friends as a second home or as a rental investment.

Please feel free to give me a call or just return the enclosed card.

Sincerely,

Deanie Zelkin
Coldwell Banker
Dillon, Colorado

P.S. If you are considering the sale of your property, let me know if you would like me to prepare a Comparative Market Analysis for you and send you details on my aggressive, guaranteed, Best Seller's Marketing Plan.

1-25 New purchasing agent

In today's fast-changing business world, sales reps must continually establish relationships with new purchasing agents. Write to new agents immediately to introduce yourself and your company. When purchasing agents are appointed in the middle of negotiations, bring them up to date on the transactions. Explain why you expect the orders to go forward as planned.

Dear _____:

I wanted to get some information off to you to bring you up to date on WIOQ in Philadelphia. Some time ago I had spoken with _____, who at the time was your regional contact. He told me that you had purchased your advertising through October of this year, and that after the current contract was up, he would be interested in considering WIOQ as one of your radio stations in this market.

I am sending you updated information to give you a better picture of what is going on at WIOQ. Our emphasis is on reaching the 25- to 34-year-old adult, as you can see by the most current rating information. As a matter of fact, WIOQ has the highest percentage of 25- to 34-year-old listeners of all the radio stations in the Philadelphia market! We're even slightly ahead of _____ with men 25 to 34. I have attached a rate card for your perusal.

I will be getting back to you in a couple of days to go over this information and to discuss your upcoming plans for radio advertising in the Philadelphia market.

I am looking forward to working with you in the near future.

Sincerely,

Alan Caplan
WIOQ
Philadelphia, Pennsylvania

P.S. I think you might be interested in knowing that other tire retailers in the market, who currently are on the air on an ongoing basis with WIOQ, are _____ and _____.

1-26 New purchasing agent

Dear _____:

Congratulations on your new position as purchasing agent for Nationwide Stationers.

I represent the DayTimes line of appointment books and calendars. We carry items for business, personal and student use. Our nifty new "hot spots" designs are much in demand across college campuses. Once you see the samples I'm sure you will want to place an order for your outlets before fall semester starts.

I'll call you Monday to set up an appointment. In the meantime, I'm sharpening my pencil. I think you'll be pleased at what I can offer Nationwide.

Sincerely,

1-27 New purchasing agent appointed in middle of negotiations

Dear _____:

Congratulations on your new assignment as purchasing agent for Milburn.

We have been negotiating a contract to supply next year's requirements for neoprene inserts. Your engineering staff approved our compounds, and we extended a bid November 1. _____ called a week later and assured us that we could expect a contract in the mail by the 30th.

Taking over as quarterback in the middle of the game is tough, but I urge you to go forward with the order as planned. We can deliver high-quality products on the flexible schedule Milburn requires.

Sincerely,

1-28 New purchasing agent appointed in middle of negotiations

Dear _____:

I just learned that you have taken over _____'s responsibilities as purchasing agent for Print Away Corporation.

Our firm has been negotiating to design, develop and manufacture the printer control unit for your new midrange printer. I showed John the preliminary sketches in March. He was quite impressed and promised to take the necessary steps to issue a formal contract.

Although he has left the firm, I hope you will go ahead with the contract as soon as possible. The dates we discussed were quite aggressive, and we need to begin prototype development by May to meet your deadline.

Control Sys, Inc. has worked with Print Away on several projects over the past several years. I'm confident you will be pleased with our performance in delivering this new component.

I look forward to meeting with you and going over the plans, deadlines, pricing and financial arrangements we had worked out with John. I'll call you the beginning of the week to set up an appointment.

Best wishes in your new assignment.

1-29 Clients in new territory

When you join a company or take over territory from another sales rep, you must send your customer and prospect list a letter of introduction. Begin by stating your name and position. Assure readers you will be their connection with the company and that you value their business.

Dear _____:

Just a quick note to say hello and introduce myself. I am your new sales representative with U S WEST Cellular. My name is Yvonne O'Meara; and I am the person who has replaced ____. ____ has moved on to pursue other opportunities.

I have learned several things in the past month, but the most important thing is that customer service has the highest priority when representing US WEST Cellular. I would like to hear from you if you have any comments or questions. I will be your link to being 100% satisfied with our products and service.

I am very excited about my new career in the cellular industry, and I look forward to working with you throughout the next few years.

Very truly yours,

Yvonne O'Meara
U S West Cellular
Des Moines, Iowa

1-30 Clients in new territory

Hi!

My name is ___and I am your newly appointed IBM Marketing Representative. I am committed and feel confident that together we can pilot and fully exploit the challenges of the 1990s.

Please consider me as your window and guide through the library of IBM's product/technology information, industry expertise and data processing services. I am your resource to help ensure that information systems are purchased for and used as a competitive advantage.

I, or an IBM Business Partner, will be contacting you in the next few weeks to further understand what concerns you currently have and what challenges you will face in the 1990s.

In the meantime, if you have ANY questions, concerns or just want to talk, please call me at ___. I look forward to working with you in the next decade.

Sincerely,

IBM Corporation
Denver, Colorado

Advice from the sales experts

Externalize the postulate that compendious and rudimental locution selection is invariably augmentative to a successful commercial missive.

What does that say? Who knows? Who cares?

Some business letters are almost that bad. Too many big words that require a dictionary to understand. Too many complicated sentences that are difficult to follow and much too long.

The opening sentence can be "translated" into somewhat simpler English, such as this: "Always remember the precept that a concise and simple phraseology choice is forever a positive asset in a business letter."

But that's still a poor (and boring) way to say: If you want to write a good business letter, keep it short and simple!

No one wants to waste time wading through a rambling, lengthy letter. And who wants to read a letter filled with high powered words that make the letter difficult to understand and confusing? The shorter and simpler your letter is, the more likely it is to achieve the action you desire.

Walter L. Bond
Former Executive Vice President
Tupperware International
Kissimmee, Florida

Chapter Two

Reintroduction Letters

Keep lines of communication open to prospects you have met and to the clients you have worked with in the past. Reintroduction letters remind prospects of a meeting or association that occurred some time ago and keep them abreast of changes in your career or your company. They provide brief details on the services or products you now offer. The message is: I remember you. I'm still here to help you.

2-1 Former clients of company

Dear _____:

I learned last week that you have been named Director of Research and Development at ____, and I wanted to convey my congratulations to you. I spoke with ___ and ___, and they also informed me that the grilled, fully-cooked fillet is doing well.

Despite the fact that Golden West is not currently an active supplier to the ____ system, we continue to view you as a good customer, and a company with which we want to maintain a long-term partnership. I hope to have the opportunity of talking with you soon. As we at Golden West expand our capabilities, I believe we will be able to offer some products that you will find very interesting.

Again, congratulations and much success as you approach your new job. Hope to see you soon.

Sincerely,

Rick Mende
Golden West Foods, Inc.
Bedford, Virginia

2-2 Former clients of company

Dear _____:

It's been a while since the Coran Financial Group has reviewed your portfolio.

I know you're still interested in long-term growth and safety for your investments. We can help you. We have assembled the finest team of investment experts in the area. They are dedicated to helping you realize your future financial goals. And they will provide you with the kind of service you expect—and deserve.

We specialize in Ginnie Maes, corporate and municipal bonds, and U.S. Treasury securities. Of course, we can also advise you on stocks and index options. You will find our rates extremely competitive.

One of our investment counselors will be in touch with you in the next week to give you more details about the investment opportunities that we can offer you.

Sincerely,

2-3 Former clients of company

A letter letting former customers know about changes at your company can lead to future business. They've dealt with your company in the past. Now is the time to give them a reason to do business with you again.

Dear _____:

A lot has changed at C&G since we last provided you with feeder assemblies for your copiers. We've instituted new training programs for our assemblers and technicians, purchased new equipment to speed production, and redesigned our final line inspection and test procedures to provide 100-percent defect-free quality.

I'd like to come by and talk with you about our new capabilities. I'm confident we can provide high-quality, on-schedule delivery of feeder assemblies at prices that will help you stay competitive in the copier marketplace.

I'll phone next week for an appointment. I look forward to once again supplying your requirements.

Sincerely,

2-4 Former clients of company

Dear _____:

Have you outgrown that desktop computer we sold you three years ago? Now is an excellent time to trade in that system for technologically advanced, state-of-the-art equipment. With any system you select, we will include two software programs of your choice free.

As you know, Long's Peak Computers provides complete computer service, such as setup, installation, training and support. We will work with you until you are as familiar with your new equipment as you are with the old.

This offer is good until April 15. Come in and make your selection!

Sincerely,

2-5 Clients from previous company

Your clients at a previous company will follow you, if you show them the way. These letters acquaint former clients with your current products or services. Since you have already established a rapport with them, you can open with a more familiar or humorous remark. Let your personality shine through.

Dear _____:

You're probably surprised by the new name on the letterhead. Changing jobs after five years at Soft Times wasn't easy, but the opportunity for greater challenges and growth here at Computer Experience convinced me to make the switch.

I still provide the same consulting services as in the past. In addition, I can offer Computer Experience's large client computer center. It's like having an extra computer room in your office, fully staffed and maintained. It allows you to handle jobs you couldn't tackle before if your own computers were running at capacity. We also have experienced systems analysts to handle programming assignments. No reason now to let jobs stack up because of other priorities.

Sam, this resource is a big reason why I joined Computer Experience. I'd like to stop by your office and give you the details. I'm confident I can show you ways to improve your service — and save money at the same time. I'll be in touch on Monday for an appointment.

Best regards to Millie,

2-6 Clients from previous company

Dear _____:

No, I haven't sailed into the sunset — just changed mastheads. As of September, I became the Northeastern Marketing Specialist for ____ Boating Equipment Company.

I intend to stop by your showroom within the next couple weeks to show you what we can supply. I've enjoyed our association in the past and hope that we can enjoy an even stronger relationship now that I'm with ____.

Sincerely,

2-7 Clients from previous company

Dear _____ :

I did it. When we spoke a month ago, I mentioned I was thinking of a career move. Things happened faster than I expected, and I'm delighted to tell you that I now represent Corporate Impressions. Even better, I will be working with businesses in my old service area.

One reason I made the switch to Corporate Impressions is that I believe their national network provides greater exposure, flexibility, and stability for our clients.

I'd like to talk with you about CI and show you how you can increase profits by making the switch to CI with me. You know you could count on me at ____. I promise to continue that tradition when I represent your interests at CI.

Sincerely,

2-8 Chance acquaintances

Chance encounters on airplanes, at meetings and dinner parties may set the stage for future sales. Send a note shortly after the meeting or at a time specified by the potential client.

Dear _____ :

I was delighted to have a chance to get to know you and Nancy at the ____. Your war stories on ____ entertained us royally. Beth is still chuckling about ____.

As I told you, I represent ____. I believe our products may have application in your manufacturing process. I wonder if you could spare me a few minutes to fill you in on our line and show you our catalog. I think you'll be pleased at what we offer. I'll call your office next week to arrange an appointment.

Again, it was a pleasure to meet you. Please give my best to Nancy.

Sincerely,

2-9 Chance acquaintances

Dear _____:

St. Louis. March 19__. The Ritz-Carlton. We met during a seminar on environmental factors in office design. I was seated to your right at the lighting seminar (the person with the bright red University of Miami sweatshirt).

At the time, your firm was about to break ground on a new building in Atlanta. You suggested I get back in touch with you in a year regarding your furniture requirements.

Sheldon Office Furnishings has focused on office ergonomics for more than a decade. We carry products developed for people, not for space—products that reduce fatigue and discomfort and promote creativity and productivity.

I'd like to meet with you to discuss our line of desks, chairs, tables and other office furnishings. From what you told me of your building concept, I'm confident our furniture would provide just the right inside touch.

Sincerely,

2-10 Chance acquaintances

Dear _____:

Hope your flight to Milwaukee was smoother than the one we shared between Newark and Chicago!

Despite the "bumps," I enjoyed the opportunity to hear about the new fitness centers you'll be opening in the Milwaukee area. As I mentioned during the trip, my company manufactures a full range of exercising equipment, from jogging treadmills and stationary bikes with electronic consoles, to massagers, trampolines, and cycle and flexing exercisers. Smaller articles are also part of our line — items like barbell-dumbbell sets and dual action jump ropes that your clients will expect.

Our products are made of steel, wood, and skid-resistant vinyls that keep on performing year after year, even with heavy use.

I'll be in Milwaukee the last week in April and will call you to arrange a time when I can stop by with some information that will fill you in on the excellent design and overall quality of our exercising products.

Our company and your new company would make a great team!

Regards,

Tips to sharpen your writing skills

Don't overload letters with weak verbs such as "is, am, are, have and has." Instead, choose action verbs that say exactly what you mean.

Examples:

Our company is the distributor for . . .
Our company *distributes* . . .

This product has many advantages.
This product *offers* many advantages.

Our product is the leader in the industry.
Our product *leads* the industry.

Chapter Three

Appointments

Before you can make the sale, you must make the appointment. A brief, friendly letter that either precedes or follows a telephone call is an efficient way to secure an appointment. Telephone calls alone don't do the trick. So much is going on in the office that once the person hangs up, he/she may forget your message. Letters grab—and hold—the prospect's attention and serve as a reminder of when you will be coming and the purpose of your visit

3-1 Ask for appointment

Letters that open doors must be friendly, concise and quickly tell clients how they can benefit from your products or services. Keep them brief.

> Dear _____:
>
> Thanks for your time on the telephone. As you suggested, I will call you the week of July 24 to arrange a time to get together and discuss any upcoming projects you may have for marketing, advertising and/or public relations services. I look forward to the opportunity of working with _____.
>
> Sincerely,
>
> Sandra E. Lamb
> Marketing Communications
> Denver, Colorado

3-2 Ask for appointment

> Dear _____:
>
> We would like to discuss with you how Marketing Communications may assist you in obtaining positive high-profile publicity in the Denver marketplace.
> Marketing Communications has been extremely successful in achieving this for its clients at great economy. I shall call your office in a few days to arrange a time to discuss this further.
>
> Sandra E. Lamb
> Marketing Communications
> Denver, Colorado

3-3 Ask for appointment

> Dear _____:
>
> Thank you for your time on the phone last week discussing the marketing and public relations of the _____. As I mentioned, Mar-

keting Communications is a full-service marketing, public relations and advertising agency with an extensive amount of expertise in health care.

You mentioned that you may consider promotion of some Continuing Medical Education programs. Marketing Communications would like to discuss the possibility of our assisting you in this area. Our experience includes developing multiphased and multimedia continuing medical education programs including interactive computer programs.

I have enclosed a background piece on Marketing/Communications for your review, and will contact you next week to see if we might get together briefly and discuss the possibility of our working together.

Sincerely,

Sandra E. Lamb
Marketing Communications
Denver, Colorado

3-4 Ask for appointment

Dear _____:

You are one busy person. I've tried several times to make an appointment by phone without success.

Here's the bottom line. Seeing me for a half-hour could save you thousands of dollars this year alone. Our firm has just developed a new diskette that provides the reliability of top-name brands at a fraction of the cost.

Considering your usage, that translates into big dollar savings for your firm.

Now, how about that appointment?

Sincerely,

3-5 Ask for appointment

Dear _____:

I'd like to meet with you to explain a new software package that puts the expertise of a financial specialist at your fingertips. In minutes, you can determine the effects of factors such as growth rate, volume pricing and special bids, cash flow and indebtedness, taxes, and financial acquisition method histories.

The programs are easy to learn and easy to use. And easy to explain, so I won't take much of your time. I'll call next week for an appointment.

Regards,

3-6 Ask for appointment

Dear _____:

It was a pleasure speaking with Dr. _____ recently regarding programmable PCA Therapy and, in particular, your interest in the BARD Family of PCA instruments. BARD manufactures a wide line of PCA instruments for both IV and epidural administration. I have enclosed some information regarding the BARD PCA, as well as some sample protocols. Please use the enclosed sample protocols in whatever way you see fit.

I would recommend your serious consideration of the PCA-1 for hospital use. If you are considering or doing epidural administration, the ambulatory PCA shown has an advantage in that a reservoir capacity of 100 and 250ml is available. The PCA-1 is extremely easy for the nursing staff to use, and uses a 50ml prefilled syringe or a 60cc plastic syringe prepared by the pharmacy, should you choose this option.

I will call you on December 18 to set up an appointment for sometime in January. It would be most helpful if you could be ready to begin an evaluation during our January meeting.

Sincerely,

Denny C. Dickinson
Bio-Medical Resources, Inc.
Broomfield, Colorado

3-7 Ask for appointment

The most important element in letters asking for demonstration appointments? Specificity. State the time you would like the appointment and what you will demonstrate.

Dear_____,

Recently, I tried to reach you on the phone without success. The reason for my call was to acquaint you with RELA, Inc. and its capabilities. A brochure describing these capabilities and other relevant collaterals are enclosed for your review.

RELA is a contract designer, developer and manufacturer of electronic and electromechanical-based products and systems. RELA is capable of taking a client's product or system idea from the earliest concept stage through hardware and software design and development, mechanical and industrial design, printed circuit board design, prototype development and manufacturing. For the client that does not require the complete development package, RELA offers any portions thereof.

RELA services clients of all sizes, ranging from members of the Fortune 500 to startup companies.

Because we believe that RELA's expertise could make it a valuable outside resource for your organization, we would welcome an opportunity to make a presentation of these capabilities to you and interested associates.

To talk about the possibility of this presentation, I plan to phone you in the days ahead.

Cordially yours,

RELA, Inc.
Boulder, Colorado

3-8 Ask for demonstration appointment

Dear _____:

Spring showers make it tough to keep golfing greens trimmed to perfection.

Until now, that is.

Our new GreenSpring mower was designed specifically to handle the toughest conditions. Small and rugged, this rider mower provides the best cutting action possible for damp grass.

Talking about it doesn't cut it, however. Let me bring the Green-Spring by for a demonstration at 2:00 this Tuesday afternoon. You'll be amazed at what you see.

I'll call to confirm.

3-9 Ask for demonstration appointment

Dear _____:

With the emphasis again this year on AS/400 Office Software, we are trying to find ways to educate our customers and Business Partners on how AS/400 Office can be used not only as a Word Processing tool, but also as a way to enhance their application software.
I would like to meet individually with you to:

1. Explore how AS/400 Office and Application Programming Interfaces (APIs) can be used in your software packages.
2. Review examples of APIs.
3. Review resources available to assist in writing APIs for your software.

If you are interested, please give me a call at ____ to schedule an appointment. I look forward to hearing from you.

Sincerely,

IBM Corporation
Denver, Colorado

3-10 Ask for demonstration appointment

Dear _____:

As you may be aware, Amdahl Corporation has become a leading supplier of large ____ -compatible processors over the last ten years. Our Denver area customers have installed ____ Amdahl mainframes with cumulative savings approaching $____ when compared to ____ alternatives. Among the prominent local companies enjoying these savings are:

(List customers.)

Recent accomplishments include being the first (and only) plug-compatible manufacturer to deliver 370 Extended Architecture. The attached ComputerWorld article confirms the advantages of Amdahl's compatibility at one of our customer's installations. I have also attached a summary of additional advantages our customers receive when compared with the ____ alternative.

Please call or have your secretary call me at _____ to arrange for a complete update on available mainframe, peripheral storage, and communications products and services Amdahl now offers in the Denver area. The update should take one hour. Would you be kind enough to provide me with two optional meeting dates, to make sure I can accommodate your schedule.

Sincerely,

Amdahl Corporation
Denver, Colorado

3-11 Ask for second appointment

Dear _____:

The company's bean-counters are at work putting together a new—and I believe substantially better—discount if you go ahead with the larger order this month. I'll be back your way next week and could stop by Wednesday at 10:00.
Can we get together?

3-12 Ask for second appointment

Dear _____:

When we met last week, you said you needed time to consider our proposal for supplying ____'s product needs.
Can we get back together next Monday, at 1:00? I can answer questions and address any issues that you've thought about since our meeting.
I'll confirm with Donna.

3-13 Ask for closing appointment

Letters asking for that critical closing appointment must emphasize the benefits to the client. The first sentences emphasize the fact that it is in the client's best interests to close the deal.

Dear _____ :

The clock is ticking. Only a few days remain to sign the contract without jeopardizing your ship schedule.

I called Joan and set up a meeting with you on Monday, the 3rd. If I can answer any questions before then, please call me. As soon as I have the contract in hand, our machines will begin stamping out flanges for your master assemblies.

I understand how important meeting your government contract deadline is, and I urge you to give us the signal to begin work by the 10th of this month.

Sincerely,

3-14 Ask for closing appointment

Dear _____ :

I trust you've had time to consider our proposal to provide cleaning services for your office complex at _____ Wilshire.

As I mentioned, we take extra steps to insure that your offices receive the finest cleaning possible. Our supervisors evaluate the products and techniques to best handle your needs. They accompany our cleaning professionals the first week to see that everything is handled correctly.

What's more, they check with your personnel each month to be sure services are satisfactory.

I hope I've convinced you that we have the power and enthusiasm to mop, wax, dust and buff your complex better than anyone else. I'd like to stop by with a contract on Tuesday, December 3, at 9:00, so that we can start brightening your office environment the first of next month.

Sincerely,

3-15 Let clients know of plans to be in their area

A good way to let your clients know you will be in their area is to send preprinted post cards.

Dear _____:

    I will be in your area during the following dates: ____
Please mark your calendar. I am looking forward to working
with you.

Regards,

John Speas
Wrangler
Portland, Oregon

Advice from the sales experts

When I write letters asking for an appointment, I always give the customer a reason to see me. The question in the customer's mind is: "What can this salesperson do for me?" I begin my letters by introducing myself and giving the name of my company. Then I tell about what I'm offering and how it can help the customer. By the end of the first paragraph, he/she has the answer to the question.

I ask for the appointment by giving the customer a choice. I tell when I will be in the area and offer two or three dates when I am available for a meeting. I let the customer know that, if those dates don't work, I'm willing to find another mutually convenient time. The trick is to ask for the appointment in such a way that the customer has a difficult time saying no.

John Speas
Manufacturer's Representative
Wrangler
Portland, Oregon

Chapter Four

Further Letters Regarding Appointments

Besides paving the way to appointments, letters can handle other appointment matters, such as confirmation, change of date or time, even cancellation. Clear, concise letters reduce the chance of misunderstandings.

4-1 Confirm appointment

Dear _____ :

I know how busy dentists are during the day, but I think you'll find it worth your time to look at the _____ line of dental supplies. I'm on your calendar for Tuesday, October 21, at 8:00. I assure you I'll take only a few minutes.

Best regards,

4-2 Confirm appointment

Dear _____ :

We are very happy that you will be able to meet with us on June 20 at 9:00 a.m. Our staff is prepared to discuss the following concerns with you:

How agencies use numbers to calculate reach and frequency.
How we identify the unique selling points of cable television in this marketplace.
How we identify the most valuable customer studies.
How we use our demographic information.

We're confident that once we've explained this information, and answered your questions, you will see the value of joining our family of cable television advertisers. We believe we can enhance your exposure in this market by 75%.

Regards,

4-3 Confirm appointment

Dear _____ :

Friday, March 16, at 2 p.m. is fine for me. I'll block out as much time as we need to go over your order and make sure we've tied everything down.

See you then!

4-4 Confirm closing appointment

Dear _____:

I'm delighted you've decided to carry The Lighter Side brand of light fixtures. I'll drop by your office at 11:00 Monday morning, the 16th, to have you sign our dealership contract.

Best regards,

4-5 Confirm closing appointment

Dear _____:

The big day is getting closer. Just wanted to confirm our appointment for the 19th at 2:30. The contract was signed by our officers yesterday, and I'll carry it back to New York for your signature.
I look forward to a long and mutually beneficial association.

Sincerely,

4-6 Inform that you will bring additional person to appointment

Dear _____:

Just a note to let you know that Sara Moran, a new member of our chemical marketing team, will join me for our meeting next Tuesday.
Sara has a degree in chemical engineering from MIT and will be able to answer any questions you may have on our chemical compounds and their effect on the environment.
I'm looking forward to meeting you and explaining how Chem-Perf solutions can make a difference at your firm.

Sincerely,

4-7 Supply information prior to appointment

Send clients important information before the appointment and write ahead to ask them to bring specific materials to the meeting. It can save time and make the meeting more productive.

Dear _____:

Color me excited! Enclosed is the contract to supply Gatlin Cosmetics' lipstick tube requirements over the next three years.

I'll be in Atlanta for the signing on November 2. Josh's detail work on the Stars of the 30s tube is beautiful. I can't wait to see it in the stores. The gold-tone tubes will start rolling off the lines February 15; silver-tone, March 1.

Call me if you need anything.

4-8 Supply information prior to appointment

Dear _____:

When we spoke Friday, you mentioned you would like to review technical information on our 39443 series monitors before we meet with your purchasing staff. The enclosed package should answer most of your questions, but I'll be in the office all week if you have any others.

Thanks again for considering the J&S line of monitors. I look forward to our meeting on the 30th.

Regards,

4-9 Supply information prior to appointment

Dear _____:

Here's the information I promised when we spoke on the phone yesterday. The brochure will give you a good idea of what our patio tables, chairs and lounges look like—the colors are surprisingly true-to-life. You'll find all the details on size, materials, strength, and durability in the six-page pamphlet. Needless to say, we're proud of the fact that consumer groups consistently give our patio products excellent ratings.

See you on Tuesday!

4-10 Ask client to furnish information for appointment

Dear _____:

After visiting your accounting department, I've already noted several aspects that I believe can be simplified, saving you time and money.

For our meeting on Wednesday, would you provide us with an estimate of the volume of transactions currently handled by your accounts payable and receivable clerks. Much of the repetitive, number-crunching activities can be handled by our existing software. I don't see a need at this time to develop any special programs. Once we have the volume, we can tell you what your costs will be, based on a two-year payoff program.

I look forward to seeing you on Tuesday.

4-11 Confirm change of appointment

Dear _____:

Thanks for calling, Mike, and letting me know you'll be unavailable for our meeting Monday. I'm able to reschedule as you asked. See you at 10:00 in your office on Wednesday, the 12th.

Sincerely,

4-12 Confirm change of appointment

Dear _____:

Rich just called to let me know you had to leave town this week. I asked him to put me on your calendar at 9:30, Tuesday, the 14th. Hope you have a successful trip to Atlanta. I look forward to seeing you when you return.

Sincerely,

4-13 Thank client for appointment

Remember to say "thank you" after an appointment. Your letter should reinforce an important idea: Your company is market-driven. You stand ready to assist your clients in meeting their business goals.

Dear _____:

May I take this opportunity to thank you for the time we spent discussing the possible advantages that would be gained by having American Seating position itself as a resource to ____.

As we discussed, our representatives will continue to work with you in setting up an educational platform with your facilities people. ____ will be pleased to make available a list of American Seating clients, as well as dealer organizations, that can assist you in both products and services.

I'm looking forward to working with you and ____ with respect to projects and/or services where American Seating's unique resource capabilities can be demonstrated.

Once again, it was a pleasure meeting you, and I look forward to seeing you in the near future. Please call upon me at any time if we can be of assistance in any way.

Sincerely,

Frank L. Baudo
American Seating Company
New York, New York

4-14 Thank client for appointment

Dear _____:

Thank you for taking the time to talk to me about the _____ Balloon Festival.

I appreciate your honesty concerning our products. I look forward to speaking to you next week regarding your patch needs.

If at any time we can be of service concerning your Corporate Image needs, please call me.

We are dedicated to quality and service.

Sincerely,

Marilyn K. Reichenberg
Initial Stitch, Inc.
Boulder, Colorado.

4-15 Thank client for appointment

Dear _____:

On behalf of our interview team, I would like to convey our appreciation for your participation in our market research effort.

Your input was invaluable to us and gave us significant information that will help us deliver programs and products to best meet the needs of customers like yourself. The information you provided will have a direct impact on a number of specific design decisions in forthcoming releases of our products. Furthermore, it will help us extend our portfolio of product offerings and shape the direction of our program strategy.

Thank you again for your time and willingness to share your views. Please extend my thanks to the other members of your organization who participated in the visit.

Regards,

Bob Millradt
Hewlett-Packard Company
Ft. Collins, Colorado

4-16 Cancel appointment

Dear _____:

I'm on your calendar for 9:00, Wednesday, May 16, to show you our engineering software package. The product literature has been delayed at the printers and won't be ready until the 21st. I'd like to reschedule our meeting for 10:00 a.m. on the 22nd.

Sorry for any inconvenience. I think you'll find the package worth the wait.

Sincerely,

4-17 Cancel appointment

Dear _____:

I'm sorry to have to postpone our 10:00 appointment Tuesday, March 9. Are you free Friday, March 20, at 10:00?

I'll call to confirm.

4-18 Cancel appointment

Dear _____:

I owe you one.

I'm sorry I can't make our appointment on Wednesday, June 23. I've been called out of town unexpectedly and won't return until the following week.

As soon as I get back, I'll call to set up another meeting. Let's talk over lunch at the Oak Room. My treat.

Regards,

4-19 Cancel appointment

Dear _____:

We're scheduled to meet this Monday at 9:00. I'm sorry I have to cancel this appointment. We're reorganizing our product line, and I believe it will be more beneficial to meet after plans are final. I'll call you soon to set another time.

Sincerely,

4-20 Respond when client cancels appointment

Dear _____:

I'm sorry to hear that you weren't feeling well on Tuesday. I do hope that you are better now.

Enclosed are a couple of articles on the state of cable advertising and how some agencies are using it for their clients.

Our sports programming has some of the best professional and college sports offered on television. I hope this information will help inform you on what's available on cable for your clients.

If there is anything I can do for you, please call me.

Sincerely,

Tim Kilbride
Denver Cable Interconnect
Denver, Colorado

4-21 Inform others of closing appointment

Dear _____ :

Just to let you know—the meeting with ____ of Body Build will be in Milwaukee next Tuesday, April 3. I'm confident we've answered his questions about durability and power on the X13 model. I believe we'll close the deal with an order for ten or more machines at the March discount price.

Keep your fingers crossed!

Tips to sharpen your writing skills

Use simple verbs:

instead of	*choose*
are able to	can
is having	has
will be going	will go
is planning	plans
has a tendency to	tends
appears to have	has
make progress toward	progress

Chapter Five

Announcements

May I have your attention, please! In announcement letters, you want clients to stay tuned to news about yourself, your company and your products. These letters convey even negative information with a positive tone. They generate excitement and reassure clients that what's happening means good news for them.

5-1 Change of career

Dear _____:

I hope you'll be as excited as I am when I tell you I've left the computer field to become sales associate at NutriBank. The health food industry is set to explode in the 90s. People are becoming more concerned about the impact of nutrition in their lives. I'm fired up about contributing to a more healthful nation.

Sue and I have been on the NutriBank program for two months, and we both feel more energetic and creative. I know you work at staying fit, so I thought you'd be interested in the enclosed pamphlets outlining the program and benefits of NutriBank. Let me know if I can provide any other information. I'll touch base by phone in a week or two.

You know I'm convinced, Mike, or I'd still be a computer jock.

Sincerely,

5-2 New career in sales

Starting a new career in sales? A letter to your friends can tell them about your sales position and ask for their help.

Dear _____:

Two years ago, when our children started leaving the nest, I began thinking seriously about my "next" career. My goal was to pursue a field which was personally challenging and provided the stimulation of working with people. Residential real estate seemed appealing; therefore, I obtained a real estate broker's license. I plan to make residential real estate my full-time career and would like to make buying and selling homes a good experience for people, for I know what it's like on both sides of the fence.

In January, I accepted a position with Moore and Company Realtor because it is a caring, professional company which provides honest real estate services. With over 25 agents in the Boulder office and 21 offices throughout the state, Moore and Company also provides me with a large and very effective sales force to help sell my residential listings.

As with any type of sales, word-of-mouth advertising is essential to succeed. I am writing this letter to let you know of my new career and to ask you to keep my name in mind if you or anyone you know may be interested in buying or selling a personal residence or investment property.

I look forward to talking with you.

Glenda Hilty
Moore & Company
Boulder, Colorado

5-3 New associate

Letters introducing new members of the firm or advising clients that another representative will be handling their account should make it clear that the change is subject to their approval. Also, personal information about the new reps helps clients feel more comfortable dealing with them.

Dear _____:

I'd like to introduce you to our new associate Tom Byers. Tom graduated from Princeton and spent two years with a brokerage firm in Los Angeles, where he set records for several of his clients.

Tom has the Midas touch when it comes to marketing treasuries, municipals and mutual funds to money markets. Since his strengths match your financial needs so well, I would like your consent in transferring your portfolio to his care.

Tom will call in a few days to set an appointment to meet you. I know once you've spent time with him, you'll agree that he has the financial savvy to look after your investments.

Sincerely,

5-4 New associate

Dear _____:

As you know, _____ are leaving Boulder. At Free Spirit Travel, we shall miss them both as highly valued employees and as friends, and we wish them well.

Your business is very important to us, and we want to continue to provide you with the excellent service that you have been accustomed to receiving. I have discussed your needs with them and selected the experienced Free Spirit travel agent we think is best suited for your travel arrangements.

_____ has been assigned to your account. She has a great deal of experience with both corporate and leisure travel and is already handling a number of our most important clients. Her business card is enclosed. All of our VIP accounts, of which you are one, are always covered by me if their primary travel consultant is not available.

Naturally, you should continue to expect daily ticket delivery, knowledgeable information regarding international travel requirements, and thorough management of all your travel needs. If you should ever find any kind of lapse, however small, in Free Spirit's service, or if you wish to work with a different travel agent, I sincerely ask that you let me know at once. We will be more than happy to accommodate you.

Thank you for your past business, and be assured Free Spirit stands ready to handle all your future travel needs.

Sincerely,

Susan Kelley
Free Spirit Travel, Inc.
Boulder, Colorado

5-5 New distributor

Dear _____ :

Great news! We now have a distributor in Charleston. Wing Forest has been in business there for 20 years and has earned an outstanding reputation for quality and service.

With a distributor close at hand, you will receive fast service when it comes to providing information, answering questions, and supplying merchandise off the shelf.

Your current orders will be shipped from the factory, but in the future, please direct your orders to: (Name/Address).

We are confident you will be pleased with the added convenience of having a direct distributor in your area.

Sincerely,

5-6 Change of company name

Dear _____:

Just so you know when you get your next bill—Carden Photographic Products has changed its name to The Maine Photographer. We provide the same line of products as in the past—at the same low prices. And we still make one-day deliveries.

Nothing in our relationship will change. Except the name on the check.

Sincerely,

5-7 Change of company name

Dear _____:

Mike's Tents is now called The CamPro Store. When Mike started the business in 1955, he sold only tents. Today we handle a full line of outdoor camping equipment—everything from tents to coolers to sleeping bags to flashlights. Our new name better reflects the wide range of products we handle.

Our credit terms are the same as before, and as always, you'll receive personal, friendly service.

We look forward to seeing you again in our showroom.

Sincerely,

5-8 Change of company address

Dear _____:

Just a note to let you know I have moved from the wilds of Nederland to a new home and office in the Boulder area.

I hope all is well with you and look forward to working together on future projects.

Sincerely,

Kevin Seitz
Graphic Designer
Boulder, Colorado

5-9 Change of company address

Dear _____ :

    The moving vans are loaded and rolling toward our new facility at 12 Market Street. The building is much larger, so we'll be able to keep more stock on hand to fill even your emergency orders. Come by any time. The coffee pot is on.

Sincerely,

5-10 Change of company address

Dear _____ :

    After nine years at Oakfort Place, we're moving to Minneapolis to be closer to the majority of our clients. We're located at 610 Larson in the heart of downtown, with free customer parking around back. Please change your records. We don't want your mail to be delayed.

    I believe you'll find the new location very convenient. When you're in the neighborhood, stop in and let me buy you a cup of coffee.

Sincerely,

5-11 Change of your address

Dear _____ :

    I've pulled up stakes in Verona and am moving across the river to Oakmont.

    You can reach me at the address and phone number shown below.

    (address/phone number)

    Although I'm on the road a lot, my machine answers 24 hours a day, every day—and I generally check in twice a day. I urge you to leave messages for me at any time.

    I look forward to assisting you in whatever way I can.

Best regards,

5-12 Change of product line

News of changes to your product line or service should stress benefits to your clients. Whenever appropriate, point out that your clients helped you make the decision. Reinforce the idea that yours is a market-driven company.

Dear _____:

You'll be happy to hear that your comments have prompted action at our factory. From now on, Wear-Easy cotton T-shirts will contain 30% polyester. When our retailers let us know their customers complained about excessive shrinkage, we listened. The new shirts have the look and feel of all-cotton, but the washing and durability characteristics of polyester. Even better news? Costs of the shirts remain the same.

Wear-Easy designers are at the drawing board working on designs for the ____ season. From what I've seen so far, the vibrant colors and bold designs of these shirts will knock your socks off. I know you'll want to order plenty so you don't run out mid-season.

Thanks for your past comments on Wear-Easy shirts. Keep them coming. You're the reason we're setting the pace in the T-shirt industry.

Sincerely,

5-13 Change of product line

Dear _____:

No, John, it isn't a typo. We have recently changed distributorships and now supply Palmer pipe fittings.

Our decision was based on comments we received from you and other clients. Palmer offers the highest quality and most extensive line of fittings in the marketplace. You can now order all your requirements from us. Quality and workmanship are guaranteed, as always.

I'll stop by next week to go over the catalog and price list and help you select stock for your showroom.

Sincerely,

5-14 New models and accessories

Dear _____:

Just when you thought you'd seen the ultimate in motor start-ers, I've got a surprise for you—the Falcon 390A all-electronic model.

Operation is silky smooth, making it an ideal driver for the medical equipment you manufacture. We've eliminated moving parts and sealed all the circuitry inside a casing. Result? Parts don't wear out, and circuits resist shock and are protected from moisture and dust.

Once you review the enclosed brochure, I know you'll be impressed with this latest addition to our line. I'll call you so we can get together and talk about what jobs the 390A can handle for you.

Sincerely,

5-15 New models and accessories

Dear _____:

We now have what you've been wishing for—the new Basco Tri-Panel Door in both tub and shower sizes.

The new doors, available in three tub and shower sizes, also come in a variety of glass options:

- All obscure glass
- All clear glass
- Etched, mirror, etched
- Mirror, mirror, mirror
- Etched, etched, etched

I know you'll be pleased with the very competitive pricing. I'll stop by next week to show you the brochures and accept your order for this new stock.

Sincerely,

The Shapes Company
Elk Grove Village, Illinois

5-16 New models and accessories

Dear _____:

Just a quick note to let you know that the popular Swanstone shower floors are now available in AGGREGATE colors: gray, granite, bermuda sand, midnight galaxy and rose granite. All come in popular sizes.

Swanstone vanity tops and bowls are also available in AGGRE-GATE colors and six new sizes, including offset bowls and longer counters.

I'll call you soon to answer any questions you may have and enter your order for next month's requirements.

Sincerely,

The Shapes Company
Elk Grove Village, Illinois

5-17 New models and accessories

Dear _____:

Hooray! No price increase for noncorrectable cartridge ribbons—just new model numbers.

Please make the following model number changes in your catalog. We're ready to accept your orders for these sharp, easy-to-install ribbons. I'll call you to check on your requirements this week.

Sincerely,

5-18 New services

Dear _____:

I am taking the liberty of sending you a copy of a sales brochure for a new company under the umbrella of Ogden Allied Services.

About 18 months ago, we formed a corporation called Ogden Allied Abatement and Decontamination Services and recently became licensed in the State of California to perform this service.

_____ is the director of this group and he has assembled a staff of people who are extremely proficient in this area. Because their offices are just down the hall from mine, I have had the opportunity to spend time talking with them. Quite honestly, I am impressed with their dedication and desire.

Because of that, I would like to help them out. If you or someone within your organization develops a need for asbestos abatement services or decontamination services, we would consider it a privilege to be included on your bidder's list. _____ would be happy to give you any additional information you believe is necessary, as it relates to this service.

I am reluctant to impose upon you, but I believe it may be of good service to let you know that there is another viable organization available in the state to provide these services. Thank you for your assistance.

Sincerely,

Robert Warner
Ogden Allied Aviation Services
Los Angeles, California

5-19 New services

Dear _____:

Western Freelance Services, Ltd., is pleased to present Jeanne Varnell in her illustrated programs for clubs, schools, churches, museums and historical societies, and for special occasions.

A fourth-generation native, Jeanne is known by her friends and the readers of Sentinel Newspapers as a spinner of entertaining and documented, little-known historical true stories. Now Western Freelance is helping make Jeanne's sparkling wit and vast knowledge of history available to the public.

Colorado's Grand Old Houses and *Ten Early Forts in Colorado* are two of her most popular programs. Color slides, old photographs and antique memorabilia add dramatic realism to Jeanne's people and places in these one-hour programs.

We, her friends, have been treated to this Colorado native's own brand of historical humor for years. Now we can share her with our favorite groups. Call or write us today to book *Colorado's Grand Old Houses* or *Ten Early Forts in Colorado* for your favorite group.

I look forward to hearing from you.

Hassell Bradley
Western Freelance Services, Ltd.,
Denver, Colorado

5-20 Discontinuation of product or service

News that you are discontinuing a product or service must be delivered with tact. Clients may be attached to the product or service no longer available. The letter should state exactly the reasons for the decision and soften the blow, whenever possible, with an explanation of actions you have taken to minimize inconvenience for the client.

Dear _____:

It is with deep regret that Ogden Allied must advise you of our decision to discontinue our Tanker Fueling activities at LAX effective March 31, at 2359 hours.

The age and condition of our tanker fleet makes it impossible for us to project an operation in the near future that is up to what we consider to be our normal high standards of service and safety. Rather than possibly subject our valued customers to future service deficiencies, we have chosen to discontinue our operation.

In order to assure that this action does not cause __ undue hardship, we have made arrangements with ____ to take over your tanker fueling operation at any time between now and April 1, if you so desire. He has assured us that he will maintain Ogden Allied's price levels for at least an additional 90 days.

Ogden Allied sincerely appreciates the opportunity to have served you, and would look forward to being of further service in areas of mutual interest.

Sincerely,

Robert L. Warner
Ogden Allied Aviation Services
Los Angeles, California

5-21 Discontinuation of product or service

Dear _____:

I'm sorry to tell you that, starting February 1, we will no longer be able to remove snow from sidewalks, steps or porches at the Mesa Professional Building.

In order to provide our clients with faster and more efficient service, we find it necessary to concentrate on large areas, such as driveways and parking lots, where we can clear the snow with our large snow-plowing equipment. You may wish to contact The Snow Shovelers to handle smaller areas.

In the meantime, we will make sure your driveway and parking lot are clear, no matter how deep the snow!

Sincerely,

5-22 Discontinuation of product or service

Dear _____:

Goodby hardware. Hello software. It's a popular tune today, and CompuTrex Consultants believes it's time to join the band.

Our clients have been asking us for more and more software solutions. We decided to focus our efforts in this area so we can serve you better and more economically.

We will complete all open contracts, but effective immediately will accept work only for software design. We have the best design team in the country when it comes to systems integration, and you can count on us to provide outstanding service for all your software-related needs.

Sincerely,

Tips to sharpen your writing skills

Use strong verbs:

instead of	*choose*
facilitate	ease, help
utilize	use
impact	affect
rationalize	decide
interface	work together

Chapter Six

Follow-Ups

Unlike handshake-type letters that introduce you, follow-up letters are a chat over coffee with good friends. They are written to clients or prospects with whom you have already established a relationship. Letters written to keep in touch should be short, while letters supplying hard information may be as long as necessary. Even then, your readers will appreciate your coming to the point quickly. Their time is valuable.

In these letters, take a moment to visualize the reader before writing. Use the same language in your letter that you would use if you were speaking face to face. Some will be quite informal, while others may retain a businesslike flavor.

6-1 Stay In touch

Dear _____:

   As we enter a new decade, the last of an incredible century, the opportunities are virtually boundless.
   The enclosed articles explore the issues of free enterprise in a global marketplace in the coming decade.
   I hope you will find the issue educational and also profitable to _____ as you address your corporate strategies for the 1990s.

Sincerely,

IBM Corporation
Denver, Colorado

6-2 Stay In touch

Dear _____:

   Just a note to remind you we are still very much interested in working with you on a per project or total services basis. As we discussed a few months ago, Marketing Communications has produced cost-effective, high-quality results for medical instrumentation companies. We have some innovative ideas for _____. Incidentally, the _____ ad is very good.
   I shall call your office next week to discuss possible projects.

Sincerely,

Sandra E. Lamb
Marketing Communications
Denver, Colorado

6-3 Stay In touch

Hello again!

   After a very hectic summer, I find myself in need of inventory. If you have been considering selling your property, please allow me the opportunity to show you how Century 21 Summit County Real

Estate and Claude Casey can give you the service and results that you deserve.

Dillon has been a very active market throughout the summer, and I believe it will continue right into the fall and winter months. If you have been considering putting your property on the market, please call me.

The snow will soon be here to stay, and that means the skiers will be arriving. That also means we will soon be in our winter selling season with all the opportunities that provides. If you would like a market analysis for your records, please call me at _____.

Looking forward to hearing from you!

Claude Casey
Century 21
Frisco, Colorado

6-4 Stay in touch

Dear _____:

_____ mentioned to us your interest relating to specifications for bid. We have taken the liberty of putting together some information that we would be happy to expand upon if you so desire.

An item not included in the specification information is our suggestion that _____ not "go to bid," but rather solicit comparative proposals. When you consider that Ogden Allied has been in place for five years and our costs are developed primarily on labor, our bid would be similar to our budget. If you also consider that the service levels have been satisfactory for the past five years, it would seem appropriate to solicit comparative proposals, rather than put the job out to bid.

Sincerely,

Robert L. Warner
Ogden Allied Aviation Services
Los Angeles, California

6-5 Stay in touch on anniversary of purchase

Dear "Feathered" Babies,

I'm writing to wish all our Double Yellow Head Amazon babies a Happy First Birthday. It was just 12 months ago all of you were "featherless" and eating every two hours.

This has been an exciting year for many of you. Heidi fell into a bucket of soap suds while her mom was cleaning. Both Heidi and Mom survived the ordeal: one, cleaner; one, more careful. Poor Maverick sampled some lead from a stained glass ornament and almost went to birdie heaven. Lead is fatal to a parrot. But observant parents and a knowledgeable avian vet pulled him through. Chico is ahead on talking ability, with a whopping 50 words.

Remember, the babies' flight feathers will be growing in during the next few months. Please bring them in for a free birthday cut and grooming. Every year some babies escape, so come in when two or three feathers are fully in. This is also a good chance for you to get some of our nutritious, fresh seed and look through all the neat toys.

Exciting new arrivals are here for viewing. Many families want a "his" and "her" bird or a baby playmate for their present pet.

We again thank you for your care and love of the babies we raise and hand feed. We give them a good start in life, but you are the ones who develop and nurture them into happy adults.

Lovingly,

Rosie's Bird Farm
Boulder, Colorado

6-6 Acknowledge chance encounter

Dear _____:

Greetings from Colorado! I enjoyed our chance meeting during my recent trip to New York. Thank you for the shared cab ride to the Waldorf. I hope that your trip to Hong Kong went well for you.

Following my return to Boulder, I called _____ as you suggested. Due to her imminent departure from New York, I was unable to talk with her. She returns this week, and I will call her as soon as possible.

Thanks for your help. I look forward to my conversations with
_____ and hope to meet you both during my next New York trip. In
the meantime . . . I will ski a run for you in Colorado!

Sincerely,

Jackie Northrop
China Coast
Boulder, Colorado

6-7 Affirm conversation

Dear _____:

This letter is a follow-up to our conversation of December 19
regarding the products offered by LIFECARE for aeromedical transport.

I have taken the opportunity to enclose a brochure that fully
outlines the products and services offered by our company. I might
point out, in particular, that the PLV-102 is well suited for aeromedical
transport and is, in fact, the ventilator that we sell for such purposes.

I am asking our Seattle District Manager, _____, to contact you
by phone and make arrangements to assist during his next regularly
scheduled trip to Portland. _____ can spend more time getting to
know your company and can teach you more about LIFECARE.

I will be looking forward to receiving the materials you promised.

Sincerely,

LIFECARE
Lafayette, Colorado

6-8 Affirm conversation

Dear _____:

This is a follow up to our recent phone conversation. As promised, I'm pleased to enclose a copy of RELA's capabilities brochure
and collaterals in areas in which you had expressed interest.

As I mentioned on the phone, RELA is a contract designer, developer, and manufacturer of electronic and electromechanical-based
products and systems. RELA is capable of taking a client's product

or system idea from the earliest concept stage through hardware and software design and development, mechanical and industrial design, printed circuit board design, prototype development and manufacturing. For the client that does not require the complete development package, RELA offers any portions thereof.

RELA services clients of all sizes, ranging from members of the Fortune 500 to startup companies.

Because we believe that RELA's expertise could make it a valuable outside resource for your organization, we would welcome an opportunity to make a presentation of these capabilities to you and interested associates.

To talk about scheduling a presentation, I plan to phone you in the days ahead.

Cordially yours,

RELA, Inc.
Boulder, Colorado

6-9 Reaffirm company credentials

These letters instill confidence in clients or prospects. They convey unique information about your company or product. They aim to convince readers that you are the best qualified company, with the best products in the marketplace, to handle their needs.

Dear _____:

You may have noticed an article in the July 19 issue of the *Wall Street Journal* reporting on _____ 2nd quarter revenue gains. In this article it is stated that ". . . has landed in a price war on mainframes and that its main combatant, Amdahl, has taken to giving mainframe computer prospects Amdahl coffee mugs and telling them it's worth $1,000,000.00, if they just leave it on their desk when their _____ salesman comes to call."

We have competed with _____ in the large mainframe market for over a decade. We have learned over these years that it takes more than price to earn your business. Amdahl has consistently had the best rated customer service in the computer industry. The reliability and serviceability of our products have "raised the bar" for our competitors. We use the latest technology in delivering products that are innovative, yet fully compatible with Data Processing Industry Standards.

If you would like additional information on Amdahl Corporation and the wide variety of products and services we offer, please contact your local account executive, ____, in our San Francisco office, at ____. He will be happy to stop by and drop off your $1,000,000.00 coffee mug!

Sincerely,

Amdahl Corporation
Denver, Colorado

6-10 Reaffirm company credentials

Dear _____:

Thank you for the time you gave to ____ and me to discuss the benefits of the Valleylab Force 1B electrosurgery system.

When you choose Valleylab for your electrosurgery needs, you are making the right and best choice. Valleylab is the leader in contemporary performance and safety features, and has been for almost 20 years.

I'm enclosing a Valleylab Systems brochure and the most current Pfizer annual report. As we discussed, Pfizer purchased the assets of Valleylab in 1983 because Valleylab was a *very profitable company.*

Besides performance, the most important feature of the electrosurgery system is the Return Electrode Monitoring System, or REM. It provides protection to the patient against an unintentional grounding pad burn. We have enough confidence in the REM system that we offer the most comprehensive indemnification, a copy of which is also enclosed.

Thank you again for your time. We appreciate your choice of Valleylab to serve you and your patients.

Sincerely,

Valleylab, Inc.
Boulder, Colorado

6-11 Reaffirm company credentials

Dear _____:

It was a pleasure talking with you last week. As I stated, Marketing Communications is a small, full-service marketing, advertising and public relations agency specializing in technical as well as consumer product accounts. We have achieved extremely effective results for our clients using a personalized program, heavily weighted in the public relations area.

I am going to be in Florida the end of the month and would like to talk with you about the possibility of your using our agency services on a per-project basis.

We are enjoying the B/PAA and hope to become more involved this year. We are also hoping, of course, that we will see some more positive change in the Denver marketplace.

The new energy products sound like an exciting endeavor, and we'll watch your progress as you get them into the market.

Would you have time to meet with me on January 30 or 31? I will call your office on Wednesday to schedule a time.

Sincerely,

Sandra E. Lamb
Marketing Communications
Denver, Colorado

6-12 Reaffirm company credentials

Dear _____:

Once people discover _____, its natural beauty and fun ski slopes bring them back. We would like to help you get out a compelling message about _____ to skiers across the country.

As we discussed, our agency specializes in the recreation industry and knows how to reach the people you're targeting—active, physically fit 18- to 35-year-olds.

We've already got some ideas under our ski hats for you. I'll call next week to set up a time when we can talk.

Until then, happy swooshing!

Sincerely,

6-13 Reaffirm company credentials

Dear _____:

This month Valleylab is celebrating National Quality Month. To promote Quality Month, a special edition of our company newspaper was published. _____, for the Valleylab Surgical Products Division, submitted an article which announced Valleylab's ranking in your recent Vendor Evaluation.

Attached is a copy of the article. I think you will agree it highlights Valleylab's commitment to provide our mutual customers with the highest quality products.

Sincerely,

Valleylab, Inc.
Boulder, Colorado

6-14 Reaffirm information discussed at appointment

Getting back to your prospect after an appointment is the name of the sales game. The underlying message in follow-up letters is always the same: I'm interested in being of service, in supplying your business needs. I'm interested in your business.

Dear _____:

It was good to see you again. I appreciate your taking time to look at our product samples and to talk about our future direction with the _____ fillet. We are excited about the opportunities that exist for our two companies to build the partnership we have established. I assure you that we will constantly strive to provide you with the highest quality products available at competitive prices so that "Fast Food with Style" will be an ongoing reality for _____.

We look forward to phasing in at _____ and getting started on the other opportunities that have been identified. Thanks again for your time, and I look forward to talking with you again soon.

Sincerely,

Rick Mende
Golden West Foods, Inc.
Bedford, Virginia

6-15 Reaffirm information discussed at appointment

Dear _____:

I enjoyed meeting with you last week and learning about the new medical center you are constructing. As I mentioned, our firm has handled the interior design for three local medical offices. We understand your professional needs to combine quiet good taste with a comfortable environment.

Because of the unique window wall facing the Flatirons, you expressed concern about lobby decor. I think you'll agree we've come up with a creative solution.

In order to submit a formal proposal, we will need a copy of your architectural drawings. I will call you next week to arrange to pick them up.

I believe that together we will be able to create the kind of interior environment you will enjoy working in for many years to come.

Sincerely,

Marc Interiors
Boulder, Colorado

6-16 Reaffirm information discussed at appointment

Dear _____:

Thank you for the opportunity to meet with you today regarding water filtration for your restaurant.

Following our conversation, I wanted to formalize the proposal I had given you.

(Pricing information)

_____, I commend you for wanting to serve the best possible products to your patrons. As I demonstrated, the NSA filters will have a substantial effect on the taste of your water, ice cubes, coffee, tea, soft drinks, and all your other water-mixed beverages. In fact, many restaurants using NSA appliances are saving 15–20% on their coffee and concentrates—possibly enough to offset the investment in the NSA products.

You mentioned the importance of using a filter that had the capacity to handle a commercial workload. NSA stands behind the products for commercial applications with a three-year warranty/re-placement program. This assures you that the cost of each 100S filter will not exceed ____ per month of use.

Awareness of water quality and taste is at an all-time high. I am enclosing several articles for your review. They speak directly to the importance of water to our health. Your patrons will appreciate your awareness and concern for their health when they learn you are serving filtered water and related filtered beverages.

Thanks again for your consideration. I will check back with you on Friday as you suggested.

Sincerely,

Steve Wherry
NSA Filters
Boulder, Colorado

6-17 Reaffirm information discussed at appointment

Dear _____:

Thank you for the time and courtesy you gave ____ and me during our visit on Friday. I was pleased to see that we were able to relate several of Amdahl's features to your future needs. To summarize, I thought that the most pertinent features of Amdahl equipment to ____ are as follows:

(Technical details)

I trust that as we proceed with our discussions, additional benefits will be recognized. In the meantime I look forward to meeting with ____, you and your staff to provide you with a complete update on Amdahl. Enclosed is an Amdahl Education Catalog. You can read the descriptions for the course schedule that I left with you.

Again, thanks for your time and interest. I look forward to hearing from you.

Sincerely,

Amdahl Corporation
Denver, Colorado

6-18 Provide additional information following appointment

Dear _____:

I am writing as a follow-up to our visit last week when we discussed the Barrett Centrifugal Oil Extractor and the McKenzie Engineering Model E Chip Separator. Barrett Proposal No. 20890 has been submitted to _____, as you requested.

I spoke with the folks at McKenzie about using the Model E to separate teflon parts and chips. I was told they were shipping, that very day, a Model E to a customer who also machines teflon parts (smaller than the ones you showed me—if that's possible!). This customer was reducing eight hours of manual labor to 20 minutes of Model E work. In order for it to work properly with teflon though, you must remove the oil from the material first. The most effective way to do that is to centrifugally spin chips and parts (remove 97–98% of the oil), and then de-grease in 1,1,1.

McKenzie will run separation tests for you. They will need shoe box sized samples of the de-greased chips and parts for the ones you want them to test. Separated work will, of course, be returned to _____. Please send to:

(Name/Address)

Please keep me posted as to when you will be shipping the parts, so I can alert McKenzie. And thank you for your interest in the Barrett and McKenzie products.

Sincerely,

Forrest D. Venz
Engineered Products Service Company
Tustin, California

6-19 Provide requested information

Dear _____:

IBM has just announced a contingency plan to protect your investment within your company. Thank you for your interest in the IBM Business Recovery Services.

Information technology and systems have developed rapidly over the past several years. The processing and delivery of information has expanded management's dependence on the availability of information systems. Effective contingency planning is one way management can reduce the impact on an organization resulting from an unplanned interruption of data processing.

The IBM Business Recovery Services offering provides you with the capability of recovering your critical business data and processing applications in times of emergencies.

IBM's Business Recovery Services capitalizes on our own internal recovery experiences, our Information Systems expertise, and our Systems Management skills.

We look forward to being your organization's Business Recovery vendor.

Sincerely,

IBM Corporation
Denver, Colorado

6-20 Provide requested information

Dear _____:

Thank you for requesting information on the Clarion Harvest House Hotel in Boulder through "Meetings and Conventions."

I have enclosed a fact sheet to introduce you to our 15-acre hotel property. Surrounded by Boulder and at the base of the Flatiron Mountains, the Clarion Harvest House offers year-round options for conference, business and leisure travel.

I am interested in learning more about your specific meeting needs so that I may respond with a proposal of rates and availability. Our 1989 corporate rates are:

(Pricing information)

Group rates are available upon request.

Three points I would like you to remember about the Clarion Harvest House in Boulder as a meeting destination:

- Accessibility—Competitive fares and schedules from across the country into Denver's Stapleton International Airport.
- Value—Exceptional accommodations and amenities at reasonable prices as a strong "secondary" meeting market.
- Environment—15 acres of gardens, patios and recreational amenities with a mountain stream running through the middle. Boulder is a truly unique city surrounded by spectacular Rocky Mountain scenery.

I encourage you to contact me directly if I may be of further assistance.

Yours truly,

Lisa Saro
Clarion Harvest House
Boulder, Colorado

6-21 Provide requested Information

Hi _____:

In answer to your fax, mock-crocodile and embossed are the same. The color samples I have forwarded to you for mock-croc are still the best current choices. There is a stone washed mock-croc that I showed you in Los Angeles. At the time you thought the colors were not strong enough. They are all faded earth tones.
Let me know if I can provide any other information.

Best regards,

Susan S. Colpitt
China Coast
Boulder, Colorado

6-22 Provide requested Information

Dear _____:

Thank you for visiting the LIFECARE booth at the International Symposium on Current Developments in Duchenne Muscular Dystrophy in Aachen, West Germany. I am enclosing a copy of the Negative Pressure Ventilation Clinician's Guide. This guide has clinical articles and product information.
I will ask our distributor to contact you to see if he can be of further assistance. Our distributor is:

(Name/Address)

Sincerely,

LIFECARE
Lafayette, Colorado

6-23 Provide requested information

Dear _____:

I'm sending the pertinent information on our appliqued belts. If you are interested in them, let me know immediately and I'll send samples of available background colors and additional designs. You could provide your own designs, but there might be a slight extra charge as new patterns must be cut.

I am leaving for the Far East in early September, at which time I plan to place a consolidated order for several companies. It would be a good time to include your order.

If you have any questions, please call me at _____. It was very nice to meet you, and I hope that the show was profitable for you.

Best regards,

Susan S. Colpitt
China Coast
Boulder, Colorado

6-24 Provide prices

Dear _____:

Thank you for the time and courtesy that you gave me during our recent meeting.

I am pleased to offer you VPA pricing on Amdahl disk equipment with a unit commitment of only _____ Amdahl DASD units. The purchase prices and maintenance rates are as follows:

(Pricing information)

As you are aware, Amdahl's prices are always competitive, but reliability and support are the cornerstones of our business. I have enclosed Amdahl DASD product information for your staff to review.

Thank you for this opportunity to serve _____. I look forward to working with you and your staff.

Sincerely,

Amdahl Corporation
Denver, Colorado

6-25 Provide prices

Dear _____:

Enclosed please find the sample luxury robes and towels. Following are our prices.

Style KIM 88 Deluxe 12-1/2 oz. Martex Terry Velour Kimono, one size fits all, 42" length, 3/4 length sleeve, adjustable belt loops, 8-track stitch on facing, sleeves and pockets.

Cost to you would be _____ plus shipping and embroidery.

We are looking forward to working with you and providing you with superior quality and service.

With warm regards,

Marilyn Kay Reichenberg
Initial Stitch, Inc.
Boulder, Colorado

6-26 Respond to prospects who have contacted company

These are hot prospects. They have already indicated interest by contacting your company. Your letter should show appreciation and state clearly that you are willing to work with them.

Dear _____:

Your Fashion Adventure is about to begin.

Thank you for your inquiry about handling our line of high-fashion footwear. We are familiar with your network of boutiques and believe that the shoes we produce would complement the garments and accessories you already offer your customers.

I'm enclosing a catalog showing styles in our summer collection. All the shoes reflect the flair and personal style of their designers. Notice, for example, the elegant beaded floral and dragonfly designs by Yakiko Iato and the gold, silver and bronze metallic collages by Sam Baldwin.

I look forward to talking with you in a few days to start you on your way to a new Fashion Adventure.

Sincerely,

6-27 Respond to prospects who have contacted company

Dear _____:

Thank you for calling Century 21 Executive Realty and letting us be the first to welcome you to Houston, Texas! I am sure you will find that we can more than adequately handle your real estate needs on your upcoming move.

Enclosed, to familiarize you with the Northwest Houston area, is our Home Buyer's Guide. I am also enclosing information on the homes available that meet the requirements you have given me.

Please let me know on what date you will be visiting Houston to search for your new home. Prior to your arrival, I will preview homes in order to make the most of your limited time, and set appointments for your inspection of the better homes.

Please keep in mind that working as a real estate agent is my livelihood. I ask for your loyalty and, in turn, I promise to diligently work for you in securing the home you desire.

Sincerely,

Jenny Moraitis
Century 21
Houston, Texas

6-28 Respond to prospects who have contacted company

Dear _____:

Thank you for calling the Clarion Harvest House Hotel. We would appreciate the opportunity to host your Christmas party on December 20, __.

The Clarion Harvest House offers beautifully renovated banquet space and meeting facilities, in addition to professional service and excellent food.

We specialize in catering to each group's specific needs and desires. Please refer to the enclosed menus for an idea of the many cuisine items we offer. We are always happy to custom-tailor a menu for you, should you desire something not listed here.

After you've had the chance to consider this information, please contact me to further pursue these arrangements, or if you have any questions. We would love to have you!

Sincerely,

Kerri Ginsberg
Clarion Harvest House
Boulder, Colorado

6-29 Respond to prospects who have contacted company

Dear _____:

Thanks for asking about our new fluid power lines.
I'm sending you a package that includes the design specs on the particular model you mentioned. After you have had a chance to review the material, I'd like to bring some samples by your office for closer examination.

Sincerely,

6-30 Respond to prospects who have contacted company

Dear _____:

Enclosed is some literature on some of our products. I will have the area representative contact you as well. I enjoyed talking with you and look forward to helping you organize your new heart program.

Sincerely,

Kip A. Stastny
Sarns 3M Health Care
Ann Arbor, Michigan

6-31 Respond to prospects who have contacted company

Dear _____,

Thank you for your inquiry about RELA. A brochure describing RELA's capabilities and relevant collaterals are enclosed for your review.

Briefly, RELA is a contract designer, developer and manufacturer of electronic and electromechanical-based products and systems. RELA is capable of taking a client's product or system idea from the earliest concept stage through hardware and software design and development, mechanical and industrial design, printed circuit board design, prototype development and manufacturing. For the client that does not require the complete development package, RELA offers any portions thereof.

RELA services clients of all sizes, ranging from members of the Fortune 500 to startup companies.

Because we believe that RELA's expertise could make it a valuable outside resource for your organization, we would welcome an opportunity to make a presentation of these capabilities to you and interested associates.

To talk about the possibility of this presentation, I plan to phone you in the days ahead.

Cordially yours,

RELA, Inc.
Boulder, Colorado

6-32 Respond to contacts from advertisement

Dear _____:

Thank you for your inquiry for information from A & A Manufacturing Company ("Gortite"). The catalog data you requested was recently mailed to you under separate cover direct from the factory. I'm sure you noted that A & A manufactures a complete line of custom-engineered covers and cable and hose carriers for machine tools, industrial robots, automated handling equipment and other precision machinery.

If you are considering covers or cable carriers for an application, please call us. We will be glad to discuss them with you and, if necessary, visit your facility to do the dimensional detail work needed to provide you with a quotation.

Again, thank you for your interest in our products, and we look forward to hearing from you.

Sincerely,

Forrest D. Venz
Engineered Products Service Company
Tustin, California

6-33 Respond to contacts from advertisement

Dear _____:

Thank you for responding to a recent VisionMark advertisement and for your interest in our product identification capabilities. A color brochure and a sample plate illustrating some of the effects you can achieve through the deep etch process were mailed to you under separate cover direct from the factory. I'm sure you noticed that VisionMark products provide a sharp, three-dimensional look with exacting, fine line detail—detail which allows you to display your company name and logo with pride.

I want to emphasize a couple of points which I think will be of interest to you. We have the ability to produce plates at an attractive price in any quantity you desire. And, there are NO PERMANENT TOOLING CHARGES. A small one-time art work charge of $60 is all you invest.

Call us so we can talk, or send us your P.O. for $60 along with a sample or drawing of the plate you want us to make. We'll run it through our art department and send you a first article prototype of your nameplate. Certainly a small price to pay to see how your logo would look on a deep etched zinc plate rather than paper, plastic, mylar or silk-screened aluminum.

Our services at Engineered Products are available to assist you in your product signage needs. We look forward to hearing from you, and working with you!

Sincerely,

Forrest D. Venz
Engineered Products Service Company
Tustin, California

6-34 Ask to be placed on bid list

Dear _____:

We provide a full line of modular encoders and would very much like to do business with Kassar Equipment. Would you please let me know how we can be placed on your bid list for next year's requirements?

Thanks for your help. I look forward to working with you.

Sincerely,

6-35 Thank client for stopping by

Dear _____:

Thank you for visiting Sanford Homes at Highlands Ranch. We appreciate your interest.

I am certain you will discover the unlimited benefits of living in a well-planned community built with the Sanford Homes' quality and prestige. The "Hartsel" is a very lovely home, one I know you would thoroughly enjoy.

If I can be of assistance to you in any way, please call me. I do look forward to seeing you again in the near future.

Sincerely,

Cheryl Pope
Sanford Homes
Denver, Colorado

6-36 Thank client for business

Dear _____:

Just a quick note to thank you for bringing the Meadows Club board here to the Clarion. I hope everything went well for your dinner, as well as for your meeting.

Sincerely,

Katie Nunnery
Clarion Harvest House
Boulder, Colorado

6-37 Thank client for information

Dear _____:

Thank you very much for the letter and the telephone call last week. The information that you passed along helped me a great deal. The Regional Sales Manager for the Western Region, _____, may contact you in the future regarding some follow up on the situation. Please call me whenever you would like.

Regarding the Service Contracts for _____ and _____, as I mentioned on the telephone, the contracts for both hospitals expired in April and have not been renewed as of this date. If you have any further questions or if we can be of any assistance, please let me know.

Thanks again, and Happy Holidays.

Kip A. Stastny
Sarns 3M Health Care
Ann Arbor, Michigan

Tips to sharpen your writing skills

Use specific nouns:

instead of	*choose*
vehicle	car, train, plane
	(Porsche, Amtrak, Continental)
room	office, library, kitchen
deadline	Tuesday, 4 p.m.
product	desktop publishing software
service	free instruction

Chapter Seven

Special Offers

Clients usually welcome special offers. After all, they're gifts. Some offers motivate clients to order by a certain date. Others encourage clients to order extras. Still others are intended to reactivate accounts. Whatever the case, state the exact nature of the offer and the date it expires.

7-1 Special offers

Dear Winter Enthusiasts:

Is your family ready for fresh powder, blue skies, loads of sunshine and lots of family fun? Well, Circus Circus, Reno's largest downtown hotel and casino, and our new "Snow Bunny Special" are waiting for you!

Under the Big Top you'll find 1,625 beautiful guest rooms, three great restaurants, the largest permanent midway with lots of excitement for the kids and, of course, the 24-hour action that Reno is known for. Just what you and your family need to make this year's ski season unforgettable.

With our new "Snow Bunny Special," which is available Sunday, October 29, 19__, through Tuesday, February 13, 19__, we're offering what's first in family fun to the entire family, whether you ski or not, with a coupon package that includes midway passes, gaming coupons, discounted ski lift tickets and much more.

Circus Circus is within minutes of some of the best skiing on the West Coast and beautiful Lake Tahoe. What more could you ask for?

We'll make it easy. When calling our toll-free number to make your advanced reservations, just mention that you want our new "Snow Bunny Special." Group reservations (10 or more rooms) can be made by calling _____.

Here's to making your winter vacation a "hopping" good time. We look forward to seeing you soon.

Sincerely,

Gerhard Scheiner
Circus Circus
Reno, Nevada

7-2 Special offers

Dear _____:

As you know, in an effort to operate in the most efficient manner possible, U S West Cellular is restructuring airtime pricing. The new Optimum Plan will have multiple and volume discounts, with even greater discounts for ten or more telephones. It will bill in thirty-second increments after the first minute.

Details of the new Optimum Plan are expected to be integrated into our billing network no later than first quarter. U S West Cellular will credit your account for _____ per month. These credits, which start this month, are our commitment to insure your satisfaction until the new plan is in effect.

U S West Cellular is committed to being the "Value-Added" carrier. We are adding a cell site in Cottage Grove. Equipment is in, and we are working out the formalities. The cell site is expected to be operational within the next six weeks. U S West Cellular has also been granted the wireline license by the FCC to provide cellular service in Albany and Corvallis. Equipment has already started to come in, and locations for cell sites have been approved by our engineering department. We are progressing at a rapid pace and expect to be operational by the end of the first quarter. We hope you will find the addition of more cell sites up and down the I-5 corridor to be a definite advantage.

U S West Cellular greatly appreciates the opportunity to be of service and looks forward to a long, successful relationship as we continue to provide for your special needs.

Sincerely,

Phyllis Pearsall
U S West Cellular
Eugene, Oregon

7-3 Special offers

Dear _____:

I would like to make you aware of two significant offerings IBM is making to our S/36 customers. The first offering is a guaranteed buyout or trade-in of your S/36. The IBM Credit Corporation is making this offering based on replacement with an AS/400. I believe that the trade-in table looks good for all models of the S/36. This offering may or may not be applicable to your business right now, but consider the following:

- If you are considering a new computer or an upgrade, the timing couldn't be better.

- If you are no longer able to depreciate your S/36, a trade-in and new equipment may be financially beneficial.

- The recent announcement of new AS/400 models, sized for S/36 users, makes migrating less costly and easier than before.
- You can move to IBM's latest technology without significantly increasing your business computing expenses.

Secondly, a financial analyzing tool has been made available to me that might interest you. This Lotus-based tool creates a financial comparison between a S/36 upgrade and an AS/400 purchase. In many instances, a new machine may be a more cost-effective route. The input variables cover all cost areas for operating your computer system. The key variables are purchase prices, resale values, maintenance costs, electrical costs and depreciation percentages. My thought is that if you have been toying with the idea of upgrading, it could be worthwhile to model your situation on this financial analyzer.

I would like to discuss with you how either or both of these programs may apply to your operation. If you are interested or would like additional details, please give me a call at _____.

Sincerely,

IBM Corporation
Denver, Colorado

7-4 Special offers

Dear _____:

Thank you for taking advantage of our offer for two weeks free delivery of the *Rocky Mountain News*.

This free sample of the *News* is provided with the compliments of your apartment management to help you save money, stay informed and live better.

- SAVE MONEY with the ads, coupons, consumer information and financial advice.
- STAY INFORMED with Colorado's complete news from all over the world, nation, state and metro area.
- LIVE BETTER with the daily features and pullout sections about the things that are most important to you. . . health, entertainment, food, fashion, autos, homes and much more.

You can continue delivery of the *Rocky Mountain News* beyond the initial two free weeks *and save 50%* by just mailing the enclosed order card.

Subscribe now and get *two months'* delivery of the *News* for the price of *one month's* delivery. This special subscription offer is available only through selected apartment communities, so act now.

Sincerely,

Fred Cook
Rocky Mountain News
Denver, Colorado

7-5 Special offers

Dear _____:

We have been offered several near-new AVI Model 200A Infusion Pumps. Since you are presently renting pumps, I thought you might have an interest in these pumps. We propose renting them to you at a rate of _____ per month for a period of two years, at which time ownership would pass to the hospital.

These pumps, I am told, are less than a year old and have been used only sparingly. If this proposal interests you, please let me know by Monday, January 29. Pumps are limited and are available only on a first-come, first-served basis.

Should you have any questions or require further information, please contact me at any time.

Sincerely,

Denny C. Dickinson
Bio-Medical Resources, Inc.
Broomfield, Colorado

7-6 Free offers

Dear Ramshorn Guest,

During the month of March, we are offering one free night's lodging for every two nights you stay with us. Think of it! This might be the chance you've been waiting for to take a long weekend away from the kids. Spend Friday and Saturday nights at Ramshorn Lodge, and we'll throw in Thursday night free. Or, spend two nights and come back later for your free one-night stay.

Either way, we know you'll enjoy once again the comforts of Ramshorn Lodge. Spacious, beautiful rooms with king-sized beds and jacuzzi baths. Our elegant dining room that specializes in wild game dishes. Dancing until midnight to the Four Quarters . . . all in the magnificent setting of Kinosha Lake.

Call us soon for your reservation. (Come on and do it now. Pamper yourself!)

Sincerely,

7-7 Exclusive offers

Dear _____:

Business executives and professionals such as yourself are excited about a new noncancellable disability income protection plan from Mutual of Omaha.

Why? What makes this plan so special?

1. It's designed exclusively for the professional person who earns a high income and needs high limit protection, with up to $10,000 a month in benefits available, depending on the plan you select and qualify for.
2. Your coverage cannot be canceled and premiums cannot be changed—up to age 65.
3. A guaranteed insurability option lets you increase your coverage regardless of any change in health.
4. Another option gives you automatic cost-of-living increases keyed to the Consumer Price Index so your coverage can keep up with inflation.

Even if you have substantial savings and investments, your income is still your most important asset. And your benefits under Mutual's Disability Income Protection for executives and professionals are tax-free under current laws.

I'll be in touch soon with more details about this exciting new plan of protection.

Sincerely,

Clifford Schultz
Mutual of Omaha Insurance Company
Omaha, Nebraska

7-8 Keep-factory-busy offers

The following offers create a sense of urgency. Clients must act right away. They include letters to keep the factory busy, trial offers, close-outs and fire/flood sale. Include a statement about the reason for the offer.

Dear _____:

We've got the winter time blues. People aren't interested in garden rakes when they're shoveling two feet of snow off the driveway. To keep our factory running full swing, we're offering our valued accounts special, deep discounts. Enclosed is a price list you won't believe. The catch is, you must order by October 30 and accept shipment within 60 days. Payment is due on receipt. We can't extend credit on this special offer.

Look over the values and enter your orders today.

Sincerely,

7-9 Keep-factory-busy offers

Dear _____:

Our April projections show that the torsion spring manufacturing line will be running much lighter than usual that month. To keep volume steady, we are offering a few long-time customers a special discount on orders placed for April manufacture.

Would you please look at your requirements to see if you can place an order for at least 10,000 torsion springs, any size, by February 1? By doing so, you may deduct 15% from your normal pricing.

Thanks for considering this matter. I'll call next week to work out the details.

Sincerely,

7-10 Extra Incentive offers

Dear _____:

Have you outgrown your desktop computer? Now is an excellent time to trade in your old computer for technologically advanced, state-of-the-art equipment. With any system you select, we will include two software programs of your choice.

As you know, Long's Peak Computers provides a wide range of computer services, such as set-up, installation, training and support. We will work with you until you are as familiar with your new equipment as you are with the old.

This offer is good until April 15. Come in and make your selection!

Sincerely,

7-11 Trial offers

Dear _____:

The chefs at Marko have been in the kitchen for months developing a nutritious, low-calorie, high-fiber frozen entree to appeal to health-conscious Americans. Yesterday the lid came off "Coq o'Nut" —breast of chicken with several varieties of nuts, berries and vegetables—and it's a taste sensation!

Talking about it isn't enough. I am making arrangements to have a trial pack included with your next delivery at no charge. Once you experience Coq o'Nut yourself, I'm convinced you'll want it to be a regular part of your order.

I've entered a special introductory price on the order sheet accompanying the trial pack. You can take advantage of the lower price until February 10. (Be prepared. You may want to order a truck load.)

Bon appetit,

7-12 Closeouts

Dear _____:

Gordon's Cabinets no longer manufactures the oak contemporary bathroom cabinet, model 631. We have discontinued the model because it is very similar in size and materials to models 630 and 632.

We have two dozen units left and are liquidating them at a 40% discount. Since the 631 is a beautiful, well-constructed cabinet, as you know, you may be interested in picking up some for your customers at this bargain price. Let me know by next Friday how many models I should tag for you.

Regards,

7-13 Fire/flood sales

Dear _____:

You may have heard about the fire at our Montrose factory. Although it damaged part of the west building, our inventory was not affected.

We have to close the factory for two weeks, however, for repairs. Our misfortune can be your advantage. I can offer you a 20% discount on any forged-steel, cast-steel and stainless-steel flanges in stock. To qualify for the discount, you must place a minimum order for 50 flanges by May 25.

I know you can appreciate this great opportunity to cut your manufacturing costs. Let me know your requirements right away. I'll put a hold on the number you want.

Sincerely,

7-14 Factory overruns

Dear _____:

Here's a deal you'll want to connect on. We overran 3,000 standard 2" connectors. We don't want to carry them in inventory past the end of the month, so we're willing to offer an extra 20% discount if you place an order by the 15th. Let me know if I should write it up!

Sincerely,

7-15 Factory overruns

Dear _____:

Whoops! Our textile factory turned on the machines and forgot to turn them off. As a result, we are overstocked with 45-inch red, purple and gold silk scarves in the flamingo motif. Since you ordered two dozen of these scarves in September, I thought you might like another dozen at 50% discount. I'll be out your way on Friday and will stop in to see if you're interested.

Regards,

7-16 Seasonal offers

Dear Retailer:

It's that time of the year again. I'm sure you have been busy and I hope your Holiday season has been a successful one.

Immediately following Christmas, Wrangler will be breaking with our Father's Day line and early-bird flannel shirt line. Because of some circumstances that happened last year with flannels, I am going to work this season a little differently. Last January 20, the flannel shirt line started to sell up and by the 30th it was gone.

I had acquired some additional territory last year and with inclement weather and the early sell-up of our line, I was unable to cover everyone's flannel shirt needs. The flannel line again is very strong and prices sharp, so I foresee the same thing happening again.

Therefore, I have taken the liberty of reserving your flannel needs for you. You are by no means obligated to the styles or quantities. They can be canceled or revised if needed. This is merely an effort to secure your flannels for Fall 1990.

I will review these reserve goods with you when I show you the remainder of the line.

Regards,

Jim Charlebois
Wrangler
Bismarck, North Dakota

7-17 Seasonal offers

Dear _____:

Some exceptional property values are listed for sale in Marina Place, and with winter upon us, some motivated sellers have recently reduced their asking prices, providing excellent buys in what appears to be a rising real estate market in Summit County.

For example:

(Specific home details)

The time is right. The price is right!

If this year's trend to higher prices continues, coupled with our declining inventory, you could see comparable properties selling for considerably higher prices next summer.

I can show you exceptional value properties in any price range, from $65,000 up. If you want to profit from today's reduced prices while the opportunity lasts (or if you have a friend in mind), call me at Coldwell Banker. Exceptional value properties are my specialty.

Sincerely,

Teresa Turrou-Bressert
Coldwell Banker
Dillon, Colorado

7-18 Holiday offers

Dear _____:

Fresh powder will soon top the Rockies, and the sounds of Christmas will echo across Colorado. Now is the time that businesses such as yours select season mementos for special clients and friends.

Two new booklets from the series, "Discovering Historic Colorado," can make holiday giving an easy task this year.

Under the Golden Dome: Colorado's State Capitol is the only history of this beautiful building. It is popular history that brings together the fascinating stories of how the capitol came to be in Denver and of the diverse groups of people who made it a reality—from the gentleman architect, Elijah E. Myers, to the homesteader Henry C. Brown, who donated the land and then tried to take it back.

The Tivoli: Bavaria in the Rockies recounts an era in Denver rich in German tradition, when streets bustled with the energy of hardworking and farsighted immigrants. The days are gone when shopkeepers greeted each other in German along Larimer Street; but many contributions of these pioneers—businesses, buildings, emphasis on physical fitness and self-improvement—benefit Denver today. Not the least of their contributions is the complex of brewery buildings known as the Tivoli.

The books contain many historic photographs, some of them never-before-published pictures from private collections. The covers are beautiful, full-color original photographs.

Additional information concerning the books, authors and pricing is enclosed. We hope one or both of these books will answer your holiday needs.

Sincerely,

Colorado & West
Boulder, Colorado

7-19 Letter that thanks client for participating in special offering

Dear _____:

Thank you for taking advantage of our special "2-for-1" apartment subscription offer.

As you know, your newspaper carrier will collect from you directly for your first month's delivery of the *Rocky Mountain News.*

Use the enclosed coupon to pay the carrier for your second month's delivery. Give the coupon to the carrier when he/she stops by to collect, or enclose it in the billing envelope the carrier leaves with your paper.

Thank you again for subscribing to the *Rocky Mountain News.* Please call us at _____ if you ever have any questions about your delivery service.

Sincerely,

Fred Cook
Rocky Mountain News
Denver, Colorado

Advice from the sales experts

Always write your letter from the reader's point of view. What you think about the subject is not important. What you think the reader thinks about the subject is very important.

In business, most people read letters mainly from their own viewpoint. How does this letter affect me, my job, my responsibilities, my company?

Therefore, it is only natural that, to be effective, your letter should be written from the reader's point of view. This means putting yourself in the reader's shoes when you write. And supplying the information that the reader needs to take the action that you want to achieve.

Walter L. Bond
Former Executive Vice-President
Tupperware International
Kissimmee, Florida

Chapter Eight

Discounts

Discounts break down client resistance. Letters clinch the sale. They put discount information in the hands of buyers at their offices. The message, as with other special offers, urges them to order quickly. These letters can be short, straightforward announcements. They can also give you a chance to be creative. Important point: State clearly the discounted price and how long it will be in effect.

8-1 Limited timed discounts

Dear _____:

We're making Valentine's Day special for our clients.
Beginning February 1 and running through February 28, you may purchase any Judy Ann Hair Care Product at an extra 10% discount. Stock up on shampoos and conditioners that move the fastest off your shelves. You may want to pass along this sweet discount to your retail customers. Valentine sales should zoom.
I plan to stop in next week for your order, but I wanted you to know about this special discount in advance. I knew you'd want time to figure out how much extra stock you want to order.

Sincerely,

8-2 Limited time discounts

Dear _____:

Your pet is one of our cherished clients.
If you bring in your dog during April to be bathed, groomed and clipped, you will receive a 25% discount. It's our way of saying "thank you" for allowing us to look after your dog throughout the year. We enjoy providing pets with the tender, loving, personal care that makes them look and feel their best.
Call now for an April appointment. The Satin Coat professionals are ready, as always, to treat your dog like royalty.

Sincerely,

8-3 One-time-only discounts

Dear _____:

You've been waiting for a deal like this. Get out an order form and start writing.
We are prepared to offer Singal Merit a one-time-only 25% discount on 4" x 5" x 12" extra-padded cartons. Yes, they are the ones you normally use. The discount is in effect only until the 20th of this month. Send us your order today. This special is too good to pass up.

Sincerely,

8-4 Quantity discounts

Dear _____ :

I enjoyed meeting with you yesterday. After seeing your offices, I'm confident that Straight Arrow Office Products can furnish you with the type of computer desks that will fit comfortably in your space and will eliminate eye and shoulder fatigue of your employees.

As I mentioned, our policy is to give our clients an across-the-board discount of 20% on orders totaling $500 or more. You mentioned interest in purchasing six retractable computer stands, which cost $300 each. The bill would come to $1,800. At 20% off, your price would be $1,440.

The desks you picked out are the most popular we carry. We have plenty in stock to fill your requirements at the present time. I can't guarantee the price if we run out and must reorder. Each time we receive a new shipment, costs seem to jump. I urge you to place your order in the next few days.

Sincerely,

8-5 Quantity discounts

The P.S. can be an effective sales letter device. Studies have shown that readers scan the P.S. before reading the body of the letter. Make your P.S. count.

Dear _____ :

At last there is a booklet to make your field trip to the Colorado State Capitol more meaningful and enjoyable and your study of Colorado history richer.

Under the Golden Dome: Colorado's State Capitol, from the series, "Discovering Historic Colorado," contains 48 pages and is full of historic photographs, some of which have never before been published.

The only history of the state capitol, the book brings together the fascinating stories of how the capitol came to be in Denver and of the diverse groups of people who made it a reality—from the gentleman architect, Elijah E. Myers, to the homesteader Henry C. Brown, who donated the land and then tried to take it back.

The lively accounts prompted former Governor Lamm to state: "This booklet is both educational and entertaining. Learn and enjoy!"

Students who study the book before touring the capitol have a greater appreciation for what they are seeing. And a personal copy makes a great souvenir of their trip for years to come.

The book retails for ____ but with orders of 25 or more, your school may purchase it at the special price of ____. Please call me at ____ to place your order.

Sincerely,

Colorado & West
Boulder, Colorado

P.S. A second book in the series, *The Tivoli: Bavaria in the Rockies*, recounts an era in Denver rich in German tradition, when streets bustled with the energy of hardworking and farsighted immigrants. Not the least of their contributions is the complex of brewery buildings known as the Tivoli. *The Tivoli* retails for ____. We can offer it to your school at ____.

8-6 Discount structure

Dear _____:

Welcome to Conrad Office Products! We are pleased to tell you your charge account has been approved and you may start using it immediately.

You will be happy to learn that you are eligible for a discount ranging from 10% to 25% on office supplies, depending on your monthly purchase volume. The appropriate discount will be automatically applied to your account balance each month. To receive the discount, you must pay off your account in full by the 10th of each month.

The discount is offered on all supplies, such as paper, ribbons, notebooks and other stationery items. Furniture purchases and service are excluded from this offer.

If you have any questions, please call and ask for me personally.

Sincerely,

8-7 New customer discounts

Dear _____:

Thank you for opening a charge account with Jones Dry Goods. Enclosed is your charge card and a certificate entitling you to a 10% discount the first time you use the card. You may buy any number of items, but please have the sale rung up at one time, so that you receive the discount on all your selections.

Through the year, we will mail you notices of special sales for charge account customers only. We hope you will enjoy these special privileges. We know you will be happy with the merchandise you purchase from Jones. We stand behind everything we sell. Should you, at any time, be dissatisfied with a purchase or the service you receive, please call me personally. Our reputation depends on satisfied customers.

Sincerely,

Advice from the sales experts

Prices are a vital component of the final sales process. However, my experience has proven that the initial purchase price has a smaller role than the value I can help the purchaser attach to the item.

When I am proposing to clients that they purchase $10,000 worth of software, I place all the benefits before them, taking great pain long before I mention the price, to help them envision the time and cost savings this purchase represents. By the time the actual dollar figure is raised, their reaction is often one of relief rather than distress. They are impressed that such an incredible program even exists. The price tag becomes secondary. The important fact is they can purchase the software immediately. They do not have to wait years while it is developed.

We offer a "subsequent purchases discount system" at our company. Once clients purchase a system, allowing us to recover our costs, we discount their additional purchases. This approach lets them know we appreciate their investment in our company and value their continued business.

Downplaying the "grand total" allows our clients and our sales people to focus on the real issue: the quality of the product, not the price.

Julie Ann DeSa Lorenz
Vice-President, Marketing and Communications
On-Line Instrument Systems, Inc.
Jefferson, Georgia

Chapter Nine

Price Increases

Nobody likes price increases. Letters help soften the blow. When clients understand the reason for an increase and believe that your company has made every effort to hold prices down, your chances of retaining their loyalty go up. Your letters must convince clients that the quality and benefit of your products or services deserve the higher price tag. Always state the effective date of the increase.

9-1 Future price increases

Dear _____:

I know you're aware that our business is tied to the oil industry. Most of our upholstery fabrics are manufactured from oil byproducts, which accounts for their durability and strength. Unfortunately, when oil prices increase, so do our costs.

Despite increases in costs over the last two years, we have held the line, not wishing to raise the price we charge our clients. Unfortunately, our material costs are now 20% higher than they were two years ago. Our only choice is to adjust our prices by a like amount.

By adjusting prices, we can continue to produce the superior quality fabrics your customers expect from you.

The new pricing goes into effect with orders shipped after May 1, allowing you six weeks to purchase stock at today's prices. Please call me if you would like to increase quantities on orders already being processed. We assure you that even though prices are increasing, our products still offer you and your clients the best value in the marketplace.

Sincerely,

9-2 Future price increases

Dear _____:

Yesterday I took my Lamborghini in for an oil change. Imagine my shock to learn the price had shot up 60 percent!

Which should make you feel better when I tell you we've had to raise the prices of our "Sew Bear" kits a mere 10 percent. I'm including the new price list that will go into effect the first of the month. One comforting note—there's still time to place your next order under the old prices.

While I'm kidding about the Lamborghini (or maybe I should say dreaming), I'm serious when I say that, even with the price increase, the quality and design features of our "Sew Bear" kits make them the best value on the market.

Warmest regards,

9-3 Future price increases

Dear _____:

I am writing this note to confirm our discussion earlier this week on the forthcoming rate increase for _____ Theaters. New rates will be _____ for 60-second spots, and _____ for 30-second spots. These rates will become effective for all orders running after November 1, 19__. They will also be guaranteed for a period of six months beginning November 1.

Thank you for your cooperation. I'm looking forward to a successful year for _____ Theaters and WIOQ.

Sincerely,

Alan Caplan
WIOQ
Philadelphia, Pennsylvania

9-4 Future price increases

Dear _____:

This letter confirms our discussion in our meeting of October 5. Golden West Foods will continue to pack the label formed onion ring to meet the requirements of your system. We make this commitment in recognition of our very valuable business relationship and our desire to do our part to maintain that relationship.

As we also discussed, December 1, the price of the onion ring will be _____ per case, or _____ per pound, F.O.B. Waynesboro, Va. Freight will be _____ per case from Waynesboro to Landover, for a delivered price of _____ per case.

Also, the film will arrive at our Bossier City Plant around mid-October. Production will take place the week of October 28. In order for you to buy product before the price increase goes into effect, let us know how much you want, and we will make sure you get it.

I believe Golden West can continue to provide _____ with the value to which you are accustomed. If at any time you have concerns regarding the quality of the product or service you are getting, please call. We look forward to a continuing, mutually beneficial business relationship.

Sincerely,

Rick Mende
Golden West Foods, Inc.
Bedford, Virginia

9-5 Future price increases

Dear _____:

Here is the new price list for bathroom cabinets. Please note that all the listed cabinets have plate glass mirrors and electrical fixtures that wire into an outlet box. The prices become effective June 5.

Oak-framed and solid pine-framed cabinets: $49.95
Sliding door, 2 adjustable interior shelves: $69.95
Sliding door, 2 adjustable interior shelves, one fixed shelf: $79.95
Sliding door, 2 fixed shelves: $99.95
Swing door, 3 interior adjustable shelves: $29.95

Dark-pine-framed cabinets: Add 20% to price.

Frameless mirrored, interior adjustable shelves: $59.95

I believe you will agree that the durability and craftsmanship of our cabinets still make them a good bargain, even at these slightly increased prices.

Sincerely,

9-6 Immediate price increases

These letters should indicate pressing issues which require raising prices with little or no advance notice. Assure clients that quality, popularity, reliability and other characteristics will keep the product strong in the marketplace despite the increase.

Dear _____:

As you know, the Southwest has been experiencing drought conditions for four years. As a result, costs of some natural materials used in our products have increased dramatically.

We all hope the rains come soon to alleviate this condition. Until that happens, we must adjust published prices on our spring line by 10%. When you place an order, you will receive a confirmation showing the correct price.

Our products remain popular because of the natural fibers and leathers we use. The slight increase shouldn't dampen the public's enthusiasm for them.

I look forward to seeing you on my swing through Santa Fe in September.

Sincerely,

9-7 Immediate price increases

Dear _____:

You'll be happy to hear that back orders on the popular line of ART-CRAFT polyurethane lacquer bedroom and dining room furniture are now filled. New orders can be shipped immediately.

At the same time, I must tell you that, effective the first of this month, pricing on the line will increase 6%. As you know, costs on this line are tied to energy costs. We didn't raise prices last year; and although energy costs have slowed a little, we find we must adjust prices to be able to maintain the current level of quality.

Enclosed is a new price sheet. In spite of the slight increase, we believe strong sales will continue for the line because of the excellent design and proven durability.

Sincerely,

9-8 Immediate price increases

Dear _____:

Over the past six months, we have experienced materials and labor cost increases from our suppliers above the rates expected. This, plus an increase in operating expenses, requires us to raise prices by 5% effective immediately. New prices are contained on the enclosed sheet.

We are taking this action to assure that our customers continue receiving the highest quality products—on schedule.

In the current competitive environment, we know you will understand that we still offer outstanding quality for the price.

Sincerely,

Tips to sharpen your writing skills

Keep letters fresh with new ways of saying old things.
Examples:

Please don't hesitate to call . . .	Call our company and ask for me personally.
Feel free to call . . .	I look forward to your call.
I enjoyed meeting with you . . .	I enjoyed hearing about your business.

Chapter Ten

Cover Letters

Cover letters are more than wrappings for brochures, catalogs and other information. They reinforce the importance of the materials they accompany. They can direct the client's attention to an important feature of your product or service, one that would be of special interest to him/her. They can also lead to the next step in the selling process by telling what you plan to do: call for an appointment, stop by at some specific time, or pass your client's name on to your distributor.

10-1 For brochures, catalogs, other information

These cover letters guide readers to specific information in the literature you're enclosing. What information will interest your clients most? What items do you especially want them to notice? Point out these elements in the cover letter. Your clients will be grateful for saving their time.

> Dear Governor _____:
>
> Enclosed for your review is a description and analysis of Writing to Read by an independent educator who visited 30 schools using the Writing to Read program. This article is a succinct description of the program and can be used readily as a reference document.
> Also enclosed are some of the latest documented outcomes, which demonstrate that Writing to Read and Principles of the Alphabet Literacy System (adult version of WTR) successfully increase reading and writing skills.
> I would like to thank you for your investment of time to review the Writing to Read program and to meet with ____. I am convinced that your investment and continued interest will reap dividends for the ____ educational system in the near future.
>
> Sincerely,
>
> IBM Corporation
> Denver, Colorado

10-2 For brochures, catalogs, other information

> Dear _____:
>
> Enclosed is the brochure on the sample that you will receive from us tomorrow. Note the detail work on the front of the bags. The photos give you a general idea of the look. The fabric is so exquisite, however, that pictures don't do it justice.
> We will know by Monday if any colors other than black are available. I'll call you then so we can enter your order in time for the fashion mart show.
>
> Sincerely,

10-3 For brochures, catalogs, other information

Dear _____:

This month Valleylab is celebrating National Quality Month. To promote Quality Month, a special edition of our company newspaper was published. ____, of the Valleylab Surgical Products Division, submitted an article which announced Valleylab's ranking in your recent Vendor Evaluation.

Attached is a copy of the article. I think you will agree it highlights Valleylab's commitment to work with _____and provide our mutual customers with the highest quality products.

Best regards,

Valleylab, Inc.
Boulder, Colorado

10-4 For brochures, catalogs, other information

Dear _____:

This year's line of soft-sided luggage features bright, bold designs, to make it easier for passengers to identify their bags at airline carrousels. Bags are individually painted, and no two designs are alike. A special coating protects the art work through years of use.

Enclosed is a catalog showing styles available. I'll bring along samples so you can see the gorgeous new look of this line.

Sincerely,

10-5 For brochures, catalogs, other information

Dear _____:

Enclosed is some information on both the Sarns 9000 and the Sarns Touch and Record Information System. I hope it will help you choose the options that you would like to have.

The S.T.A.R. system is the only stand-alone information system available that has a "touch screen" for use during a case and provides a work station for use both before and after a case using the keyboard.

The 9000 system is the only perfusion system with a "touch screen" and built-in flow meter, blender, and automatic battery backup.

I enjoyed talking with you on the telephone today, and I'll keep my ears open for perfusion positions here in Michigan.

Sincerely,

Kip A. Stastny
Sarns 3M Health Care
Ann Arbor, Michigan

10-6 For brochures, catalogs, other information

Dear _____:

Thank you for stopping by our booth at the Mexico Hospital Expo '90 in Mexico City last month.

As promised, here is the information on positive pressure ventilation, along with relevant articles and application procedures. I hope this is adequate information for you. If I can be of further help, please call me.

At the present time, we do not have a distributor in Mexico, but we are actively seeking a company to represent us. If you have any recommendations for a company that has expertise in respiratory medicine and has a strong reputation for excellent after-sales service, I would be interested in hearing from you.

Again, thank you for your interest in LIFECARE and our products.

Sincerely,

LIFECARE
Lafayette, Colorado

10-7 For brochures, catalogs, other information

Dear _____:

Enclosed is literature on some of our products. I will have the area representative contact you as well. I enjoyed talking with you and look forward to helping you organize your new heart program.

Sincerely,

Kip A. Stastny
Sarns 3M Health Care
Ann Arbor, Michigan

10-8 For specifications

Good Morning Nancy and Terry,

The manufacturer for your sample order has requested a drawing and specific instructions. I thought it wise to fax this to you to be certain that we are in agreement as to your specifications.

If this is correct, let me know ASAP, as they are awaiting a fax from us. They have guaranteed shipping within two weeks.

Have a great day!

Jackie Northrop
China Coast
Boulder, Colorado

10-9 For samples

These letters draw attention to particular characteristics of the samples. They also explain your reasons for sending the samples.

Dear _____ :

Enclosed is the pink Karung that seems to be the correct color for you. We can get just enough to fill your order. Please let me know if it is acceptable to you.

At the moment we are having more difficulty acquiring the correct color and quantity of top-grain cowhide. The color on the cowhide can be changed slightly, but the color must go from light to dark, and this seems to be a problem. If the pink cowhide turns up by tomorrow, I will let you know.

Best regards,

Susan S. Colpitt
China Coast
Boulder, Colorado

10-10 For samples

Dear _____:

We have just received the leather swatches for your belts:

#1602 Buckingham—Navy
#3621 Kent—White
#1603 Windsor—Ivory
#1619 Merton—Camel

I'll call Monday to see if these samples meet your approval. We will need to know if you like the matte finish or if you will require a higher sheen finish for the leather.

Susan S. Colpitt
China Coast
Boulder, Colorado

10-11 For samples

Dear _____:

Enclosed are three walnut chips showing the shading we can get on the table tops. Notice that the lightest chip shows more of the grain, which makes a busier looking finish. The darkest shade is also the smoothest, and I believe might be the best. Let me know what you think.

Regards,

10-12 For samples

Dear _____:

Enclosed are three belts and two extra buckles. As we discussed, we can manufacture buckles to your specification. This would offer you exclusivity but would probably be more expensive, depending on the quantity ordered. Mold charges per buckle range from ____ to ____, and this cost must be spread out over the number of buckles ordered.

I am enclosing a fourth belt with a beaded buckle. I've located the factory in China that does the beading. They also do evening bags to match. My Taiwan manufacturer can do a better job on the other material. The prices that we quoted on the No. 10 and 20 belts are on a Net 30 basis (with credit references), delivered to your distribution center. If you wish to do business on a Letter of Credit basis, we can offer an additional discount.

China Coast has its own office and staff in Hong Kong with quality control inspectors in Korea, Taiwan, China and the Philippines. We will enjoy working with you.

Sincerely,

Susan S. Colpitt
China Coast
Boulder, Colorado

10-13 For samples

Dear _____:

Enclosed are some yarn samples. If any should inspire your designers, I can request enough for samples. Of course, there are thousands of other yarns available. This is just a small sampling. I have requested a hank of the silk tape for you, too. It should arrive by next week.

Best regards,

Susan S. Colpitt
China Coast
Boulder, Colorado

10-14 For requested information

Dear _____:

Enclosed is the information you requested. You'll see that it contains all the measurements, including depth, on the chairs you're interested in. I believe these chairs would fit nicely into your waiting room, providing ample seating without giving the room a crowded appearance. Please phone with your verdict.

Sincerely,

10-15 For requested information

Dear _____:

Enclosed is the information you requested on the Bard Infus OR.

Product No.	Description	Price
6461500	Infus OR Pump	$_____

(Additional products listed)

Special Offer

Until November 15, _____, we are offering a three-year extended warranty and two additional smart labels at no charge in exchange for a three-year commitment to buy anesthesia sets. This is a value of _____ if purchased separately.

Rental

Pump—month-to-month—no equity $_____
Label—month-to-month—no equity $_____

Lease

Purchase Labels Separately
12 month $_____
24 month $_____
36 month $_____

No Cap Program

Bio-Medical Resources will provide to the hospital three Bard Infus OR at *NO CHARGE.*

Hospital agrees to purchase _____ anesthesia sets per month for _____ at $_____ each.

Pumps have three-year extended warranty and ownership by the hospital. Three labels per pump provided at no charge.

The last alternative may have real appeal by allowing the hospital to acquire pumps with no capital investment. If this alternative is of interest, let's pin down the actual predicted usage, which could reduce the anesthesia cost. Please discuss with me.

If you have any questions, call toll free at _____.

Sincerely,

Denny C. Dickinson
Bio-Medical Resources, Inc.
Broomfield, Colorado

10-16 For video or promotional material

Dear _____:

There's a lot of quality and heritage that goes into every Wrangler jean and shirt. I'm sure you, as a valued PRCA dealer, know that. For nearly a century we have been committed to producing the best-fitting, best-looking and longest-wearing authentic western apparel in the industry. That's still our commitment.

The enclosed video will prove valuable in communicating the quality and heritage of our core western products to your sales staff. Fabric, fit, construction and authenticity—all these features are pointed out in the video. Whether reinforcing Wrangler features to your seasoned sales professionals or training new sales personnel, this video will be of great value!

It's a fact that sales people who know about a product are more motivated, enthusiastic and productive. Now, as the holiday rush begins, is a perfect time to conduct a seminar with your sales staff, using the video to help educate and motivate your personnel.

Thank you again for your support. All of us at Wrangler extend our best wishes for a healthy, happy and prosperous holiday season and New Year.

Sincerely,

Brian Goldberg
Wrangler
Greensboro, North Carolina

10-17 For video or other promotional material

Dear Travel Agent:

The enclosed video gives only a glimpse of Montana's breath-taking scenery—from sun-swept plains of wheat to spectacular mountain peaks. It also shows the splendid accommodations and services your clients can enjoy at Alpine Meadows this summer. Everything from golf and tennis to horseback riding and river rafting is waiting for them. Take a minute to view the tape. You'll be refreshed just watching.

Sincerely,

P.S. Please return the video in the prepaid container within two weeks.

10-18 For price list

Dear _____:

    When I stopped by your store last month, you mentioned how receptive your customers were to the fiberglass tubs.
    You'll be happy to hear that we now have a fiberglass tub available in the Mermaid model. I'm enclosing a brochure and price list. I'll call you soon to see if you'd like one for your showroom.

Sincerely,

10-19 For proposals

Cover letters for proposals offer the opportunity to direct your client's attention to important items in the proposal. Is there a deadline? Say so. Is the proposal divided into sections? Say so. Is your product exceptionally outstanding in some respect? Remind your client of that fact.

Dear _____:

    Thank you for the opportunity of allowing Ogden Allied Aviation Services to submit this proposal to perform aviation services for _____ at Los Angeles International Airport. We believe that _____ can benefit substantially by taking full advantage of Ogden Allied's unique capability to provide a total airport services product.
    Enclosed is a detailed proposal encompassing all of the requirements for a management staff and Ramp Services. Our program is designed to offer our customers quality services in a professional and cost-efficient manner. This proposal is separated into sections which outline our overall qualifications and our service and pricing package for Los Angeles. We trust that the information submitted is sufficient for your review and will convince you that Ogden Allied can furnish _____ with excellent service at competitive prices.
    Ogden Allied is prepared to utilize all of our sizable resources to ensure that your Ramp Services operation at Los Angeles is second to none. The Ogden Allied corporate strength and commitment promised to _____ is built on a strong management team of experienced, successful airline services personnel who have an established record in all the proposed functions; a training and qual-

ity control program that has consistently provided dependable professionals; a strong financial foundation which provides Ogden Allied with the capability to support any and all service requirements for these functions; and last, a corporate dedication to the attainment of a superior level of performance that separates Ogden Allied, and our clients, from other competitive organizations.

All of this will come together to maintain the value, image and marketability of _____ at Los Angeles. This, combined with the information offered in our proposal, we hope will clearly demonstrate to you that Ogden Allied would be a great service partner for your Ramp Services operation at Los Angeles International Airport.

Sincerely,

Robert L. Warner
Ogden Allied Aviation Services
Los Angeles, California

10-20 For proposals

Dear _____:

Enclosed is a 3390 DASD proposal to replace the existing 3380 Js and Ks on ICC leases. Upgrading to the new DASD technology is not only financially attractive, but will also provide improvements in performance. There are migration considerations which are currently being discussed and planned for with you and members of your staff.

The ICC rates quoted for the 3390 DASD and the termination charge are firm through June 20, _____. Some of the other figures are estimates and may vary slightly at time of installation. The analysis is valid assuming installation of the 3390 DASD occurs by July 1, _____.

Please let me know if you have any additional questions.

Sincerely,

IBM Corporation
Denver, Colorado

10-21 For proposals

Dear _____:

Valleylab, Inc. respectfully submits the following proposal for the CUSA* System 200 Ultrasonic Surgical Aspirator.

Since its introduction in 1978, the CUSA has maintained the standard for excellence in ultrasonic surgery. Today, the System 200 is the most advanced ultrasonic surgical aspirator available.

We hope the information provided in this proposal will help you select the best ultrasonic system for your hospital's needs—the CUSA System 200 from Valleylab.

Sincerely,

Valleylab, Inc.
Boulder, Colorado
*CUSA is a registered trademark of Valleylab, Inc.

10-22 For proposals

Dear _____:

Thank you for the opportunity to present the special capabilities and services of Initial Stitch computerized embroidery.

For your convenience, the USOC logo on the enclosed paper tape is now on disk file in our facility and ready for your use.

Also enclosed please find our contract sewing charges for the United States Olympic Committee logo.

I look forward to hearing from you and am grateful for the opportunity to serve your embroidery needs efficiently and with exquisite quality.

Sincerely,

Marilyn Kay Reichenberg
Initial Stitch, Inc.
Boulder, Colorado

10-23 For unsolicited proposals

Dear _____:

We appreciate your allowing Ogden Allied Aviation Services to submit an unsolicited proposal to perform Passenger Services for _____ at Los Angeles International Airport. As discussed, Ogden Allied is vitally interested in entering the passenger service area and is submitting proposals to a selected number of airlines, preferring to propose an excellent concept to an excellent air carrier.

We have developed a program for _____ that is designed to emphasize training, quality of selection of employees, recurrent training and management.

We have included information not specifically germane to the passenger service proposal, such as total organization charts, to give you an overall view of Ogden Allied and the Western Division and, more specifically, the Southwest Region for which I am responsible.

Throughout this proposal we have attempted to relate to you, as honestly as possible, our plans and commitments. We have a reputation of providing what we commit to. Your consideration of this proposal is greatly appreciated.

Sincerely,

Robert L. Warner
Ogden Allied Aviation Services
Los Angeles, California

10-24 For training materials

Dear _____:

Enclosed is a copy of the Sarns 3M Sales Trainer Guide. It will give you an idea of the curriculum that we follow when training a new sales representative.

If you have any questions, please call me.

Kip A. Stastny
Sarns 3M Health Care
Ann Arbor, Michigan

Tips to sharpen your writing skills

Eliminate duplicate nouns:

instead of	*choose*
the level of wages rose	the wages rose
the volume of demand	the demand
the area of retraining	the retraining
the amount of material	the material
the process of retooling	the retooling
the issue of inflation	the inflation

Chapter Eleven

Proposals

Proposals put your company on the front line of the sales battle. Take your best shot. Proposal letters—whether they ask permission to submit a formal proposal or actually present the proposal information—aim for the sale by supplying prospects with persuasive information about your products and services.

Proposal letters often contain lengthy descriptions and supporting data. Keep the reader's attention through a variety of techniques:

- Point out benefits quickly.
- Be sure details are important to prospect.
- Use unexpected or colorful words and phrases.
- Eliminate all unnecessary statements.
- Present material in interesting format.
- Divide long proposals into sections.

11-1 Ask to submit proposals

Dear _____:

As fall colors set the countryside ablaze, I'm reminded that it's the time your company traditionally places purchase orders for the coming year.

We would very much like to bid on your requirements for seals, gaskets, and weatherstrips. The enclosed brochure describes our entire line. Our quality is first-rate, and we can compete on cost with any other supplier.

I'll call you in a few days to discuss quantities so we may provide an accurate bid on your requirements.

Sincerely,

11-2 Ask to submit proposals

Dear _____:

I appreciate your meeting with me and allowing me to introduce Marketing Communications. We would welcome the opportunity to bid on an upcoming project or campaign. I believe we can fit into your present program best in the areas of ads, technical writing and completing public relations activities.

If you change your philosophy about using a number of agencies simultaneously instead of one, we could offer you the following:

1. Economy, a great savings in the number of dollars spent.
2. Well-coordinated efforts which increase the impact of your advertising and public relations dollars, eliminate duplicate efforts and anticipate and recommend new approaches.
3. Innovation, creativity and expertise, using Denver's leading talent for each specific project.
4. Savings in time and effort expended by personnel.
5. Immediate responsiveness to needs.

I believe we have the right "fit" in technical writing, health care industry knowledge, and creative talent.

We will continue to check with you about projects. Again, it was a pleasure meeting you, and we look forward to working with you in the future.

Sincerely,

Sandra E. Lamb
Marketing Communications
Denver, Colorado

11-3 Ask to submit proposals

Dear _____:

I enjoyed meeting with you last week and learning about the new medical center you are constructing.

I have discussed the project with my partners, and I'm pleased to say we all agree this is "our kind of project." As I mentioned at our meeting, we are interested in submitting a formal proposal. To do this, we will need a copy of your architectural drawings. I will call you next week to arrange to pick them up.

I believe that, together, we will be able to create the kind of interior environment you will enjoy working in for many years to come.

Sincerely,

Marc Interiors
Boulder, Colorado

11-4 State proposal

Dear _____:

It was a pleasure seeing you recently in San Diego. We appreciate the opportunity to quote on your Skycap service needs.

Ogden Allied provides a consolidated Skycap service for several airlines at San Diego, with approximately _____ Skycaps working the curb for this consolidation. Our rates are _____ straight time and _____ overtime and holidays (six), which are New Year's, Memorial Day, Fourth of July, Labor Day, Thanksgiving and Christmas. As you know, in this consolidation, the hourly rates are used to develop a unit cost; and each airline pays based on its passenger volumes.

As we discussed, Ogden Allied does not favor a dedicated Skycap service to _____ intermingling with the current consolidation, because the integrity of the service level to all carriers, including your own, could be jeopardized. We believe that it would be in your best interests to join the consolidation. It would be necessary to increase the weekly hours by _____. Your airline would have access to Skycaps across the facility, which would enhance the service level tremendously to your passengers.

If you are interested in joining this consolidation, Ogden Allied would consider it an honor to provide this service to you.

Sincerely,

Robert L. Warner
Ogden Allied Aviation Services
Los Angeles, California

11-5 State proposal

Dear _____:

We are pleased to submit this proposal to provide Janitorial Services for your Administrative Offices, VIP Lounge and Operational facilities at the Tom Bradley International Terminal at Los Angeles International Airport.

We will provide all labor, supervision, equipment and materials required for the performance of the service in accordance with the enclosed janitorial specifications provided by you.

The employees assigned to your facility will be attired in a distinctive and stylish uniform to insure that they represent _____ in the most positive manner.

The cost for this service will be a flat fee of _____ per month, guaranteed for one year. This price does not include restroom supplies, nor does it include additional airport taxes or business fees that may be assessed in the future.

If you have any questions regarding our staffing, wages and benefits, we would be most happy to discuss them at your convenience.

We appreciate the opportunity to submit this proposal for your consideration. Should you accept our proposal, we will prepare an agreement for your signature.

Sincerely,

Robert L. Warner
Ogden Allied Aviation Services
Los Angeles, California

11-6 State proposal

Dear _____:

Thank you for your continued confidence in Valleylab electro-surgical systems and for this opportunity to submit the following quotation for a Force 4 Electrosurgical System. As we have discussed, this quotation will reflect_____discount as well as a trade-in allowance for your hospital's oldest Valleylab unit, model SSE2K.

As requested, I am furnishing quotations for direct purchase, installment purchase and accessory purchase programs that would allow the hospital to receive the new equipment without spending capital equipment funds. Instead, the equipment would be paid for through the cost of Valleylab accessories purchased under the plan.

Option 1: Direct Purchase
Option 2: Installment Purchase

(Details for Options 1 and 2)

Option 3: Accessory Purchase

Valleylab would agree to provide the equipment quoted above, with the stated trade-in included. Payment for the equipment would be through the purchase of the Valleylab E7506 and E7507 PolyHesive Patient Return Electrodes, which are currently used. This allows the hospital to acquire the equipment without spending valuable capital equipment funds, since the equipment payments would be included in the cost of the accessories.

Current average usage of E7507 and E7506 at your hospital is _____ per month. Since it is not in the hospital or Valleylab's best interest to overstock your hospital on these products, I have computed a three-year Accessory Purchase Plan based upon the purchase of _____. Therefore, a total of _____ cases would complete the hospital's obligation to this agreement.

(Additional pricing details.)

The Accessory Purchase Agreement requires that an annual standing order be placed for one case of _____ and one case of _____ each month. If the hospital requires additional product during any month, extra product may be ordered. It will be billed at the same price as that of the Accessory Purchase Agreement. If extra orders are placed, then the hospital will meet its case obligation sooner, and the contract will end before the actual due date.

For your review, I have enclosed an Accessory Purchase Plan Prospectus which summarizes the features and prices of this program.

If you have any questions regarding this quotation, or if I may ever be of service to you in the critical areas of electrosurgical equipment, accessories or service, please call me.

Sincerely

Valleylab, Inc.
Boulder, Colorado

11-7 State proposal

Dear _____:

Ogden Allied Aviation Services is pleased to submit this proposal to continue providing Passenger Screening Services at John Wayne Airport.

We have taken the liberty to incorporate the provisions outlined by _____ and have located those prerequisites in Section IV of our proposal.

Ogden Allied has provided Preboard Screening Services at John Wayne Airport since May 1986. During this time, providing high-quality Preboard Screening has proven to be a unique challenge for the carriers serving the airport and for Ogden Allied. Orange County has for years experienced one of the lowest unemployment rates in the country. It is presently at 2.9%, which has resulted in an employee turnover rate in 1989 of 267%, or an average of twelve employees per month.

In spite of this situation, it is our belief that a more than satisfactory service has been maintained. During 1989, 47 of 48 (97.9%) FAA tests have been passed, and there have been few incidents of unsatisfactory passenger service.

This performance has resulted from a strategy developed and implemented cooperatively by the participating airlines and Ogden Allied, in which the emphasis has been placed on developing and maintaining an effective CSS work group. While the PBS employee has been paid _____ per hour, the CSS group has been paid _____ per hour and has been provided with a health insurance program. This has created a situation in which the CSS work force feels to be a participating member of supervision and management.

In order to continue the effectiveness of this program, further improvements must be made in 19__. The present wage rates at Los Angeles International Airport are ____ per hour for PBS and ____ for the CSS group.

The planned wages in this proposal for John Wayne Airport are ____ for PBS agents, ____ for the CSS group, plus the CSS health insurance program which adds ____ to the CSS rate.

In addition, the per-hour rate we offer for the CSSs and the Preboard Screeners includes a newly implemented Corporate profit-sharing plan, as well as the basics of uniforms and maintenance, parking, vacation and holidays.

The expected growth in the size of the function would normally require additional supervision. We believe the quality of the CSS program negates this need, and the only addition to our planned staffing would be a clerical position necessary to support a workforce of more than ____ people.

We are aware that our proposal will not be the least costly, but we sincerely believe that it will be the most cost effective in the long run. Improved wages and benefits will result in a more stable and effective workforce. That will result in a continued high quality security and passenger service.

Thank you for the opportunity to provide this proposal to continue serving you at John Wayne Airport.

Sincerely,

Robert L. Warner
Ogden Allied Aviation Services
Los Angeles, California

11-8 State rent-to-buy proposal

Dear _____:

We have been offered several near-new AVI Model 200A Infusion Pumps. Since you are presently renting pumps, I thought these pumps might interest you. We propose renting them to you at a rate of ____ per month, for a period of two years, at which time ownership would pass to the hospital.

These pumps are less than a year old and have been used only sparingly. If this proposal sounds like something in which you may be interested, please let me know by Monday, January 29. The supply is limited, and pumps are available only on a first-come, first-served basis.

Should you have any questions or require further information, please contact me at any time.

Sincerely,

Raymond G. Palandri
Bio-Medical Resources, Inc.
Broomfield, Colorado

11-9 Decline to submit proposal

When you can't furnish a proposal, a letter serves as a good public relations gesture to keep you in the prospect's mind for future needs.

Dear _____:

It was good seeing you again yesterday after a two-year absence, and I look forward to working with you on various plant engineering projects as they arise at _____.

I have reviewed your specification relative to the centralized spray mist system you're currently considering, and what our principal, LSP Industries, can do for you. Hans, this really isn't the type of thing that LSP does. They're primarily involved in the manufacture of the spray mist equipment itself (what you refer to as your "Bijurs"), and not the design of hydraulic systems. I will therefore submit a No Bid for this project.

Thank you for the opportunity to quote. Should you have any questions or require additional information, please advise.

Forrest D. Venz
Engineered Products Service Company
Tustin, California

11-10 Follow up when your proposal has been rejected

Dear _____:

I've been watching for some signs of _____'s new ad and P.R. campaigns since our meetings several months ago and have not seen anything except a couple of mentions of _____ people in the press. Has there been a change in plans, timing or direction? I still believe that the prime window in the marketplace is now, and this is passing quickly.

If there have been changes in your ad and P.R. plans, I would again suggest that _____ consider working with Marketing Communications to achieve a consistent, high-profile public relations program; or work with us on a per-project or total-services basis. I believe together we can arrive at a very effective and economical approach —quickly.

I'll call your office next week to see if any further discussion is in order. Or, please call me sooner, if you like.

My husband and I are working with _____ as we discussed. It's a very educational and beneficial experience.

Sincerely,

Sandra E. Lamb
Marketing Communications
Denver, Colorado

Advice from the sales experts

I take a respectful attitude when asking for the order. I always presume clients want to purchase from me. Rather than asking, "When will you place your order?," I verify that all questions and objections have been answered to their satisfaction and then simply ask if I should send the quotation. Any hesitation from them means they will get an "informal quotation" from me. An informal quote is written on high quality white paper and uses the words "informal,""proposal"and"nonbinding."

Assured that I am in no hurry for the order, these more cautious purchasers often respond with a telephone call asking for the "formal quotation, because purchasing requires it."

Julie Ann DeSa Lorenz
Vice-President Marketing and Communications.
On-Line Instrument Systems, Inc.
Jefferson, Georgia

Chapter Twelve

Orders

Four words taped to a sales rep's mirror or car dash? "Ask for the order." Although other letters may include such a request, those in this chapter are written specifically for that purpose.

12-1 Ask for the order

Dear _____:

I've reviewed the production times for the belts that you're considering. Since we've eliminated all leathers not currently in stock in Taiwan, the belts can all be finished in the time we discussed.

We need verbal orders from you by Monday, March 27, so that we can start ordering the raw materials. We then need color swatches and size breakdowns by Monday, April 3. This time schedule should allow us to get color samples to you for approval and, later, a finished sample (before we start production). On this schedule, we can have the belts in your warehouse by June 15.

Sincerely,

Susan S. Colpitt
China Coast
Boulder, Colorado

12-2 Ask for the order

Dear _____:

I trust you've had time to decide on the diskettes for your Wall Street location.

As we've discussed, reliability is your No. 1 priority. The literature I sent should help convince you that our diskettes provide absolute reliability.

Our inventory control people tell me we have 5,000 in stock for immediate shipment. If you'll send your P.O. today, you can have them in your office by next week.

Best regards,

12-3 Ask for the order

Dear _____:

When I visited in March, you said you'd be putting orders out for air filters by May 15.

Can I count on you for the thousand A34-476 models we discussed? Please send the order to my attention, and I'll see that it gets top priority.

Sincerely,

12-4 Ask for the order

Dear _____:

Have you decided on the basketball uniforms for next season? The design you selected should set your team apart on any court.

I'd like to have your order by the 15th of this month, so we can vend out the monogramming and have the patches in our hands before it's time to sew the garments together.

Call me if there's a snag. Otherwise, I'll expect your order in the mail.

Here's hoping the Lady Panthers take state again this year.

Sincerely,

12-5 Ask for the order

Dear _____:

Enclosed is the melon suede color swatch for sofa 3355. Please phone me with your reaction tomorrow. We are really in a time crunch on these sofas.

To meet your deadline, I must put in the order by Friday at the latest.

The leather for style 3375 is in stock and does not need to be redyed, so it will be exactly the same as your sample.

Sincerely,

12-6 Ask for the order

Dear _____:

I'm sending you the lightweight silk sweater I told you about, along with the price list.

We use only the finest silk yarns in these sweaters. This accounts for the vivid coloring, sheen, and soft texture. These sweaters are wonderfully comfortable! What's more, even though they have a delicate look, they are very durable.

The designs are classic, not faddish. The style will last as long as the fabric. The cost runs somewhat higher than that of other silk sweaters, but the quality can't be beat.

I'll call you next week for your order.

Sincerely,

12-7 Ask client to sign and return contract

Letters asking clients to sign and return a contract must give specific instructions, leaving no doubt as to what the clients must do to receive the orders on time.

Dear _____:

Thank you for selecting the Clarion Harvest House Hotel to host your event.

Enclosed are two copies of the Engagement Contract. Please read through this information carefully to insure that all arrangements we have discussed have been confirmed. Mark any changes in red ink, sign one copy and return it to me in the envelope provided. The second copy is for your files.

If regular mail time will not allow me to receive your signed copy three days before your function, please call me directly with any changes.

I'm looking forward to working with you. I am confident you will enjoy every aspect of our hotel!

Sincerely,

Kerri Ginsberg
Clarion Harvest House
Boulder, Colorado

12-8 Ask client to sign and return contract

Dear _____:

I know you'll be pleased with the baseball caps you picked out this year. The bright red color and snappy lettering should be a hit with your boosters.

As you can see, the enclosed contract contains all the specifications we discussed. Please sign and return the contract and we will start imprinting "Go Knights" immediately.

Thanks for teaming with Graphic Gear.

12-9 Ask for additional order

With order in hand, you're ready to move on to the second deal. These letters let clients know why they will benefit from placing an additional order immediately.

Dear _____:

Thought you might like to know that the gold-tipped frame, #5422, is selling out in frame shops across the metro area. Seems one of these frames was featured in a *Lifestyles* photo spread. After the current run, the factory isn't scheduled to produce this frame again until September.

Would you like to place an additional order to be sure you don't run out? I'll give you a call next week.

Sincerely,

12-10 Ask for additional order

Dear _____:

That promotion you ran on ceiling fans sure paid off. When I stopped by the store, I learned you had sold all but two. Can you use another dozen? I've set them aside for you, but I'll need an order by Tuesday to hold them beyond that date.

Best wishes,

12-11 Ask for additional order

Dear _____:

I was pleased to hear how much your client liked the silver-and-gold frames we supplied.

You mentioned you would like to carry additional models but were concerned about the quality of the hinges on two samples I showed you. I am sending two new models so that you can examine the hinges closely. Keep in mind that these samples are made of very inexpensive material and have no felt backing. The frames you will receive, of course, will be sterling silver.

Sincerely,

12-12 Ask for additional order

Dear _____:

To confirm our conversation of the yearly promotion for _____: Our rate will be _____ for 60-second spots and that rate will be guaranteed for the full year. We will be running a total of 100 60-second spots per month between the hours of 6 a.m. and midnight. The schedule will begin sometime in March.

Now to move on to what I believe is one of the most exciting promotional concepts to come out of this radio station. I have already received the approval of our program director to put together a full one-year sponsorship for _____ of one of our most popular features: "The Album for Lunch." This program, in which a classic album is played in its entirety, airs weekdays at noon and has broad appeal. In order to tie this feature in with a weekly traffic-building program, we would like to give away the featured album each day, Monday through Friday. The host for the program would call a designated person at your store, who would then pull a winner's name from one of the ballot boxes located in each _____ department of all _____ stores. The winner will be announced at the end of the first side of the featured album. This means we would give away a total of 260 featured albums a year.

The sponsorship would work as follows: _____ would, in addition to the 100 spots per month, purchase one spot per day in the "Album for Lunch" at a rate of _____. This would increase the monthly budget to approximately _____. For the additional $___ a month, _____ would receive a total of five promotional announcements a day, Monday through Friday, as a sponsor of "Album for Lunch." In addition, _____ would receive an opening and closing billboard each day.

In addition, we would work out an arrangement to put very attractive signs in all the stores promoting your sponsorship and involvement with "Album for Lunch."

We have never done an ongoing promotion of this magnitude. I believe it will generate a tremendous amount of attention and excitement for _____.

I am looking forward to getting your feedback on this concept, and am hoping that WIOQ and _____ can bring together their mutual energies to establish a very strong relationship in the coming years.

Sincerely,

Alan Caplan
WIOQ
Philadelphia, Pennsylvania

12-14 Ask for additional order

Dear _____:

I am sending two frames to you so that you can examine the hinges closely. Keep in mind that these samples are made of very inexpensive material and have no felt backing. Your orders, of course, will be of superior quality.

We have already placed your sample order. However, we could change it if you decide on another style in the next few days. Please contact me soon if there will be any change. The prices would be the same, and the quotes should be in our office tomorrow. I will fax them to you when they arrive.

Sincerely,

Advice from the sales experts

Think before you write. This is deceptively simple. It is also the prime reason behind successful letters. So what should we think about before we write or dictate?

To whom am I writing?

No matter what you want to accomplish, the content of your letter should be tailor-made to the person receiving it. An established client requires different facts from those you would write to a prospective client.

What action do I want this letter to trigger?

Direct your letter toward the purpose of achieving a desired course of action. This could be anything from a luncheon appointment to a multi-million dollar purchase order.

How can I best ask for the order?

Plan the best way to make it easy for clients to take the action that you want to happen. Ask yourself: How can I make it easy for them to say yes? How will they benefit? What can I offer that is better, faster, more cost-saving than the competition offers?

Do I need to follow up?

Decide in advance if your letter requires follow up. If so, establish who, when and how as you write it, and follow through accordingly.

Walter L. Bond
Former Executive Vice-President
Tupperware International
Kissimmee, Florida

Chapter Thirteen

Order Follow-Ups

Congratulations! You landed the sale. You'll want to thank the client, confirm the order, explain changes, and handle other details with follow-up letters. Clients need reassurance they have spent their money wisely. Regardless of the specific reason for writing, assure them they have made the right choice. These letters cement the relationship.

13-1 Welcome new client

Letters welcoming new clients allow you to reaffirm the benefits of your product or service. They also assure clients you are committed to the new relationship.

Dear _____:

    Congratulations and welcome to the elite clique of OLIS clients! We sincerely hope your first days with your newly modernized Cary 17 Spectrophotometer have been fruitful and enjoyable.

    As I am certain Dr. DeSa impressed upon you and your colleagues during his installation visit, your OLIS Spectrophotometry System should perform without problems for a very, very long time, making the need for service of any nature highly improbable. However, at any point at which you have concerns about the software or computer's operation, you should notify us right away, and we will do whatever is necessary to get the system back to 100% integrity.

    Also, while our manuals could be better, they do include all the information which you will need to find and correctly use features of the OLIS Operating System. If you notice inconsistencies or if you have suggestions for improvements, please let me know. Suggestions for manual (and software) betterment are always enthusiastically solicited!

    I have prepared the entry for your installation, which I would like to include in our OLIS booklet. As you know, we rely a great deal on word-of-mouth advertising, and this list serves as a "silent messenger." Please look over this entry and make any suitable corrections; if no changes are necessary, you need not return anything to me. However, if you do have a moment to answer my two queries, I would appreciate your doing so and returning the page to me in the enclosed envelope at your earliest convenience.

    Of course, any verbal or written mention you could make of OLIS to your colleagues will be enormously appreciated! A satisfied user speaks far more elegantly for a product than the glossiest print advertisement can. Many of our clients first learn of us from colleagues.

    We try to keep track of the applications for our systems, and we appreciate your keeping us informed of any published articles referencing the system. If you could send me reprints, this would be ideal.

    Our sincerest welcome to you as you join our select group of satisfied users! Please contact us any time for assistance, and please assure all other users of your OLIS System that they can contact us with any big or small questions about the hardware or software.

Sincerely,

Julie Ann DeSa Lorenz
On-Line Instrument Systems, Inc.
Jefferson, Georgia

P.S. We look forward to the timely payment for this job. Your copy of the invoice is enclosed for your records. Any encouragement you could give Accounts Payable will be sincerely appreciated. All funds over our expenses for your job will be used for our never-ending research and development—your next system is guaranteed to be even more sophisticated and polished than your first!

13-2 Thank new client for order

Dear _____:

You should have no problem whatsoever justifying the buy on "Q," as even God is a heavy listener, especially during morning drive!

Sincerely,

Alan Caplan
WIOQ
Philadelphia, Pennsylvania

13-3 Thank new client for order

Dear _____:

The business relationship that ____ and Amdahl share is valued greatly by us at Amdahl. We recognize that ____ has been a key part, if not a leader, in this relationship. Your orders for the two Amdahl 5890 computers for Salt Lake City confirms your position. These computers will be delivered in November and December, making them the first Amdahl 5890s within ____.

We at Amdahl take tremendous pride in being part of organizations like yours and attempt to provide the industry's best service and support to retain our position. Your orders confirm your confidence in us, and we appreciate that.

Thank you for your business. We will continue to work hard to earn your confidence and make your Amdahl decisions great ones.

Sincerely,

Amdahl Corporation
Denver, Colorado

13-4 Thank new client for order

Dear _____ :

It was a pleasure meeting with you last Wednesday while visiting your new facilities.

Thank you for giving American Seating the opportunity to serve you. I'm looking forward to continuing our conversation with reference to the Leasing and National Account programs that we discussed.

____, of Commercial Design & Furnishings, will be working with you along with American Seating personnel, to make this a successful operation within the ____ Corporation.

If in the meantime, we at American Seating can be of assistance in any way, please contact us.

Sincerely,

Frank L. Baudo
American Seating Company
New York, New York

13-5 Thank new client for order

Dear _____ :

I'm so glad you decided to join our family of Wrangler retailers.

Many thanks for your order. Your shipment will arrive around February 1, in plenty of time for the big spring-summer display you're planning. One of my customers had a great deal of success with a window display of western clothes and props from local antique stores. The theme was "How the West Is Worn."

Call me if I can help you in any way. I'm sure your customers are going to be pleased to be able to buy Wrangler clothes at _____. We make a great match.

Best regards,

John Speas
Wrangler
Portland, Oregon

13-6 Thank new client for order

Dear _____:

Welcome to the Wrangler family of retailers.

Thanks for your recent order. I'm confident your customers will appreciate the fine selection of Wrangler clothing with which you can now provide them.

If you have any questions, please call me. I look forward to working with you. I know our association will be mutually profitable.

Best regards,

John Speas
Wrangler
Portland, Oregon

13-7 Thank new client for order

Dear _____:

Thank you for establishing a relationship with Central Bank of Chatfield. We appreciate the confidence you have shown in our bank.

We look forward to serving your banking needs. Please contact us regarding savings, investment services, discount brokerage services and loans. We offer many types of loans to help you achieve your financial goals, and we will work with you in designing terms and repayment options that meet your needs.

If I may assist you in any way, please be sure to call on me. Once again, thanks.

Sincerely,

Central Bank Chatfield
Littleton, Colorado

13-8 Thank established client for order

Dear _____:

Thank you for giving us the opportunity to meet more of your financial needs. Our customers are the most important aspect of our business, and we are always interested in providing more service to them.
If you have questions or concerns regarding any of our services, please contact us at once.
Again, thank you for the confidence you have shown in Central Bank Chatfield.

Sincerely,

Central Bank Chatfield
Littleton, Colorado

13-9 Confirm order

Confirmation letters state the deal exactly as you understand it, eliminating the chance for any misunderstanding.

Dear _____:

Thank you for selecting the Clarion Harvest House Hotel to host your banquet on November 9, __. I am sure that our facilities and professional service offer you the finest in hospitality.
The program is outlined below.

Proposed Program

Day	Date	Time	Function	Guests	Rental
Friday	Nov. 9	6–10 pm	Dinner	140	No charge with dinner for 100+

Tentative arrangements include a cash bar.

All food and beverage is subject to ____ gratuity. Additionally, ____ tax applies to food, beverage and gratuity.

If you would like to set up a bar for your event, there will be a ____ bartender charge, per bartender.

A final guaranteed guest count is required three working days prior to your event, on Tuesday, November 6, 19__.

Payment Information

Anticipated balance is due 72 hours prior to the event, with the final guaranteed number. Any further charges will be due at the conclusion.

Deposit

A ____ deposit, payable by June 21, 19__, is required to retain the space for you. An additional ____ deposit will be due on October 9, 19__.

Cancellation

Should cancellation occur on or after August 29, 19__, a ____ cancellation fee will be incurred unless a group of comparable revenue can be scheduled. After October 9, 19__, the cancellation fee increases to ____.

We are looking forward to working with you. If these arrangements are satisfactory, sign one copy of this contract and return it to me by June 21, 19__. Receipt of the signed copy will confirm your plans and hold the space for you on a definite basis.

Sincerely,

Kerri Ginsberg
Clarion Harvest House
Boulder, Colorado

13-10 Confirm order

Dear _____:

Thanks for your order yesterday. (The coffee was good, too.) I have you down for:

12 dozen mixed-color plaid long-sleeved shirts, sizes S, M, L, XL
6 dozen red short-sleeved shirts, sizes S, M, L, XL
6 dozen blue short-sleeved shirts, sizes S, M, L, XL

6 dozen mixed color plain short-sleeved shirts, sizes S, M, L, XL
3 dozen white long-sleeved dress shirts, sizes S, M, L, XL
3 dozen white short-sleeved shirts, sizes S, M, L, XL

The shirts will be shipped June 26. You should have them in time for your July 4 sale.
Always a pleasure doing business with you!

Regards,

13-11 Confirm order

Dear _____:

I am writing to confirm our conversation of today, and to confirm the orders which you placed. We will be running 20 spots over the period of September 16, 17, 18 and 19, from 3 p.m. until 11 p.m. These will be two per day from 3 p.m. to 8 p.m., and three per day from 8 p.m. to 11 p.m. The cost per spot for this schedule is _____ per :60, or a total of _____. We will run the same schedule for the period September 30, October 1, 2 and 3.

After this order, we will run any schedules that you would like at the same rate through the end of December, with the understanding that these spots could all run after 7 p.m. For a continued guarantee of two between 3 p.m. and 8 p.m. and three between 8 p.m. and 11 p.m., the rate for October, November and December would be _____.

Please keep in mind that at _____, you are still _____% under the current minimum rate for 3 p.m. to midnight schedules. At the rate we are going now, quite honestly, by October that rate could be another _____% or _____% higher. However, I will guarantee the rate through December for you.

I am looking forward to a successful season for the _____, with the inclusion of WIOQ as part of your advertising mix.

Sincerely,

Alan Caplan
WIOQ
Philadelphia, Pennsylvania

13-12 Confirm new agreement regarding order

Dear _____:

Just to confirm the agreement we reached in our meeting of July 12: Golden West Foods will remain an approved supplier of the _____ fillet, but will phase out of active supplier status effective with depletion of finished goods inventories (_____ cases on hand as of today). Unused raw materials will be purchased by _____ at our cost.

Golden West will commit to helping you with "emergency" supplies of _____ fillets should it become necessary for you to call on us. It might make sense for us to establish a procedure to follow in such a situation, so that we will not be caught short of materials or production capacity. I would appreciate your letting me know if you have any suggestions on how we might approach this matter.

It has been a real pleasure working with you, _____, and all the people at _____. Although we are becoming inactive on the fillet, we certainly want to keep our close ties with the organization. As Al and I indicated, we are very positive about our partnership with your company, and we look forward to working on future projects that will keep us in close touch.

Please call if you have any concerns.

Sincerely,

Rich Mende
Golden West Foods, Inc.
Bedford, Virginia

13-13 Inquire about satisfaction

Ask your clients how they like your product or service. Your interest in their well-being paves the way to the next order.

Dear _____:

This note is to thank you for allowing Boulder Toyota the opportunity to assist you in purchasing a Toyota vehicle. Your business is extremely important to me, and your complete satisfaction is even more important. The majority of our new and used vehicle customers are either repeat customers or referred by one of our customers.

You will soon be receiving a survey form like the one on the attachment, from Toyota Motor Sales, U.S.A. This survey is very important to both Toyota and Boulder Toyota. My request is two-fold: first—if you cannot complete the survey exactly as our example, please call me personally at _____. [Note: Attached sample showed "very satisfied" answers to all questions.] Secondly—please complete the survey form and return it to Toyota.

Thank you,

Darrell Wells
Boulder Toyota
Boulder, Colorado

13-14 Inquire about satisfaction

Dear Toyota Owner:

Thank you for purchasing a Toyota from the dealer listed on the front of the enclosed survey form.

Your opinions regarding your recent purchase experience are very important to us, as they will help us provide Toyota products and services that satisfy your needs. We would like you to share with us your impressions and experience with your vehicle and of the dealership where it was purchased. Please take a few moments to complete the enclosed survey.

We use the information gathered on the front page of the survey to evaluate the dealership's performance in handling your recent purchase. The data collected on the back page is used to determine your satisfaction with your Toyota vehicle.

Please return the completed survey directly to Toyota in Torrance, California, in the enclosed self-addressed, postage-paid envelope. If you have additional comments, please contact your dealership's Customer Relations Manager or our Toyota Customer Assistance Center at _____.

We appreciate your business and thank you for taking the time to share your opinions with us. Your satisfaction is important to us.

Sincerely,

A.W. Wagner
Toyota Motor Sales U.S.A., Inc.,
Torrance, California

13-15 Inquire about satisfaction

Dear _____:

When you buy a computer from Burlington Computer Systems, you are also buying service—service to you, to help you become familiar with your equipment, and service to the equipment itself.

As part of our continuing efforts to see how we are doing, would you please take a few minutes to rate our services on a scale of one to ten (one is terrible—need vast improvement; ten is excellent—on the right track.)

Service to you _____
Service to your equipment _____

Many thanks. Please stop in again soon.

Regards,

13-16 Inquire about satisfaction

Dear _____:

You've been using Cheflon pie fillings for two months now. Is everything going smoothly? We believe our recipes are the best in the industry, and I hope the service you've received equals the product. Please let me know if you have encountered any problems or have any suggestions for improvements.

Sincerely,

13-17 Inquire about satisfaction

Dear _____:

How do your people like using the financial program we installed in July? Any problems or suggestions? Don tells me that after the rash of Help Desk calls in July, things have been quiet at ____. That's good news, I trust.

Now that you're on your way with the financial program, I'd like to show you our new inventory control program. I'll call you for an appointment.

Sincerely,

13-18 Confirm shipment

When speed counts, you may want to fax your letters or send them by electronic mail. Again, keep them short. Unlike phone calls, letters provide records of the transaction.

Dear _____:

Your order of buckles, style 55–25, was shipped by air on October 14 by G & P Express, Ltd. It will arrive at your distribution warehouse on October 16. Call me immediately if it doesn't show.

Sincerely,

13-19 Explain change in order

When your product or service changes after an order is placed, write and explain the changes. Emphasize how the change will enhance the product.

Dear _____:

Enclosed is the buckle that just arrived from the Philippines. It was not painted in the impressionistic style of the buckle that I had shown you, as they could not reproduce the design detail in this medium. I believe this buckle is lovely and would be wonderful with a nappa leather belt in jade or black. Do you agree?

Sincerely,

Susan S. Colpitt
China Coast
Boulder, Colorado

13-20 Explain change in order

Dear _____:

Please find enclosed two emerald handbags, style 166. The clasps have been replaced with a brass-finished metal since we are unable to dye the stone the correct color. The metal is long-wearing and should retain its distinctive character throughout the life of the bags. In the long run, it's a better choice than the stone.

Sincerely,

13-21 Acknowledge request to expedite order

Dear _____:

I've called the factory today to hurry along your order. I've been assured that it will be sent Tuesday by overnight express. You should have it Wednesday afternoon. So far, the factory has always made good on its word, so I don't anticipate any glitches. In case the order doesn't arrive, call me right away.

Sincerely,

13-22 Acknowledge request to expedite order

Dear _____:

Your request to expedite your order #3044 just arrived. We can't ship the order next week as requested, but we can move the date up a week from what we originally promised. The order will be ready Wednesday, May 3. Would you care to authorize air shipment?

Sincerely,

13-23 Explain need for more production time

Dear _____:

In order to avoid all problems on your orders, we are asking for more production time so that color samples and finished garments can be sent for approval before production begins.

This will mean a one-week delay. If we have your verbal okay by March 27, production will get underway on April 3. This should allow us to have the stock in your warehouse by June 15, instead of June 6. Please get back to me with your okay.

Sincerely,

13-24 Explain warranty

Dear _____:

Thank you for purchasing 25 Bryce Sanders model 40 electronic typewriters.

You asked that I send a separate statement regarding the warranty on these machines. Our standard warranty does apply, and I'm enclosing a legal description for your files.

As I explained when you placed your order, we warrant the equipment to be free from defects in material and workmanship for a period of 90 days. In the event of problems within the warranty period, please return the items to us. We will decide whether the equipment will be repaired or replaced.

If you have any further questions about warranties, please call me.

Sincerely,

13-25 Explain return policy

Dear _____:

We want you to be happy with everything you purchase from Play Fair Toys. If any item you receive does not meet your expectations, please return it. Your refund or credit will be for the full purchase price (excluding shipping and handling charges). If an item is defective or we have made an error (we try very hard not to) we will also refund all postage and handling charges.

If there is any damage to this merchandise, please save the original carton and packing materials, and call your local UPS/Postmaster for an inspection. After following this procedure please notify us immediately.

To return merchandise for credit, refund, or exchange:

- Wrap return securely in a good box with strong tape.
- Be sure the package is insured and prepaid.
- Enclose the packing slip with your return.
- Please state the reason for the return below.

Please let us know if there is anything else we can do for you.

Thanks for your order.

Play Fair Toys
Boulder, Colorado

Advice from the sales experts

Writing a business letter is not a formal occasion. Almost all letters, in my opinion, are improved if they are written as if you were talking to your reader. Letters written in this style are not formal and stilted, because we don't talk that way. They also seem to have just the right tone of respect.

Read your letter before you sign it. Here is the last chance to see if it meets your standards. Take advantage of the opportunity. Don't be afraid to make changes. You want to be certain it is the successful business letter you planned to write.

Walter L. Bond
Former Executive Vice-President
Tupperware International
Kissimmee, Florida

Chapter 14

Value-Add Suggestions to Clients

Clients have the right to expect value-add suggestions from their sales reps. After all, that's what makes your services and products stand out amidst the competition. Put suggestions in writing. Letters remind clients of your good ideas when you're away from the account. They prove you are on top of situations where clients can improve their business.

14-1 Suggest displays

Dear _____ :

During the past week, I stopped in your branch stores to check on our sweaters. I was pleased to see that, generally, all the sweater styles are doing well. Lakeside, the branch with the best sales, displayed the sweaters on front and center aisles. Cottons and acrylics were in cubes, while argyles and shetlands were prominent on four-ways, with the I.D. sign up. It might be a good idea for your other branches to follow Lakeside's lead.

I'm sure we can come up with other good ideas to increase your profits. Let's discuss them at lunch.

Sincerely,

14-2 Suggest displays

Dear _____ :

When I visited the Twin Oaks Mall store recently, I noted that your Top 10 display was just inside the front door. I suggest you move it to the west wall. It would be seen as customers pass the Classic Videos aisle. Could be an immediate encouragement! Try it for a month and see if the change boosts sales.

Sincerely,

14-3 Suggest plan for turning inventory

Dear _____ :

As you know, the way to make money in the retail business is to TURN the inventory. The difference between high- and low-volume stores is not necessarily size, location or product mix—rather, it is the number of times the merchandise is turned.

Here's a plan to help you turn your inventory of Wrangler jeans twice as fast and double your profits. We have made up some model scales to guide you in reordering fast-selling jeans. All you do is count both men and boys' jeans once a month and fill the number into these scales (i.e., if the model were 3 and you counted 1, you would order 2).

Attached is a model scale for each style of Wrangler jeans. We've tested this method in 25 stores, and results were outstanding. I know it will work for you, too. Call me if you have any questions.

Sincerely,

John Speas
Wrangler
Portland, Oregon

14-4 Suggest advertising strategy

Dear _____:

It's that time of year again! The time that can make or break your entire year. I know you're interested in maximizing your sales and profits and that is why I'm sending you this letter.

With Christmas right around the corner, I strongly encourage you to advertise your Wrangler products to maximize your sales. With that in mind, your coop accruals are at the bottom of this page. We will reimburse _____ of your advertising and promotional costs up to your available accruals. Please use these accruals on Wrangler advertising before the end of the year. What you don't use will be gone on January 1. If you need more ad slicks or promotional ideas, please call me any time.

Also, please inventory your best selling Wrangler products (basic jeans, etc.) and make sure that you are adequately filled in for Christmas sales. You may want to beef up your best selling sizes and styles. You can't make money if you don't have the products to sell! Our deliveries are excellent right now, so please call me with your order.

If there are any questions or problems I can help you with, please call me at _____. Again, please get your Wrangler fill-in orders to me as quickly as possible.

Best regards,

Lory Merritt
Wrangler
Ft. Collins, Colorado

14-5 Inform that company personnel are available

Dear _____:

Sue Lansford, one of our marketing engineers, will be in your region during the last two weeks of July. Sue is willing to spend an afternoon, or even a full day, with your programmers, answering questions or solving any problems they may have with the software we delivered last month. Let me know if you would like Sue's assistance, and if so, the best day.

Regards,

Tips to sharpen your writing skills

Strong writing avoids "there is" and "it is."
Examples:

POOR	There are exceptional values located in . . .
GOOD	Exceptional values exist in . . .
POOR	There is another option that gives you . . .
GOOD	Another option gives you . . .
POOR	It is my fear that . . .
GOOD	I fear that . . .
POOR	There was agreement among the sales reps.
GOOD	The sales reps agreed.
POOR	It was a decision by the stockholders.
GOOD	The stockholders decided.

Chapter Fifteen

Terms and Payments

Business letters about terms and payments are the mortar that holds sales together. They should be concise and specific, stating exactly what you expect. "Thank you" and "please" can smooth the process of talking about money.

15-1 State terms

The length of these letters varies greatly, depending upon how complicated the terms may be. They must contain precise information.

Dear _____:

Thank you for your order. We'll be shipping the parts as promised.

Your purchase order noted terms as "Net 30 Days." Our policy is to receive payment within 10 days. Would you please alert your accounts payable department of this requirement?

Thank you for your help. Please call me if you have any questions.

Sincerely,

15-2 State terms

Dear _____:

This letter outlines our agreement for your acquisition of two new Pancretec Model 5500 and one Model 5500 which you have been renting for the months of August, September and October. Although you have been renting s/n 70494 during November, we have no billing for November and will not do so. For the three months of past rental, we will apply 50% of the rents paid to the purchase price. The transaction thus breaks down as follows:

Item	Price	12 Monthly Payments	Buy-Out
1. Model 5500	$__		
2. Model 5500	$__		
3. Model 5500	$__		

Terms and conditions are the same as your previous purchase in June.

Conditions:

1. The effective date of this transaction will be ____.
2. First and last month invoices will be rendered on November 17 and are due and payable at that time.
3. Title will remain with BMR until last payment is made.
4. Terms for other than first and last payment are net 30 days.

5. Manufacturers one-year parts and labor warranty will apply.
6. _____ is responsible for any damage caused by misuse or fluid damage.

Disposables may be purchased as needed according to the attached price list. Different sets may be mixed to achieve quantity discounts.

Tom, please review, sign below, and the deal will be done. Return one to me; the other is for your files. Please call toll-free if you have any questions.

We appreciate your business and thank you for it.

Best regards,

Denny C. Dickinson
Bio-Medical Resources, Inc.
Broomfield, Colorado

15-3 Ask for credit references

Dear _____:

Thank you for your order of six dozen hand-painted T-shirts, style 554.

We can supply you immediately with two dozen orange, two dozen red, and two dozen blue. If you wish a breakdown other than that, or if you want some shirts in green or purple, it will take us another three weeks to fill the order. Please let me know your preferences.

Before we can ship, we will need three credit references (a business credit card and two banks).

We look forward to doing business with you.

Sincerely,

15-4 Explain payment plan

Dear _____:

You asked about our payment plan for orders totalling more than $25,000.

Because we cannot carry accounts receivables for more than 30 days, we have arranged with the XYZ Credit Corporation to automatically assume outstanding accounts. Their rates and payment schedules are extremely competitive, and our customers have been pleased with their service.

The person in charge of our account is Martha Benson. You can reach her at ____. She will provide you with current interest rates and credit reference requirements.

This arrangement has allowed us to keep our prices low and still offer our customers the convenience of paying on credit.

Sincerely,

15-5 Demand payment

Dear _____:

You have managed to run past my tolerance regarding the attached invoice, which has been outstanding since February.

Our operations manager has spoken with you on several occasions, and you have told her your check is in the mail.

I spoke with you on October 23, and you told me that you would send the check that day.

While I do sympathize with your cash flow problems, you have taken advantage of us.

Here's the deal. I expect to receive your check by November 22. Failure to meet this deadline will precipitate the following actions:

1. This account will be put out for collection to an outside agency.
2. Letters will be sent regarding your unwillingness to meet your obligations to:
   a. Dun and Bradstreet
   b. Better Business Bureau
   c. Accountant
   d. Hospital

All you need do is send us a check for ____ and this matter will be concluded.

Sincerely,

Denny C. Dickinson
Bio-Medical Resources, Inc.
Broomfield, Colorado

15-6 Acknowledge deposit

Dear _____:

I wanted you to know your deposit check arrived in today's mail. We'll ship your order Monday, June 17.

Thanks for this opportunity to show how Microsens can help you improve profits.

Sincerely,

15-7 Acknowledge deposit

Dear _____:

Thank you for the room deposit covering your stay at the Hacienda from May 25 to June 5.

Our staff looks forward to your arrival and showing you why Alabama is famous for its "Southern Hospitality."

Sincerely,

15-8 Acknowledge payment

Dear _____:

Thank you for your payment on the March 16 order.

The order has been shipped and should be in your hands within the next four days.

Regards,

15-9 Answer question about payment

Dear _____:

Thanks for calling my attention to the fact that your payments were not credited to your account in January and February.

Please send me copies of your canceled checks, front and back. They will help us trace the accounts in which your checks may have been deposited. We will, of course, cancel interest due for these payments.

Hope to have this straightened out soon.

Sincerely,

Tips to sharpen your writing skills

Eliminate extra words.

instead of	*choose*
This service is an offering that capitalizes	This service capitalizes
Clients are beginning to select	Clients select
This item is being offered	We offer
The car is being displayed	The car is on display
The committee made a decision	The committee decided
The companies made an agreement	The companies agreed

Chapter Sixteen

Complaints

With your client relationship and future orders on the line, letters that handle complaints must display sensitivity to the client's problem, plus the willingness and ability to improve the situation. Letters should include both an explanation and an apology. The tone should be straight-forward and sincere. Be specific about the steps being taken to ensure the problem won't recur.

On certain occasions—and only when you know the client well and your instincts tell you it's the right approach—inject humor to diffuse an emotional situation.

Clients generally respect an honest admission of guilt. It sends a signal that you are a person of integrity, someone they can trust in future dealings.

16-1 Handle complaints about personnel

Dear _____ :

Thank you for letting me know about the problem you encountered with one of our telemarketing specialists.

As you know, we have recently retrained a large number of factory employees into positions where they deal with clients. In most cases, the transition has been smooth and successful for the individual and for the company. Occasionally, it takes an employee longer to adjust to dealing with the outside world. This was the case with the specialist you encountered.

We have counseled the employee and arranged for him to attend the next customer awareness seminar, actions we believe will improve his performance in the future.

At this time, we would like him to continue serving your account. I'll check back with you in two weeks. If you are not totally satisfied with your relationship, we will immediately switch your account to a more experienced specialist.

Thank you for your patience. We value your patronage and promise to provide you with the best service possible.

Sincerely,

16-2 Handle complaints about personnel

Dear _____ :

You're not going to believe this, but all our clerks are graduates of the "Juilliard School of Happy Customer Relations," or so we thought. Still, somebody occasionally slips up and doesn't provide the level of service we expect. I'm sorry you had to experience the slip up, but I'm glad you came straight to me about it. Be assured that heads have rolled and new procedures are now in place to prevent this type of situation from ever happening again.

_____ , you and I have done business together for more than five years. I hope you'll look at this incident for what it was — a once-only happening. Please accept my apology, and allow us to continue supplying Rockmont's container needs.

Sincerely,

16-3 Handle complaints about service

How are you going to straighten out the mess? That's what your clients want to know. Be specific. Tell them what has been done and what you plan to do.

Dear _____ :

    Following our meeting on November 17, we initiated both short-term actions and a longer-term analysis of our Los Angeles ramp and aircraft cleaning operations to ensure a continuous, highly reliable and safe service product for your airlines.

    In the short term, we have accomplished the following:

- Appointed a new manager to head the ramp operation. The manager has an extensive and successful background in the industry.
- Appointed a new supervisor who is completely dedicated to ____ during the ____ operation.
- Assigned an additional supervisor on a temporary basis to the sole function of training and quality control.
- Appointed an additional supervisor to our Safety Plus Department. The supervisor will concentrate on safety training and monitoring safety procedures on the ramp.
- Upgraded our hiring and training procedures to ensure a sufficient and well trained workforce.

For the longer term, we are analyzing the following:

- Worker, lead and supervisory pay scales.
- The Ramp Service Department's organization.
- The further dedication of personnel in certain critical job functions and operations.
- Improved training and quality assurance programs.
- Improved communications procedures.

    We will review our conclusions on these matters with Mr. ____ and his staff in order to gain his concurrence with the program, and will plan to implement further action in early ____ in order to ensure an extremely high quality of service.

    Thank you for your patience in this matter. We believe that the changes already achieved have reestablished a superior service product, and that the mutually agreed upon long-term program will maintain a service level that is representative of the high service quality image of ____.

Sincerely,

Robert L. Warner
Ogden Allied Aviation Services
Los Angeles, California

16-4 Handle complaints about products

Dear _____:

Enclosed is some epoxy to glue on the handle stones on the ornamental sea chest. Epoxy is the best type of glue for this purpose. The stones were firmly affixed when they left Arizona. I suspect that cold weather during shipment might have caused the problem, and I'm sorry you were inconvenienced by it.
Let me know if, after using the epoxy, everything isn't A-OK.

Sincerely,

16-5 Handle complaints about products

Dear _____:

I have sent a replacement for the satin-finished antique mirror, #45378, that was scratched in shipment. The damage occurred as the mirror was being placed in the packing crate. We have implemented new procedures that should eliminate such problems in the future.
Please accept my apologies for any inconvenience.

Sincerely,

16-6 Handle complaints about shipping error

Dear _____:

Your call Thursday stopped me in my tracks. I'm as concerned as you are about the shipping error on your order for 500 electronic Spellomotor games, invoice 7042. I've taken action to correct it.

In tracking the shipment, I found that all 500 units went to your Seattle distributor, instead of 100 units to each of your five distributors.

Since you mentioned that your Los Angeles dealer is out of stock, we are shipping 100 units to Los Angeles by air today. Another 300 units left our docks this morning by truck. Shipments should arrive by midweek in New York, Chicago and Dallas.

We have asked your Seattle receiving department to keep 100 units and return the balance—collect, of course.

I wish we could blame the error on alien interference with our computers, but unfortunately it was a human error in data entry. We have taken steps to ensure it won't happen again.

Sincerely,

16-7 Handle complaints about shipping error

Dear _____:

Your call this morning to let us know that you finally got delivery of your order was welcome news. We are very sorry about the mixup. We realize it caused you a great deal of inconvenience, and we appreciate your patience in working with us to straighten out the matter.

Be assured, we have taken steps to see that such snafus don't happen again. All shipping orders will be double checked to make sure they are tagged for the correct branch.

Thanks again for your help and understanding. Let's have lunch the next time I'm in Phoenix. My treat.

Sincerely,

16-8 Handle complaints about pricing

Dear _____:

I appreciate your letting me know that another agent has suggested a lower-priced disability policy than the one I recommended.

As you know, not all policies offer the same benefits, even though at first glance, they may appear comparable. Some limit the number of payments, while others delay payments for a long period after disability has occurred.

Having assessed your business situation, and your plans to retire at age 65, I believe the ____ policy would provide you with the security you need. Payments would begin 30 days after disability, and they would continue until age 65.

Let's sit down and take a look at both policies. Since I'll be in Limon next Tuesday and Wednesday, I'll call your office to arrange a convenient time to stop by. I'm confident that, with our policy, you would get much more protection for the money.

Sincerely,

16-9 Handle complaints about incorrect billing

Dear _____:

I'm sorry that our May invoice did not include the 20% repeat-order discount you deserve.

It was an accounting error. Your account has now been flagged with the correct codes to avoid any problem in the future. A new invoice is being issued to replace the one you received. Please discard the old one.

Thanks for letting me know about this. When my customers are unhappy, so am I!

Sincerely,

16-10 Handle complaints about product not arriving at trade show

Dear _____:

I am very sorry that the leather belts did not arrive in time for the fashion trade show. We really tried to get them to you, but a problem developed unexpectedly at customs. We've taken steps to prevent any such foul-ups in the future.

I trust, by now, the belts have arrived at your locations. Again, my apologies that you didn't have them sooner.

Sincerely,

16-11 Handle complaints that are not your fault

Telling clients an error that caused them embarrassment or inconvenience is their own fault won't give them a lot to cheer about and could cause resentment against you. Even so, they expect you to be honest and give them the facts. Be tactful.

Dear _____:

I'm sorry you were inconvenienced when our last shipment arrived at your docks C.O.D. I can appreciate the trouble it caused your receiving clerk.

I investigated the matter and discovered the source of the error. In your original purchase order, the box marked "Ship C.O.D." is checked with an "X." Apparently the check mark should have been in the next box down, "Ship on Account." As a result, our shipping clerk, following instructions, sent the package C.O.D.

In the future, I have asked our order expediters to alert me to packages marked to go C.O.D. Such shipments are rare, and I should be able to intercept those heading toward our established clients.

Thanks for calling me, Carl. I appreciate your confidence in us and your continued business.

Sincerely,

16-12 Handle complaints about late delivery

Dear _____:

I've checked with our shipping department and learned that your order did in fact go out before 3 p.m. on Friday. It was shipped overnight express, which means you should have had it by noon, Saturday, as we had discussed. I'm as upset as you are over the foul up, but that doesn't change the fact that you were short twelve dozen boys' pajamas for the Saturday moonlight sale.

John, I'm very sorry this happened. You can bet we will use a different overnight service in the future to make sure it doesn't happen again.

Sincerely,

16-13 Request more information

Dear _____:

Sorry I missed you yesterday when I stopped by.

Mary mentioned that you have been dissatisfied with the last shipment of heavy-duty staple guns. I was surprised to hear that, since this model has been very popular. Please drop me a note and let me know what the problem is. You know that we stand behind our products, and we'll work with you to make things right.

Sincerely,

Tips to sharpen your writing skills

Before writing a letter, ask yourself:

Who is my reader?
What information does he/she want and need?
How can he/she benefit from my ideas or proposal?

The answers will tell you how to write the letter.

Next, take a few moments to make an outline. List the information you wish to include. Divide the list into "main topics" and "sub topics." Now, arrange the list of "main topics" in their order of importance. Place the "sub topics" under the appropriate "main topics." You are now ready to begin writing. Follow your outline as you write.

Chapter Seventeen

Referrals, Testimonials and Other Client Support

Satisfied clients help you connect on other sales by providing valuable referrals and testimonials. These letters show how to ask for assistance and decline requests.

17-1 Ask for referral

Dear _____:

I was pleased to learn how much your people enjoy using the new financial software. I'd like to spread the word to others in your industry and wonder if you would be kind enough to refer me to acquaintances who may be interested in the software. I'll talk to you soon.

Sincerely,

17-2 Ask for referral

Dear _____:

We are interested in expanding our business in downtown Chicago. Since you have been a customer of Barrett Computer Systems for several years, I wonder if you would share the names of colleagues who may be interested in our networking capabilities.

We will offer free networking consultations to prospective clients, and I can offer you your choice of several software programs for each referral who becomes a customer.

I will be in Chicago in mid-April and would like to contact your referrals at that time. Any assistance will be appreciated.

Sincerely,

17-3 Thank client for referral

Dear _____:

One of your residents recently subscribed to the *Rocky Mountain News* using the order blank in our apartment welcome packet.

The enclosed certificate is our way of thanking you for distributing the packets to your new residents and for encouraging them to subscribe to the *News*.

The certificate may be redeemed directly at _____. You may also return the certificate to me (with a note and your social security number) for a check or restaurant gift certificate.

Thanks again for helping promote the *Rocky Mountain News*. If you need more welcome packets, please call me at _____.

Sincerely,

Fred Cook
Rocky Mountain News
Denver, Colorado

17-4 Thank client for referral

Dear _____:

I'm sending this letter as a follow-up to our conversation today. Thank you for referring me to _____. I shall call her on the battery line.

We would also be interested in working with you on any of your other product areas. Marketing Communications is a full-service marketing, advertising and public relations agency specializing in technical business-to-business accounts and also consumer products. (We are members of the Business/Professional Advertising Association.)

We would like to discuss with you possible outside agency representation — on a project or full-services basis. We have been very successful in achieving extremely high results for our clients. Results have been tops in both cost and results effectiveness.

I will call your office next week to arrange a time for a very short meeting.

Sincerely,

Sandra E. Lamb
Marketing Communications
Denver, Colorado

17-5 Ask client for testimonial

Dear _____:

I appreciate your remarks about how much you're enjoying your coffee and juice every morning, sans chlorine.

Would you be willing to write a letter telling about your experiences with your new water filter system? I'm preparing a package of testimonials for prospective clients and would very much like to include your remarks.

Thanks for everything, and I'm glad you're becoming accustomed to good-tasting water.

Sincerely,

17-6 Thank client for testimonial

Dear _____:

Many thanks for the kind things you had to say about our company at the seminar last Friday. Nothing is more valuable to us than knowing that we are doing a good job for our customers. It's especially gratifying when one of our customers says so in public. You have my word that we will continue to work hard to live up to your endorsement.

Sincerely,

17-7 Request client assistance

Dear _____:

Ogden Allied is preparing materials for the Annual Report. Los Angeles has been honored by being selected as the site for the Aviation Division pictures.

We would greatly appreciate your approval of Ogden Allied taking photographs on November 13, 14 and 15 of our crew while loading and unloading your aircraft. We will not interfere in any way with your service.

_____'s department will be in further contact with your staff regarding this project. Your cooperation is appreciated.

Sincerely,

Robert L. Warner
Ogden Allied Aviation Services
Los Angeles, California

17-8 Decline request for sponsorship

Dear _____:

Thank you for submitting a proposal for sponsorship of the
_____ conference.
As you know, Coors Brewing Company has recently taken a
fresh direction and is focusing on literacy. As a result of this, all
available resources have been committed to programs working with
illiteracy. Therefore, we are unable to commit to this conference.
I wish you much success in developing strategies to increase
minorities in key positions at institutions of higher learning.

Sincerely,

John Meadows
Coors Brewing Company
Golden, Colorado

17-9 Decline request for sponsorship

Dear _____:

Your funding proposal sent to _____ has been forwarded to me
for a response. I appreciate the opportunity to review your funding
request for the _____ Conference.
As you may or may not be aware, Coors is currently working
on a program to help fight illiteracy. We are working with various
organizations to teach individuals/families to learn to read. As
a result of our Literacy—Pass It On campaign, we are unable to
participate in your conference as a sponsor. We are excited about
the Literacy program and the impact it will have on future gen-
erations.
Best wishes on a successful conference.

Sincerely,

John Meadows
Coors Brewing Company
Golden, Colorado

17-10 Decline request for sponsorship

Dear _____:

Thanks very much for your letter regarding _____.
I'm sorry to inform you that we will be unable to support your efforts at this time. As you can probably imagine, we receive a tremendous number of requests for support, almost on a daily basis. Unfortunately, we can support only a relatively small number of the many deserving causes and regret that we will be unable to assist in funding your event.

Nonetheless, we salute you on your efforts to significantly improve _____. You have our best wishes for your continued success in your efforts. And thank you for thinking of Pepsi-Cola.

Sincerely,

Pepsi-Cola Company
Somers, New York

17-11 Decline request for sponsorship

Dear _____:

Thank you for inviting us to participate in your upcoming advertising campaign. Golden West, as a key supplier to the _____ system, is constantly striving to give our customers the highest quality at competitive prices. In order to do this, we must be very selective about the promotions in which we participate.

We are not currently in a position to participate in your campaign. We trust that you understand our situation, and we wish you much success in the grand opening.

Once again, thank you for the invitation. We appreciate your business and look forward to working with you in the future.

Sincerely,

Rick Mende
Golden West Foods, Inc.
Bedford, Virginia

17-12 Decline request for sponsorship

Dear _____:

Thank you for your letter and the information on this year's _____ Festival. The Festival is a wonderful way to raise funds for Boulder's fine non-profit agencies.

The Clarion Harvest House participates in many events each year, including the Chili Olympics and A Taste of the Nation. Additionally, each June we host the Chad Everett Celebrity Tennis Tournament, which benefits the Bal Swan Children's Center. Though we support the goals of the _____ Festival, we will not be able to participate with a booth this year.

But, we will be participating in the Rubber Duck Race! Last month I mailed Barbara a gift certificate for a night in our VIP Tower and Sunday brunch as a prize for the race.

Good luck in all of the _____ Festival's events. Thank you for thinking of the Clarion Harvest House.

Sincerely,

Jack Reed
Clarion Harvest House
Boulder, Colorado

Tips to sharpen your writing skills

Cut excessive words:

instead of	*choose*
at the present time	now
in the event of	if
in the majority of instances	usually
prior to the time of	before
for the reason that	because

Chapter Eighteen

Interoffice Memos Regarding Orders and Products

Dash off an interoffice memo when you need a written record for follow-up or confirmation purposes. Memos should be quick, crisp notes stating the facts or asking questions. The "Subject" line gets instant attention, so make sure it is precise and clear.

18-1 Confirm order

MEMO TO: Order Department
FROM: Sales Rep Name
SUBJECT: New Account Order

 We've landed a new account. As I asked over the phone, please ship 100 LPG valves to _____ Butane Service by the 13th. Use their order #33849. Local credit references are excellent, so please bill at the dealer discount.

 Let's make sure everything is perfect on this one. They're a very competitive dealer and could send a lot of business our way.

18-2 Confirm product in stock

MEMO TO: Marketing Manager
FROM: Sales Rep Name
SUBJECT: Cosmo Plastics Order

 Enclosed is an order from Cosmo Plastics. We had problems on their last order, and I want to be sure, this time, everything goes smoothly. Please let me know whether all items on the order are in stock. Thanks.

18-3 Confirm product in stock

MEMO TO: Order Department
FROM: Sales Rep Name
SUBJECT: Where is Part No. 933?

 You say part No. 933 is out of stock and won't be available for a month.

 Please check behind the dust bins. We had three boxes of these screws when I inquired. I want to accept an order from Stanton, but they want the parts by the 10th. Let me know what you find.

18-4 Change order

> MEMO TO: Order Department
> FROM: Sales Rep Name
> SUBJECT: Change Order Alert!

Please change the quantity of LPG valves going to ____ (Order No. W441195) from 75 to 100. The order is scheduled to ship Thursday, the 13th. Everything else remains the same.

18-5 Disagree with price increase

> MEMO TO: Marketing Manager
> FROM: Sales Rep Name
> SUBJECT: Cancel Price Increase

I don't know how we can raise the price again to ____. Every time I talk to them, the price has taken a quantum leap. I will explain that we prefer to have the ____ assembled in Taiwan, even though the cost is somewhat higher, because of the political climate of ____.

In the meantime, I'd like to hold the line with our last quote. Let me know if you disagree.

18-6 Inquire about shipping dates

On what date is the product scheduled to be shipped? Do you wish to confirm or change that date? Be specific.

> MEMO TO: Marketing Manager
> FROM: Sales Rep Name
> SUBJECT: Shipping Date on Order 1392

What's going on? Order 1392, for standard, off-the-shelf products, requests shipment no later than March 3. The confirmation states the order will go out March 15. My customer isn't going to be happy. I will need a good reason for slipping the date nearly two weeks. Please get back to me right away.

18-7 Inquire about shipping dates

MEMO TO: Marketing Manager
    FROM: Sales Rep Name
SUBJECT: Confirm Delivery Date

I can write up a very nice order for Carol Ltd.—if we can ship the merchandise by March 21. I've assured the buyer we can do so and am enclosing the order. Any problem? Let me know right away if we can't meet the deadline. Cheers.

18-8 Request brochures, catalogs, other information

MEMO TO: Marketing Manager
    FROM: Sales Rep Name
SUBJECT: 1331 Latch Brochures

The brochures you produced on the 1331 latch hit the best seller list. I'm totally out. Please send me 50 more copies right away to cover my road trip into Arkansas.

Give Jill and Roger a pat on the back for me. They did a great job!

18-9 Request brochures, catalogs, other information

MEMO TO: Marketing Manager
    FROM: Sales Rep Name
SUBJECT: Medipac Brochure and Video Tape

Please send one Medipac brochure and video tape to the following prospect:

Name/Company/Address.

I promised them within two weeks, so let me know if you can't make that deadline. I'd appreciate confirmation when you do ship. Thanks.

18-10 Request vendor support

MEMO TO: _____
    FROM: John Speas
SUBJECT: Vendor Support

I'm requesting additional funds for ____, Milwaukee, Oregon, for their "Spring Show-Stopper" promotion.

History:

____ is located in a suburb of Portland, Oregon. They have been in business 30 years and are the leading western wear store in the greater Portland area. Their 19__ volume with Wrangler was ____. They are a PRCA dealer and are on a four-week STEP count.

Promotion:

The objective is to move Wrangler products at retail and to create a higher visibility both for Wrangler and our account. During this advertising campaign, Wrangler will be advertised as the official jean of the PRCA, which should help build additional traffic and store awareness.

(Further details and costs)

My volume objective for this account is ____, and this promotion will help achieve that goal. This will be an excellent promotion, both for the account and Wrangler. The western store business is slim in this area of Oregon, and we could use the television exposure.

John Speas
Wrangler
Portland, Oregon

18-11 Inquire about delays

The most important message in memos that inquire about delays or lapses in product quality is: Our client is dissatisfied. We must act to restore satisfaction.

MEMO TO: Marketing Manager
FROM: Sales Rep Name
SUBJECT: Request to Speed Delivery

I just received confirmation for the order I placed on behalf of Jason Electronics. Delivery has been delayed two weeks from our standard commitment. Jason is a new customer, and it is imperative that we deliver as promised. What can you do to speed things up?

18-12 Inquire about lapse in product quality

MEMO TO: Marketing Manager
    FROM: Sales Rep Name
 SUBJECT: Faulty Valve Seating

The valves sent to All-Bupro have been malfunctioning because of faulty seating. We've corrected the problem in this instance, but I would like to know what procedures are being implemented to prevent the problem in the future. My customers will not tolerate problems like this, and I need to assure them we've got things under control. Let me know right away.

18-13 Inquire about shipping errors

MEMO TO: Marketing Manger
    FROM: Sales Rep Name
 SUBJECT: Order Gone Astray

Order No. 1677 destined for Rockstone, in Shreveport, ended up at Rockport in Shreveport. I assume it was a typo, but I'd appreciate your checking procedures to be sure the error doesn't happen again. Advise me of your findings. Thanks.

18-14 Inquire about shipping errors

MEMO TO: Marketing Manager
    FROM: Sales Rep Name
 SUBJECT: Order 13884 Mix-up

The subject order called for 100 Model 790A automatic shutoff valves. The customer received 100 Model 479B regulators. I can't figure out how this error happened. Replacement valves have been shipped by air, but the customer is unhappy and wants an explanation. Please check out what happened and let me know ASAP. Thanks.

18-15 Inquire about billing errors

MEMO TO: Marketing Manager
    FROM: Sales Rep Name
 SUBJECT: Carlton Music Pricing Error

Carlton Music called me about the invoice covering the last shipment. The sheet music pricing seems to be off by 10 percent. They should receive our distributor pricing. Please check and issue credit if appropriate. Let me know your findings, so I can get back to them personally.

18-16 Inquire about product modifications

MEMO TO: Sales Engineering Manager
FROM: Sales Rep Name
SUBJECT: Tolerance Change Information Request

At the last department meeting, you stated your engineers were changing tolerances in Series 3 friction clutches and brakes. What's the status? I have two orders for Series 3 parts, depending on whether we improved the tolerances. Please send me all the tech details immediately.

18-17 Inquire about product specifications

MEMO TO: Sales Engineering Manager
FROM: Sales Rep Name
SUBJECT: Rush Polymer Specs

A customer wants to know the specs on the new Reliance Series polymers: impact strength and heat and chemical resistance. Please return the information overnight express. Thanks.

18-18 Inquire about warranty

MEMO TO: Marketing Manager
FROM: Sales Rep Name
SUBJECT: Max-Vari Warranty Extension

Does our standard warranty apply to the Max-Vari Compressors? Our sales strategy is based on longer life, and customers want to know if our warranty reflects our confidence. If we haven't extended the warranty period, please put it on the agenda for next week's management review.

18-19 Recap orders for year

On what date is the product scheduled to be shipped? Do you wish to confirm or change that date? Be specific.

MEMO TO: Sales Director
FROM: John Speas
SUBJECT: Year-End Recap Sheets

Enclosed is a copy of the year-end recap sheet reflecting my results per area. In the percentage complete to goal, you will find the final numbers for first quality and for final objectives in the appropriate boxes. The Total Sales Calls box lists the average number of calls I've made per month. Thanks for all your good help in making this a successful year.

John Speas
Wrangler
Portland, Oregon

Tips to sharpen your writing skills

For emphasis, place the most important idea at the end of the sentence.

Examples:

POOR
We hope that our goal, which is the highest one we have ever set, will be achieved.

GOOD
We hope to achieve our goal, the highest we have ever set.

POOR
We still consider you a good customer, despite the fact we are no longer supplying your needs.

GOOD
Despite the fact we are no longer supplying your needs, we still consider you a good customer.

Chapter Nineteen

Salary and Territory Issues

Salary and territory letters range from simple matters of pay adjustments and errors to complex issues that may jeopardize your relationship with the company. Your letter should contain facts that will convince your company to reconsider the issue. State concerns and expectations in a firm tone. The tone results from the words you select and the details you include.

19-1 Confirm base pay

Dear _____:

I appreciated the opportunity to meet with you last week to review the base pay and commissions provided by Redley.
This is my understanding of the amounts involved.

Base pay:	$____
Quarterly Draw:	$____
Commission:	
0 – $100,000	$____
$100,000 and above	$____

Redley offers two weeks paid vacation annually, plus eleven paid holidays. Benefits include health insurance and a dental plan for me and for my family.
Please let me know if I should adjust my notes on any of this. I'm looking forward to joining the Redley team.

Sincerely,

19-2 Inquire about error in pay

MEMO TO: Payroll Department
FROM: Sales Rep Name
SUBJECT: Pay Check Error

I think the computer just cut my salary. On my recent pay check, base pay is listed as $1,000. This is in error. The correct base pay is $1,250. Please review and send me a check for $250 as soon as possible.

19-3 Inquire about error in pay

MEMO TO: Marketing Manager
FROM: Sales Rep Name
SUBJECT: Pay Error

I understood I was to receive a raise in base pay six months from starting date. Apparently no one told the computer, and the raise is a month delinquent. Would you correct this with payroll and send me a check to cover last month? Call if there's a problem.

19-4 Ask for raise in base pay

MEMO TO: Marketing Manager
   FROM: Sales Rep Name
SUBJECT: Pay Raise

I've enjoyed working with _____ the past six months. I'm familiar with the product line and clients in my territory. You can see by the activity that I've even recovered some lost accounts.

Now that I've completed the learning curve, I'd like to be considered for a raise. Would you please review my salary plan and see if you can bump up the base pay? I look forward to hearing your decision.

19-5 Inquire about error in commission statement

MEMO TO: Payroll Department
   FROM: Sales Rep Name
SUBJECT: Commission Error

Just received my March commission statement. What a shocker! Our figures are off $1,200.

Enclosed is a copy of my invoice log. Please note on page 3, line 7, the sales amount for ABC Company was $24,000, not $12,000 as shown in the statement. The invoices involved are:

ABC Company

Invoice	Date	Amount
39842	3/4	$5,000
42771	3/19	12,000
55943	3/23	7,000
Total		$24,000

Please correct the statement and issue an additional check in the amount of $1,200. Thanks for taking care of this, Steve. I know you wouldn't want me to miss out on that 40-foot sloop on sale at Niemans.

19-6 Inquire about missing bonus

MEMO TO: Payroll Department
FROM: Sales Rep Name
SUBJECT: Missing Bonus Checks

My third quarter bonus check hasn't arrived. I figure it should amount to $2,500. The second quarter check was late also. Unfortunately, my creditors don't like waiting for payment. Would you arrange to send the checks express mail in the future. Thanks.

19-7 Ask for travel advance

MEMO TO: Marketing Manager
FROM: Sales Rep Name
SUBJECT: Advance for Meeting

I am attending the Universal Standards meeting at the Peachtree in Georgia next month. Air, room, meals and miscellaneous expenses will come to $1,000. Would you please authorize an advance to reach me by May 13? Thanks.

19-8 Submit expenses

MEMO TO: Marketing Manager
FROM: Sales Rep Name
SUBJECT: Expense Account

Enclosed is my expense account covering the Universal Standards meeting at the Peachtree in Georgia. As you can see, expenses ran more than the $1,000 advance. Would you please authorize a check to cover the $200 difference?

19-9 Protest cut in territory

Cuts in sales territories often generate intense anger on the part of sales reps. Letters protesting cuts must be based on fact, not emotion. They must present facts and figures aimed at convincing management that future profits are on the line and showing that it is in the company's best interests to let you work your own territory.

MEMO TO: Marketing Manager
    FROM: Sales Rep Name
SUBJECT: Proposed Territory Changes

Should you go ahead with plans to cut my territory in half, you will see serious erosion in company profits for the next five years.

In the relationship I've built with my clients over the last decade, I am the one who assesses their business situation and matches products and services to their needs. I have built up a great reservoir of trust. To them, I am the company.

It will take years for a new sales rep to establish the kind of relationship I have with these clients. In the meantime, our competitors will be aggressively working the area. What guarantee is there that our clients will not switch loyalties? After all, while competitive products offer comparable features at comparable prices to ours, my clients continue to purchase from me because of personal loyalty. You risk losing business if you give part of my territory to a new sales rep.

Look at the figures. The territory you suggest cutting produces ____ annually in sales. Are you willing to lose even a portion of this amount, while a new sales rep gets established?

Please think about it seriously. I'll be at headquarters on Friday to discuss this.

19-10 Protest cut in territory

MEMO TO: Marketing Manager
    FROM: Sales Rep Name
SUBJECT: Proposed Territory Changes

Let me get this straight. You're decreasing my territory by 25 percent? I've worked hard at developing the potential here. As you can see from the records, sales were at $12,000 a month when I started. I've pushed them up to $32,000. I cannot agree with any cuts unless I receive other benefits in return. Please don't make any changes until we can talk in person. I'll be in Chicago next week.

19-11 Protest cut in territory

MEMO TO: Marketing Manager
   FROM: Sales Rep Name
SUBJECT: Proposed Territory Changes

I disagree with the change outlined in your recent letter. I'd lose $10,000 a year if you cut Maine from my territory, not $2,000 as you state. (See enclosed records.) I cover clients in Maine every six weeks. These visits do not impact customers in other parts of my territory. Please reconsider. I can't afford to lose that chunk of business.

19-12 Protest change of client to "in-house"

MEMO TO: Marketing Manager
   FROM: Sales Rep Name
SUBJECT: Proposed Territory Changes

I cannot agree with the proposed change of Houston Pneumonics to an "in-house" customer. I think orders will nose-dive if the account goes in-house. The account requires a great deal of personal attention. I'm there at least every other week. Please check the records. We did about $20,000 a year with HP when I took over. In four years, I've tripled that revenue.

Give me a chance to convince you that it's to the company's advantage to keep me on the account. Can we talk Monday?

Advice from the sales experts

When writing letters to my company about salary or territory issues, I keep four things uppermost in my mind:

1. Do I have the facts? It's important to take the time to gather the information you need and to make sure it's correct. You cannot expect to win your company over to your point of view without facts.

2. Is my information specific? For example, instead of writing: "My base salary isn't nearly enough and everything costs much more today," write: "The cost of living in my area rose 4% last year." Remember that the person to whom you are writing may not be the one who makes the final decision. Give that person the precise figures he or she needs to fight for you at the next corporate level.

3. Is my message professional? Leave out personal items, such as: "My neighbor, who has a similar job, makes more than I do." Or, "I have extra expenses now that my daughter has started college." This type of information will not win your case. Stick to business issues.

4. Is my letter formatted correctly? This means paying attention to such matters as spelling, paper quality and neatness of typing or printing. Always include the date, formal address, and *informal* salutation (Dear Don, instead of Dear Mr. Smith). A professional letter commands respect.

John Speas
Manufacturer's Representative
Wrangler
Portland, Oregon

Chapter Twenty

Employment

Better opportunity. Better environment. Better conditions for the family. For whatever reason, sales people change jobs frequently. Letters regarding employment issues cross the country every day. Letters seeking employment should express your personality. Potential employers learn about you from what you say and the way you say it.

20-1 Ask for position with another company

Dear _____:

I've looked at your company, and I like what I see. You have an excellent line of pharmaceuticals and continue to announce new products. I'd like a chance to sell for you.

I've worked in pharmaceutical for two years. Enclosed is a detailed resume. My sales track record speaks for itself, and I'm anxious to take on increased responsibility.

If you're interested, give me a call.

Sincerely,

20-2 Ask for position with another company

Dear _____:

Your company is aggressive and forward-looking. So am I. I believe we would make a good match.

I have been selling children's apparel in midwestern states for six years. During that time, I opened dozens of new accounts, including accounts with three national franchisers. My total sales volume increased by 10 to 15% each year. Enclosed is a resume containing specific information.

Now that I've relocated to California, I'm interested in selling for a company whose interest in quality merchandise and customer service matches my own. I will be in your area in September and would like to talk to you about a position with your sales department. I will call next week to arrange an appointment.

Sincerely,

20-3 Ask for promotion

MEMO TO: Marketing Manager
FROM: Sales Rep Name
SUBJECT: Promotion

I'd like to be considered for the position of assistant sales manager.

October marks my seventh year with the company. In that time, I have established and run some of the company's largest and most important accounts. I believe my experience in the field could be put to good use in training and managing other salespeople. Could we talk it over? How about lunch next week?

20-4 Ask for promotion

MEMO TO: Marketing Manager
    FROM: Sales Rep Name
SUBJECT: Promotion

I was surprised to look at the calendar and realize that I'll be starting my third year with Western this month. When I came on board, you stated that it normally took two and a half years for a sales rep to be promoted to senior level.

I've learned the ropes, handled the territory alone and proved my ability to generate revenue for the company. Now I'm ready to take on greater responsibilities. Can we get together next week to discuss this matter?

20-5 Inform company of job offer made to you

When another company approaches you with a sales position, which you decline, inform your manager. It won't hurt your standing to let your company know that others are recruiting you. Point out some aspect of your company's policy that influenced your decision to remain on board.

MEMO TO: Marketing Manager
    FROM: Sales Rep Name
SUBJECT: Job Offer

Yesterday, out of the blue, ____made me an offer to come to work for them. I'm happy at ____, and I said so. The plan for this year, with its raise in the commission rate, is a strong incentive to stay with this company. Thanks for playing fair. I intend to do the same.

20-6 Reject offer for employment

Dear _____:

I was flattered by your offer, but I've decided to stay with ____. Should the situation change in the future, I certainly will call you.

Thanks for thinking of me.

20-7 Reject offer for employment

Dear _____:

I enjoyed meeting with you last Thursday. Your offer of a sales position with Trugood Industries is very tempting, especially with the reduced territory and increased base salary. After talking it over, however, my family and I have decided against relocating at this time.

I would appreciate your keeping my resume on file. It's possible that we might strike a deal a little further down the line.

Sincerely,

20-8 Reject applicant

Dear _____:

We appreciate your prompt response to our advertisement.

While it is difficult to make an assessment with such a small amount of information, we believe that your qualifications and skills might be more rewarded in an environment other than OLIS.

We wish you the best in finding a company which will put your training to best use!

Again, we appreciate the opportunity of reviewing your resume.

Sincerely,

Julie Ann DeSa Lorenz
On-Line Instrument Systems, Inc.
Jefferson, Georgia

20-9 Reject applicant

Dear _____:

Thank you for taking the time to meet with us recently regarding the marketing position available at __.

Many highly qualified applicants were interviewed, and we were left with a very difficult choice. After extensive consideration, we offered the job to another candidate and the offer was accepted.

We wish you the best of luck in finding a position that will take maximum advantage of your skills and experience.

Sincerely,

20-10 Inform that no sales position is available

Dear _____ :

Thank you for your letter of introduction and for sharing your credentials with Pepsi-Cola Company. Judging from your resume, you have already taken advantage of valuable opportunities to put your skills to work.

Such initiative would make you a welcome addition to any corporation. Unfortunately, based on our current personnel needs, I am sorry to say that we do not have any appropriate openings in our department.

However, situations do change from time to time and we welcome the opportunity to contact you should a suitable vacancy occur.

Once again, thank you for your interest in Pepsi-Cola and best of luck in pursuing your career.

Sincerely,

Pepsi-Cola Company
Somers, New York

20-11 Inform that no sales position is available

Dear _____ :

Thanks for your letter. Your qualifications are first-rate, and your attitude shows that intuitive flair for selling. Unfortunately, we are unable to offer you a position at this time. I'm keeping your resume on file should a position open in the near future.

Sincerely,

20-12 Recruit sales personnel

You happen to know a dynamic salesperson your company would like to hire. The company asks you to help recruit the person. Your letter should stress your experience with the company, pointing out those aspects that you like the most.

Dear _____:

We've heard from ____ that you are the dynamic, assertive, polished professional computer sales expert we're looking for at ____. We may be able to provide you with a position that challenges your ability and gives you an unlimited horizon.

We are a start-up affiliate of ____. By joining now, you will take advantage of an opportunity of a lifetime. You'll have the opportunity to expand your client base and to grow. Our benefits compare with any Fortune 500 company, and as we grow, so do your monthly and quarterly bonuses.

We'd like to fly you in to our corporate headquarters in Tampa next weekend. You can look us over, and we can talk dollars and cents.

Sincerely,

20-13 Recruit sales personnel

Dear _____:

Enclosed are some reference materials for your perusal. The book is a good one but tends to be somewhat opinionated. The videos are of an open-heart operation and the SMO/IR, which is no longer a product as you will see it in this video.

I hope it is not premature to say "welcome aboard."

Please call me if I can be of any help. I look forward to meeting you.

Sincerely,

Kip A. Stastny
Sarns 3M Health Care
Ann Arbor, Michigan

20-14 Recruit sales personnel

Dear _____:

Thank you for applying to Oceanside. Your resume indicates you are a sales professional who can make things happen.

We'd like you to come in and discuss your qualifications with members of our marketing team. You may be the heavy hitter we're looking for.

Sincerely,

20-15 Offer sales position

Dear _____:

Fred and I enjoyed meeting you and Ruth last weekend and appreciate your both taking the time to come to Denver for the interview.

I'd like to make you a formal offer of the position as Marketing Director for our organization at a starting salary of _____ per month, effective May 1.

We have excellent benefits, which include medical, dental, life insurance and a 401(k) plan. As we discussed in the interview, we will assist you with your relocation. Please call me when you have time, and we will finalize the arrangements.

Stan, I'm excited about your joining our firm and look forward to our being able to institute a comprehensive international marketing effort for Mary Cook & Associates.

I will be out of town on business until the 23rd, but will be available to provide relocation assistance after that date.

Sincerely,

Mary Cook
Mary Cook & Associates
Denver, Colorado

20-16 Offer sales position

Dear _____:

Congratulations. You made a hit with our marketing team. I hope we impressed you as well. I'm enclosing a formal offer of employment. Starting date is June 1.

I hope you accept the offer. You're the type of person we need to expand into the southeast territory.

Sincerely,

20-17 Offer sales position

Dear _____:

   I'm happy to invite you to join the _____ team. Your base salary will be _____ per month, plus you will receive a _____ commission on all sales generated in your exclusive territory.

   Enclosed is our moving policy which explains reimbursements for relocating to Memphis. The language is somewhat legalistic, so if you have questions, call me or Doris (she's really the expert.)

   You've made the right choice, Art. We're a fast-growing company in a fast-growing industry. We're just starting to tap the potential. You can look forward to earning a healthy income.

Welcome aboard!

20-18 Welcome new staff person

Dear _____:

   I'm delighted you chose _____. It's going to be fun, crazy, and profitable, I can assure you. Call on me anytime. I'm happy to answer questions or provide whatever help you need.

Good luck!

20-19 Welcome new staff person

Dear _____:

   Welcome to the sales team. We're delighted you decided to join our staff. With your qualifications and excellent sales record, you're sure to feel at home here. Let me know if there's anything I can do to help smooth the way!

Sincerely,

20-20 Recommend retaining new employee

It's not unusual for the company to ask a sales rep to take new people around and show them the ropes. Let the company know when a new person has potential.

MEMO TO: Marketing Manager
FROM: Sales Rep Name
SUBJECT: Commendation

The new sales rep, John _____, spent the last two weeks visiting clients with me. I think we've taken on a winner!

John has a knack for meeting new people and putting them at ease. Within a few moments, they're talking to him as if he were a long-lost friend. He has a low-key, confident manner that makes people trust him and want to do business with him—a major asset in sales!

I also found John to have a good grasp of the line. When one style didn't appeal to a client, he was quick to suggest another that the client did like.

I think he'll be one of our top sales people.

20-21 Encourage new employee

MEMO TO: Marketing Manager
FROM: Sales Rep
SUBJECT: Good Job!

I enjoyed working the territory with you the past two weeks. I was impressed with your knack for meeting people and putting them at ease. Several clients let me know that they like your low-key, confident manner. You have already gained their trust.

I was also impressed with your grasp of the line. I noticed that when one style didn't appeal to a client, you were quick to suggest another one the client did like. Your ability to understand the needs of our clients and provide them with solutions should enable you to become one of our top sales people within a very short time.

Good luck as you begin working the territory on your own. Please call me if I can ever be of help.

Sincerely,

20-22 Ask for clerical/secretarial support

Too busy? It makes sense to ask for help when you need it. It's in the company's interest, as well as yours, to have you doing what you do best—selling. Be sure to state why you need the help at this time.

MEMO TO: Marketing Manager
   FROM: Sales Rep Name
SUBJECT: Request for Clerical Help

With the holiday special, the next four weeks will be the busiest of the year. I'm confident I'll be able to close major deals with new clients as well as with the usuals. But I'll need to get around to see everybody. To do that, I'll need temporary secretarial support. Could Mary give me 8 to 10 hours a week to help write up the orders during the special? Let me know by Friday.

20-23 Ask for clerical/secretarial support

MEMO TO: Marketing Manager
   FROM: Sales Rep Name
SUBJECT: Request for Clerical Help

Help. I'm bogged down in clerical work. Instead of selling, I'm filling out forms and sending off brochures two days a week.

How about hiring a sales secretary? Either half-time, or one that could work for me two days a week and handle other duties the rest of the time.

I'd like to move quickly on this, so that I can add two days of face time with prospects and customers by the end of the month. Increased sales should offset most of the expense.

20-24 Ask for sales support

MEMO TO: Marketing Manager
   FROM: Sales Rep Name
SUBJECT: Additional Sales Support

Las Vegas is booming, and my sales activity has increased over 200%. I think it's time to put on an additional sales person.

I recommend that we split the territory by accounts based on sales volume. At first, I'll keep two-thirds until the new person gets fully on board. Then we can cut it down the middle. There's plenty of sales opportunity for two people here. Right now, we're losing business to competitors because I can't get around to everybody fast enough.

Let's talk next Friday when I'm in the office.

20-25 Ask for sales tool

MEMO TO: Marketing Manager
     FROM: Sales Rep Name
 SUBJECT: Sales Letter Book

I've just seen a copy of a new book that will help increase my sales productivity. It's called *Best Model Sales Letters for Every Selling Situation* and contains 450 model letters covering everything I do. The cost is $_____—a bargain for the amount of help it will give me.

Would you please approve the enclosed purchase order so that I may put this book to work for me as quickly as possible?

20-26 Commend employee to management

You may have the opportunity to work closely with somebody else, somebody who, in your opinion, went out of the way to do a good job. Why not take a few moments to let the manager know?

MEMO TO: Marketing Manager
     FROM: Sales Rep Name
 SUBJECT: Commendation

I want to commend Sara Martin on the outstanding support she provided in getting the _____ proposal off on time.

Sara had very little time to pull together the 200-page proposal. She worked into the night checking facts and making sure everything was perfect.

The customer was impressed with the comprehensive document and subsequently placed an order.

Sara's dedication, professionalism and positive attitude helped make this sale possible.

20-27 Recommend employee for promotion

MEMO TO: Marketing Manager
    FROM: Sales Rep Name
SUBJECT: Commendation

Since _____ started working for us in January, she has taken on an increasing amount of responsibility. From supervising one person in the office, she now supervises three. She has been responsible for seeing that all contracts, orders, shipping notices are correct and out on time. The job has meant learning several new computer programs. She took classes on her own time in order to do this.

I have found Joan to be a highly responsible, competent employee who has made our job of selling much easier. While I would be sorry to see her leave our office, I believe her talents and hard work make her an ideal candidate for the administrative assistant position.

If you need further information before offering her this promotion, please let me know.

20-28 Recommend employee for promotion

Dear _____:

I would like to recommend _____ to the position of Field Sales Trainer effective immediately. During the course of the year, _____ has met the can-do criteria that we have set forth in our job description.

_____'s sales results have been outstanding. He is the only sales representative in our district to have an increase in net sales month after month.

Regarding his sales presentation skills, _____ has a solid foundation of Counselor Selling. He is direct with his accounts and shows the ability to gain commitment on every pull through call. I have observed, through field visits, his ability to have a good recap from a previous call along with a very positive intent statement. One of his strengths is his ability to close, not only for action but also for commitment to move the business forward in his accounts.

_____'s sales planning and activity levels have been solid all year. With the tremendous demands he has on his travel within the state of Nebraska, he has exhibited an outstanding ability to plan and manage this territory. _____ has been quite flexible in his planning and call cycles during the course of the year. As the company has changed some direction, _____ has shown the ability to change his direction and now is focusing on his top accounts as a priority.

_____'s product knowledge is at standard in terms of _____. He has worked very hard this year to continue to understand the entire contact lens industry. He has shown me on field visits his knowledge of not just our Toric business but also competitive products.

Regarding the "will do" criteria, I believe that a few areas need to be noted here surrounding _____'s abilities. One is his perseverance and persistence in moving the business forward. Many other reps would have quit or folded their tents in the early part of this year when the quotas were very, very high. _____ and I met on this matter, and he gave me his word that he would continue to give us 110% effort in his territory. I believe this shows the ability for _____ to see the long-term effects that he could have, not just in Nebraska but for the entire organization. This represents _____'s overall solid business experience in the medical industry.

If you need any other information surrounding _____'s qualifications for this recommendation to Field Sale Trainer, please call me.

Sincereiy,

Rick Prall
Vistakon, Inc., a Johnson & Johnson Company
Jacksonville, Florida

20-29 Report to management on poor employee performance

MEMO TO: Marketing Manager
FROM: Sales Rep Name
SUBJECT: Unsatisfactory Performance

While I was at Clarks Department Store Monday, the manager told me that she has not been satisfied with the service provided by _____.

Orders are not processed promptly, and order entry mistakes are common. Clarks insists on having another analyst handle the account. I told them we would make a change immediately.

Would you please take care of this matter and let me know who the new analyst will be.

20-30 Ask client to recommend person for sales position

Dear _____:

As a policyowner, we value your business and your opinion. And because both are important to us, we'd like to ask your help in finding the right person to fill a sales position.

The person we're looking for is honest, dedicated and enthusiastic. For the person with these qualities, the Mutual of Omaha Companies offer comprehensive training, opportunities for advancement and an income potential limited only by his or her ability and determination.

You may know someone you'd like to recommend. If so, please provide us with the name and phone number and return it in the enclosed postage paid envelope. As always, we appreciate your help and consideration.

Sincerely,

Jeff O'Connell
Mutual of Omaha Insurance Company
Omaha, Nebraska

Advice from the sales experts

The tone and style of personnel or employment related correspondence should be open and honest. State the facts and be pleasant, but keep the letters short and to the point. Use the same words you would use if you were speaking with the person; don't use trite or stilted language. If you are writing about company policies or procedures, don't use a "you're in the army now" approach. A participative, open-organizational style is best. On the other hand, don't be too laid-back. You might miss key issues or give the appearance of being disinterested. Aim for that critical balance between a formal and a casual writing style.

Mary Cook
Mary Cook & Associates
Denver, Colorado

Chapter Twenty-One

Meetings, Workshops and Training Classes

Thanks to the technological explosion, the world's knowledge doubles every year. Staying abreast of information is a critical challenge facing companies everywhere. Each day, thousands of meetings, workshops and training sessions are held. All require a variety of letters to be written, from announcements to confirmations.

Because your event must compete with so many others, your letters must not only convey information, they must also entice the prospect or client to attend.

21-1 Invite client to presentation

Dear _____ :

I am happy to invite you to a presentation titled "The Amdahl Response." It will contain an in-depth analysis of the recent competitive announcements on products and maintenance offerings and the Amdahl response to each of them. The materials presented will make you comfortable with Amdahl as your preferred choice.

On October 22, Amdahl announced its latest family of processors, the 5890, Models 200, 300 and 600. This group of products signaled the second ten years of successful delivery of innovative compatible products from Amdahl. The on-time delivery, performance, reliability and tremendous customer acceptance has placed the 5890 as the benchmark standard in the large mainframe _____-compatible market. The 5890 Model 190 was announced in January of this year with availability in March.

Amdahl single and double capacity 3380-compatible DASD devices, the 6380 and 6380E Models, are proving on a daily basis to be the industry standard for reliability, performance and environmentals.

Amdahl's most innovative feature, M.D.F., Multiple Domain Feature, has revolutionized the many ways in which to best utilize processing power.

Amdahl's support organization, PS&S, has again topped the customer surveys with being absolutely in line with Amdahl's standard of "a customer problem is an Amdahl problem."

These significant items have caused competition to react with announcements in the processor, software and maintenance areas. The "Amdahl Response" will address each of these directly.

Details and R.S.V.P. information are enclosed. I look forward to your attendance.

Sincerely,

Amdahl Corporation
Denver, Colorado

21-2 Invite client to presentation

Dear _____:

Subject: Inventory Management Executive Briefing

DO YOU NEED TO INCREASE YOUR COMPANY'S PROFIT-ABILITY??

DO YOU NEED TO INCREASE THE PRODUCTIVITY OF YOUR INVENTORY??

HAVE YOU EVER CONSIDERED REDESIGNING YOUR INVENTORY CONTROL SYSTEM??

IBM cordially invites you to attend a one-day Inventory Briefing for Wholesale Distribution Executives. The briefing features _____, well known author and consultant in the wholesale distribution industry for 20 years. The briefing will be held Wednesday, June 20, at the Hyatt Regency, Denver Tech Center. It is scheduled to begin at 9:00 a.m. and conclude by 4:00 p.m. A continental breakfast will be available at 8:30 a.m., and lunch will be served midway through the briefing.

This is an excellent opportunity for you to hear, through the use of actual case histories, a fresh and eye-opening perspective on inventory management. Learn what other companies are doing with their inventory management systems and how they are winning the battle of increasing inventory productivity and, as a result, company-wide profitability. Determine what it means to have control of your inventory and why a good computer system is mandatory for the 1990s.

If you are interested in learning more about the briefing or want to register, please contact ____. We look forward to helping you understand how the physical control of inventory can affect your company's bottom line profits.

Sincerely,

IBM Corporation
Denver, Colorado

21-3 Invite client to presentation

Dear _____:

Interest in desktop publishing is hot. We are offering a high-level class to acquaint publications managers with the capabilities and advantages of our software packages.
The class is scheduled for Monday, June 3, from 8:30 a.m. until 4:00 p.m. Enrollment is free, but is restricted to one person per company.
Please complete the enclosed enrollment form and return as soon as possible. The class will fill on a first-come, first-served basis.
I hope you will join us.

Sincerely,

21-4 Invite client to presentation

Dear _____:

The Denver Interstate Branch Office of IBM is assigned the multiple missions of new business and installed mid-range IBM and competitive systems for Colorado, eastern Wyoming and western Nebraska. With these new opportunity missions, Denver Interstate is responsible for the majority of the IBM Business Partners in their geographical area.
With the excitement surrounding the RISC System/6000*, the IBM marketing representatives are very dependent upon solutions provided by business partners to successfully close sales. These marketing reps are making numerous contacts each day with organizations that could be your future customers.
The AIX** Business Partner Branch Exchange will introduce your Business Partner company and solutions to the Denver Interstate marketing reps, so that together we can form the winning combination required in today's marketplace. Plan now to attend on June 15 between 12:30 and 2:30 p.m. in Room 104/105 at _____.
All AIX business partners are invited to attend and bring sales literature and business cards (no demonstration equipment). All the Denver Interstate marketing reps and systems engineers will be in attendance. An invitation is also being extended to the four other IBM Denver branch offices. Pizza and soda will be abundantly available to all who attend.

Call _____ now to reserve your place at the Business Partner Branch Exchange.

Sincerely,

IBM Corporation
Denver, Colorado
*RISC System/6000 is a trademark of the IBM Corporation.
**AIX is a registered trademark of the IBM Corporation.

21-5 Invite client to attend class with fee

Many classes and meetings require attendees to pay a fee. Letters regarding these occasions should point out the value clients will receive.

Dear _____:

We have arranged for _____, noted financial wizard and author of three best-selling books, to address a group of our investors on Friday evening, May 2, at 7:00 in our site cafeteria.

Dr. _____'s methods have generated excitement and envy in the Wall Street community, and I know you will want to take advantage of this unique opportunity. Cost for the lecture is $25. Please return the enclosed card, with payment, by April 20.

I hope you are able to attend.

Sincerely,

21-6 Invite client to attend class with fee

Dear _____:

We have scheduled an additional desktop publishing class. The classes close quickly, so I'm enclosing a registration form that you can fill out and return as soon as possible.

Class will be held from 8a.m. to 4p.m., March 8–12, at our main site on Capital Parkway.

Cost is _____ per person. I recommend that all three members of your department attend. The instruction is superb, as you can see from the enclosed comments. What they gain in class will more than offset the training costs.

Let me know if you have any questions.

Sincerely,

21-7 Inform about accommodations when client pays

Dear _____:

    I know you'll enjoy the convenience of Denver's Mart Hotel. You can walk to showrooms at the Merchandise Mart. And it's an easy drive to the downtown night spots. I've reserved a room for the nights of March 28 and 29. The room has a king sized bed, cable television, view of the mountains — the works. Rates are _____ per night.
    I believe you'll enjoy spending a couple of days in our showrooms and attending the special seminars on promotions that have been scheduled. It will give you a good idea of the range of products we offer and the ways in which they can benefit your customers.
I look forward to seeing you.

Regards,

21-8 Inform about accommodations when client pays

Dear _____:

    Thank you for registering to attend our weekend workshop on electronic publishing.
    We've reserved a room for you at the Sundowner. As part of the workshop, you'll be extended a 10% discount.
    Please join us for a complimentary breakfast Saturday at 8:00 in the Horizon Room. The first session, Advantages of In-house Publishing, is scheduled for 9:30 a.m. in the Greenhouse Terrace meeting room.
    I look forward to seeing you at the workshop.

Sincerely,

21-9 Inform about accommodations when client pays

Dear _____:

    Thank you for sending in your registration fee for the technical writing conference.

As you asked, I've reserved a room for you for the nights of the 13th and 14th at the Comstock as part of our company block. The discounted rate is _____ a night.

I look forward to seeing you at the conference.

Sincerely,

21-10 Inform about accommodations when your company pays

Dear _____:

So glad you can come to the printer symposium.

I'm enclosing your hotel confirmation and a schedule of events.

Of course, I put in for the penthouse suite, with heart-shaped jacuzzi and fully stocked bar, but somehow my request went astray. However, you did get a room on a no-smoking floor, as you asked. (The room fee will be deducted from your bill when you check out.)

I think you'll be impressed when you see the advances we've designed into the new Electron-50 printer and amazed by all the things it can do for your company. Printing has come a long way since Gutenberg.

See you in New Haven. . . .

21-11 Enroll client in training session

This type of letter is sent within your company or to another organization providing enrollment service for you. It spells out precisely the information the registrar needs to enroll the client.

Mary,

Please enroll my customer, Tom Jones, in the Analogy Systems training session, Tuesday, March 4, 10 a.m. Mr. Jones will be traveling to Kansas City to attend the session. Please confirm his enrollment with me as soon as possible. Call my attention to any change of date or time.

Thanks,

21-12 Enroll client in training session

MEMO TO: Education
   FROM: Sales Rep Name
   SUBJECT: Enrollment in "Linkage for Tomorrow" seminar

   Please reserve two places at the "Linkage for Tomorrow" seminar, Friday, November 1, at the conference center. My client, _____, of ComputerWhiz, will attend with me. You can send both confirmations to me, along with any workbooks or other information that we should have beforehand.
   Many thanks.

21-13 Confirm enrollment with client

When enrollment is complete, it is a good idea to confirm with your client. Let him/her know the particulars—date, place, and time. Point out the importance of letting you know if there is any change in plans.

Dear _____:

   As you've requested, I've enrolled you in the telemarketing seminar at the New York Palace on March 31.
   Although the seminar is free, we ask you to let us know if you can't attend. It's so popular, we've had to create a waiting list.
   I know you'll enjoy the seminar and find it helpful in your business.

Regards,

21-14 Confirm enrollment with client

Dear _____:

   I'm happy to confirm a spot in the spreadsheet class for _____. It took a little elbowing, since the class is so popular. If _____ can't make it, please let me know immediately. Refunds cannot be issued on cancellations received after May 20.

Sincerely,

21-15 Confirm enrollment for employee in your company

Dear _____:

This letter confirms that you are registered for the Managing a Wide Area Sales Territory seminar to be held March 3 and 4 at Oceanside Employers Council, State Street, Santa Barbara.

You will need to make your own travel and hotel arrangements.

Travel costs, as well as the $100 seminar fee, will be paid by the company. Please forward an approved Request for Disbursement to my attention for processing.

We will appreciate your critique of the course upon its completion.

Sincerely,

21-16 Confirm enrollment with training center

Dear _____:

Three members of Short Publishing will attend the desktop publishing training class scheduled for March 8–12. Their registration cards are enclosed. Since the class just opened, I assume that all three will be admitted. If this is not the case, please call me before contacting the customer.

Thanks for your help.

21-17 Provide material/agenda for session

A brief cover letter accompanying a study guide, workbook, or other materials for an upcoming program is always a good idea. It reaffirms the program's importance in your client's mind, and points out the benefits.

Dear _____:

Enclosed is the study guide, *A Competitive Analysis of Desktop Publishing,* for next week's program. Please complete the exercises and bring the guide with you.

We encourage you to take plenty of time to review the material. Your personal "payoff" in the program will be enhanced if you understand the material well enough to ask the tough questions you'll be fielding from prospects. Since there will be some numerical analysis, please bring a pocket calculator with you to the seminar.

I hope you will find the program enjoyable and beneficial.

Sincerely,

21-18 Provide material/agenda for session

Dear _____:

Enclosed is a copy of the agenda for the Sarns Technology Seminar. The next seminar is scheduled for November 1 through 3, with arrival the afternoon of the first and departure from Detroit Metro Airport the afternoon of the third.

During the seminar, we focus on the technologies used to design Sarns products, with an emphasis on the design and development of the Sarns Membrane Oxygenator. The seminar provides details as to how products are conceived, developed, and manufactured, as well as the technologies involved.

If you have any questions about the seminar or anything about Sarns 3M, please let me know. I look forward to seeing you at the Sarns Technology Seminar.

Sincerely,

Kip A. Stastny
Sarns 3M Health Care
Ann Arbor, Michigan

21-19 Provide material/agenda for session

Dear _____:

Welcome to the first annual Software Extravaganza. In one day and one hotel, you will see demonstrations of 100 different software packages to solve every business need.

Today's agenda is as follows:

8:00 a.m.–Continental breakfast in the Washington Foyer.
9:00 a.m.–Welcome in the Lincoln Auditorium.
9:30 a.m.–Breakout sessions and demonstrations.
12:00 noon–Luncheon in the Adams Room.

2:00 p.m.–Breakout sessions and demonstrations.
4:30 p.m.–Wrap up in the Lincoln Auditorium.

We are happy to be involved in Software Extravaganza and hope you will find solutions to all your application needs.

Sincerely,

21-20 Advise client class full

Class full? Be sensitive to your clients' disappointment at not making the cut. At the same time, take a positive approach. Assure them the class is worth waiting for and you will do all you can to get them in the next session.

Dear _____:

Thank you for sending in three registrations for the "Turning the Stock" seminar.

Because of high demand, the seminar filled up before your registrations arrived. We will offer it again on May 15 and 16, and I have nailed down slots for you already. The registrar will use the cards you submitted for the April session. Just call this week and let me know if your employees can make the new dates.

Sincerely,

21-21 Ask for evaluation

Dear _____:

Here's your chance to make a difference.

Please take a few minutes to fill out the enclosed evaluation form for the Barrett Telemarketing Seminar you recently attended. Simply fill in the boxes that best describe your opinions. We've also left space at the end for any specific suggestions you may have.

We want to make sure that the information we present in our seminars, and the style in which we present it, are helpful to you, our customers. We value your opinions and suggestions.

Many thanks,

21-22 Arrange class

It's your turn to arrange a special program for your clients. Even more effective than a brochure or other official announcement is a personal letter, telling your clients about the program and pointing out the benefits.

Dear _____:

Since many of my customers tell me that creating attractive and unique displays is the toughest part of their job, I have arranged a special session on displays at the April market.

Designers Susan Logan and Camille Dorster will demonstrate new ideas for showing your wares. The demonstration will be offered on Thursday, 10 a.m., and on Friday at 2 p.m. Most of their ideas are so simple you'll say, "Why didn't I think of this?" At the same time, they are imaginative and dramatic.

I saw the program in Dallas recently and was really impressed! Let me know by March 10 if you would like me to reserve a place for you.

Regards,

21-23 Invite Instructor

Letters to trainers and instructors are important public relations links. Whether you're inviting or thanking, let them know that you, and by extension, your company appreciate their talents and abilities, and their willingness to work with you.

Dear _____:

Your talk on the American-Japanese quality equation at the Rotary meeting knocked my socks off.

Would you be willing to present that same talk to a group of sales engineers on Tuesday evening, January 16, at the Windsurfer? Please be our guest for dinner, beginning at 6:30 p.m.

Sincerely,

21-24 Invite Instructor

Dear _____:

     I enjoyed your demonstration at the Dallas mart last week. Your ideas on displaying merchandise were both imaginative and practical—something most apparel managers could use.

     Would you be able to give the same demonstration in Baltimore on April 19 and April 20? The audience will be managers and buyers of women's apparel for small, high-end boutiques in the Northeast corridor.

     We will pay your regular fee plus the cost of airline travel to Baltimore. The meeting would be held at the Redstone, and we will make sure rooms are available for your stay.

     Please let me know by March 15 whether we can expect to have your outstanding program in our area!

Sincerely,

21-25 Confirm Instructor

Dear _____:

     Thank you for agreement to present a Clinical Seminar on Sunday, April 29th! Please answer the questions below and mail the completed form to the CDLA Office by Monday, April 2.

     You are scheduled to give your presentation:

— Once, to fill the entire morning (9 AM–12:30 PM)
— Repeat three times in the afternoon (1:30–2:30, 2:45–3:45, and 4–5)

     Attendees will have the option of attending one of four clinics in the morning. In the afternoon, they will have a choice of attending three out of five. Those who are presenting a morning session can begin set-up at 8:00 AM and should plan to remove their equipment promptly so the afternoon clinics have ample time for their set-up. Also, because there is an hourly rotation in the afternoon, it is important to keep on schedule.

Equipment Information:

I will need the following equipment for my clinical presentation:

( ) flip chart
( ) blackboard
( ) audio visual
    ( ) 35 mm slide projector ( ) with remote
    ( ) 16 mm movie projector
    ( ) overhead projector
    ( ) VCR/monitor
    ( ) I will bring my own

Set-up Information

( ) Work table(s) 6' each, ( ) on a riser/stage
( ) standing podium
( ) table lectern with work space
( ) electrical outlet(s)
( ) theater style seating ( ) classroom seating

Please add anything else we should know to assure a smooth flowing program on Sunday.

Gail Turner

Meetings and Management
Boulder, Colorado

21-26 Confirm Instructor

Dear _____:

I'm pleased you will be able to give us your insights on marketing at the June 6 meeting of Centennial Club. As I mentioned in our telephone conversation, the club is made up of sales men and women from various industries—everything from real estate to computers to wearing apparel. Usually, about 50 people attend the monthly meeting.

The meeting will be held at Socrates Restaurant, 4th and Pine Streets. Social hour begins at 6 p.m., with dinner at 6:30. Your talk will begin about 7 and should run no longer than 40 minutes. We can offer you a $50 honorarium.

We are all looking forward to hearing what you have to say!

Regards,

21-27 Thank guest Instructor

Dear _____:

We are pleased with the "Write with Power" seminar you conducted for our staff in June. We're already seeing evidence of the participants applying the techniques you taught. There's no doubt our communications will improve substantially.

I'm happy to recommend your course to other businesses, so that they, too, can benefit. Thanks again for a wonderful contribution to our firm.

Sincerely,

21-28 Thank In-house Instructor

Dear _____:

A+! That's the way my client rated the promotions class you put on last week. Keep up the good work.

Sincerely,

21-29 Thank In-house Instructor

Joanna, thanks for teaching the word processing course last week. My client's employees expressed appreciation for the excellent job you did. They especially liked the time you spent with them individually to answer questions.

Support like this makes our job in the field much easier.

Sincerely,

21-30 Thank staff

MEMO TO: Staff
    FROM: Frank Baudo
SUBJECT: National Sales Meeting

May I take this opportunity to express my thanks to all of you. Speaking for the field sales organization, it was the best sales meeting ever!

Everything and everyone was just great. Your hard work, creativity and enthusiasm are an example of the talent here at American Seating.

Once again, thank you and all the members of your team who helped to make this possible.

Sincerely,

Frank L. Baudo
American Seating Company
New York, New York

21-31 Thank client for sending employee to class

Another good public relations letter lets your client know that you appreciate the fact he/she sent an employee to your program. The letter should convey the idea that your client's money was well spent.

Dear _____:

Thank you for the opportunity to have____ in our Basic Training Class on the____. In class, she learned the basics of the equipment, participated in group review sessions and spent several hours on special applications pertaining to your office's workload requirements.

However, I would like to emphasize that this is a new skill being learned and, as such, is similar to any new skill—for example, learning to drive a car or to type. ____'s productivity on the equipment will gradually improve as a result of work experience and time devoted to the equipment.

Thank you for allowing us the opportunity to work with you in creating a better office system. If we can be of further assistance, please call me at ____.

Sincerely,

21-32 Announce class to media

Take the opportunity of a class or workshop to get your product's name before the public. Send a brief press release to the appropriate journal, newsletter or local newspaper. Press release letters address the five "Ws" of journalism: who, what, where, when, why (and sometimes, how.)

FOR IMMEDIATE RELEASE

　　or, if appropriate,

FOR RELEASE (Date)

CONTACT: (Your name, company, phone number)

COMPU-TYPE OFFERS BEGINNING COMPUTER CLASSES

　　Compu-Type will offer three computer classes for beginners during February. Classes include: Introduction to computers and what they can do for you; Getting around word processing; and Selecting software for basic business needs. Classes meet four consecutive Saturdays, Feb. 2 to Feb. 23, from 9 a.m. to noon. Cost is $30 per class. Reservations are required. Call _____.

21-31 Announce class to media

FOR IMMEDIATE RELEASE

　　or, if appropriate,

FOR RELEASE (Date)

CONTACT: (Your name, company, phone number)

DO-IT YOURSELF HOME REMODELING CLASS OFFERED

　　How to replace walls, install windows, and build outdoor decks will be covered in a one-day demonstration class, Saturday, April 4. The class is offered by Rawlins Lumber and Building Supplies. It will be held at the Fairview auditorium, 4th and Main.

　　Our own experts in carpentry, plumbing and electrical work will show slides and demonstrate the best methods of handling difficult remodeling tasks. The class will be geared to homeowners who wish to handle remodeling themselves.

　　The class is free, but attendance is limited. For reservations, call _____.

Tips to sharpen your writing skills

Get to the point! Your client will begin reading your letter with two questions in mind: What is this about? Why should I care? You must answer those questions in the first two or three sentences.

Give your paragraphs unity. Every sentence in a paragraph must pertain to the same idea. If another idea intrudes, set it aside. It belongs in another paragraph.

Keep your paragraphs short—no more than three or four sentences. Short paragraphs make your letter easier to read.

Help your reader through longer letters by using transitions from one paragraph to another. Begin new paragraphs with: Just as . . . ; In contrast to . . . ; Neither is . . . ; Also . . . ; On the other hand . . .

Chapter Twenty-Two

Trade Shows and Conventions

Excitement. Networking. Trade shows and conventions create atmospheres charged with energy. Sales reps learn who's who, what's new, and what competitors' products can do. Clients check out the latest products and most advanced technologies in the industry.

To help clients set a course for your booth—before they are engulfed in the razzle-dazzle of the show—write letters in advance to stimulate curiosity and action.

22-1 Invite clients to trade show

Dear _____:

Only two weeks 'til the annual furniture trade show at the Raleigh Convention Center. On March 22 and 23, you'll have a chance to see styles and fabrics that will make furniture fashion headlines during the year.

I know you'll be impressed with the products we'll unveil during the show. You'll see samples of our gorgeous, new wood and metal seating, as well as show-stopping soft seating.

Your customers will be impressed with the new treatments—weave, texture and color—we've incorporated into our line. You can run your fingers through 30 new fabrics featured in our display.

When you come by the booth, be sure to ask for the special full-color catalog I've set aside for you. The catalog is a souvenir edition, celebrating our 25th anniversary, and features an historical perspective of the furniture industry, as well as designs to take you through the next decade. I'll be there each day between 11 a.m. and 2 p.m. It'll be a pleasure to show you our new products personally.

Regards,

22-2 Invite clients to trade show

Dear _____:

The trucks are loaded and heading for Chicago. Our display at the LPG trade show this year is the most innovative ever. It gives clients a chance to see our technology in action.

Special cutaway models of our latest regulator—the Selpac J17—let you view the inside engineering, while a clear plastic mock up shows how gas flows through the unit. You can key in a variety of emergency conditions on our computer to see how the regulator's unique safety features respond.

I invite you and your associates to stop by and take a look. I believe you'll be impressed with the technology and quality of the Selpac J17 and our other products.

After hours, when you're ready to relax, join us in our hospitality suite, room 1427 at the Hilton.

See you there!

Best regards,

22-3 Invite clients to trade show

Dear _____:

Mark your calendar for March 3, 4, and 5. The biggest trade show in the software industry will be held at the Atlanta Convention Center on those days.

Demonstrations and talks-by-the-experts will set you thinking about improvements to your own operation. You'll have a chance to see such vanguard technologies as communications networking and artificial intelligence.

We've been preparing our software to accept these new technologies. Our new tax program, called SOFT-TAX, can interact with a dozen accountants via a Local Area Network or communicate with colleagues located across the country.

Be sure to stop by our booth. I'll have a packet ready for you that explains the system. SOFT-TAX promises to simplify the accountant's life.

Sincerely,

22-4 Invite clients to trade show

Dear _____:

Why take time to visit the Toy Merchandisers Trade Show in New York? Because when you're in the toy business, you have to know what's going to be hot nine months down the line.

Turn-of-the-Century Toys will be one of 500 toy manufacturers displaying wares. The highlight will be authentic dolls, cars, stuffed animals and other favorite toys from the 1890s, along with replicas we've developed for sale in 1990. They should make hot collector items as we turn the corner into the 21st Century.

The trade show begins February 2 and runs through February 7. A special memento designed to mark the occasion is waiting for you at our booth.

Just present the enclosed gift certificate when you visit.

I look forward to seeing you there.

Sincerely,

22-5 Confirm registration with client

You've registered your client for the trade show. Take a moment to send a brief letter reaffirming the date, time, and place. Your client will appreciate the courtesy.

Dear _____:

You're all set for the trade show at the Dallas Convention Center June 1 and 2. Just check in at the front desk when you arrive. Your name will be on the computer.

Looking forward to seeing you then.

Regards,

22-6 Confirm registration with client

Dear _____:

Just a note to let you know you are registered for the trade show April 16 and 17 at the Denver Merchandise Mart. Doors will be open from 9 a.m. to 6 p.m., so you can stop by whenever it's convenient. Be sure to give yourself enough time to see everything. This promises to be the year's biggest show.

Check in at the front desk, where a name tag and information packet will be waiting.

I look forward to seeing you.

Best regards,

22-7 Thank clients for attending trade show

Your clients made a special effort to attend your trade show. Let them know you appreciate it. A brief letter also gives you the chance to get your company's name before your client once again, reinforcing the idea that you are there to provide service.

Dear _____:

Thank you for visiting with us at the AAMS Show in Phoenix.

As you requested, I am enclosing a package of literature that fully describes the products and services offered by LIFECARE. You will find information on our PLV-102.

I will ask LIFECARE's District Manager in your area to contact you by telephone to offer assistance and arrange for a demonstration. Please let me know if there is anything else that I can do.

Sincerely,

LIFECARE
Lafayette, Colorado

22-8 Thank clients for attending trade show

Dear _____ :

What a great time we had at the stock show in Denver! I still admire you for going one on one with that bull. Hope you can move your arm by now.

Seriously, thanks for visiting our booth. I do hope you were impressed enough with our new line of tooled leather belts to place a blanket order for your entire chain. If you place an order by February 15, you'll be among the stores premiering the belts and will benefit from a special sales promotion we'll be running on local TV stations in cities where the line is available.

I'm enclosing another catalog and price list—in case the copies I gave you got trampled during the stock show. I'll call you next week to talk about the order.

Sincerely,

22-9 Announce show to media

FOR IMMEDIATE RELEASE

or

FOR RELEASE (Date)

CONTACT:

JUNEFEST SET FOR BUYERS FARM

Junefest, the annual regional ladies and children's apparel market, will be held at Buyers Farm, June 22-26. Clothing and accessories for the holidays will be exhibited.

Special events will include fashion shows and seminars on such subjects as Creative Accessorizing and Small Business Marketing.

Speaker for the kick-off dinner June 22 will be ____, owner of Like-Real Silk Flowers, who will discuss "enhancing the holiday atmosphere for your customers."

Buyers representing both department stores and small shops in fifteen states are expected to attend.

For further information on Junefest, please contact Herb Straight at ____.

22-10 Confirm duties and hours of booth attendants

Dear _____:

This year's convention should be a great opportunity to pull in prospects. We've made the display colorful and attractive to grab passersby, and the "gold doubloon" paperweights should keep our name in front of them when they get back to their offices. You'll be sure to generate comments by wearing the pirate hat you'll find under the table.

The clincher is to have the booth manned constantly during display hours. The following schedule divides the duty so that two people will be at the booth in two-hour shifts.

(Schedule)

Let me know of any conflicts right away.
See you there, mate,

22-11 Inform staff about special apparel

Dear _____:

As you know, each year we do something unexpected to catch attention at the medical convention. Here's our plan for this year.

All representatives will arrive together at 1:00 p.m. wearing plaid shirts, blue jeans and straw hats. The en-masse arrival should make a splash in the middle of all the suits and ties.

Please meet in the hotel lobby at 12:45 and pick up your hat. I think it should be great fun—and you can bet we'll be the most comfortable.

Sincerely,

22-12 Thank company staff

Thank you notes are the best public relations investment you will ever make. They pay continuing dividends. After a successful trade show, let the company staff know you appreciate their efforts. They'll be willing to work even harder the next time.

Dear _____:

It was a winner! Your staff put on an extraordinary show this year. Everything from the physical arrangements to the workshops and banquet were outstanding. Congratulations to everyone who contributed.

Sincerely,

22-13 Thank trade show staff

Dear _____:

Enclosed is the Cross Pen that we spoke about at the Society of Thoracic Surgeons meeting in Baltimore. Thank you for all the hard work and effort that you put into making the convention a success for Sarns 3M. It is reassuring to know that we can attend a convention and do our job of demonstrating and selling our products to customers and not have to worry about having a great looking booth, because you do that.

Thanks again for all your help and support. I look forward to working with you again in the near future.

Sincerely,

Kip A. Stastny
Sarns 3M Health Care
Ann Arbor, Michigan

22-14 Order booth space, other requirements

Dear _____:

As we discussed by telephone this morning, the Western Sports Show will require booths with varying amounts of space, since both apparel and sports equipment will be exhibited.

We will require thirty (30) draped tables (6' long) for the equipment. They should be set up with enough space around them so that buyers can examine pieces of equipment. In addition, we prefer to have these booths at the south end of the mart, close to the overhead door. Some of the equipment, such as canoes and snowmobiles, will have to be brought in at the dock.

The other fifty-four (54) smaller booths will be used by apparel distributors. They should measure 5' x 6' x 3' and can be arranged throughout the rest of the floor area.

All the booths require access to an electric outlet or extension cord. We would also like at least two folding chairs per booth.

The show will open at 6 p.m. October 2. Exhibitors will be setting up throughout the day, beginning at 10 a.m. The show will close October 4 at 6 p.m., and exhibitors will tear down and be out of the space by 10 p.m.

Please let me know of any problems in setting up the booths as we have requested.

Sincerely,

22-15 Confirm booth space, other requirements

Dear _____:

Here is the deposit to cover our firm's booth space for the International Geophysics Symposium February 19–22.

We require a 6' x 6' space, with an electrical outlet accommodating four plugs. The space must have wall support for a large display board. We also need a 4' table and two chairs.

Please let me know of any problems in fulfilling these requirements.

Sincerely,

22-16 Order brochures/handouts for show

Dear _____:

As you know, the Western Sports Show will be held the first week in October. We are counting on a great deal of interest in our new fiberglass canoe. Since the canoe itself will not be ready in time for the show, it is essential that brochures containing photographs and descriptions be available for prospects to see.

I will need 300 to 400 to distribute during the show. Do you foresee any problem? Let me know right away if you do. Whatever it takes, the brochures must be there.

Thanks,

22-17 Order brochures/handouts for show

Dear _____:

Please deliver 500 copies of our brochure #331, "Facts about Futura Frames," to my attention, in care of the Harrison Conference Center, Lake Bluff, Illinois. Mark "Hold for Arrival June 3."

The brochures will be key in our display. I'm counting on you to make sure they arrive on time and in mint condition.

Thanks for your help.

Sincerely,

22-18 Request demonstration equipment

Dear _____:

I'd like a cutaway of the Model 440 SCUBA regulator to demo at the Waterways Meeting and Trade Show March 7. Would you arrange with the model shop to highlight the moving parts by painting the shell candy apple red. Enclosed is a sketch of what I have in mind. Let me know if you run into any problems. I'd like to have the model in hand by March 1.

Thanks to all the wizards in the back room who manage to come through with brilliant work each year. I'm counting on you again.

Sincerely,

22-19 Report on show to management

Dear _____:

We really got our money's worth at the World Communications Conference this year! More than 500 people stopped by the booth during the four days. I met with more than a dozen people who expressed solid interest in our line. Best of all, I brought home two contracts.

On a scale of 10, I'd rate the show a 9+. Let's go again next year.

Sincerely,

22-20 Report on show to management

Dear _____:

The Winter Fair was not worth our investment. The audience was oriented toward consumers, not operators. Only three contacts may eventually result in small sales. Let's drop it in the future.

Sincerely,

22-21 Establish rapport with other vendors at show

Dear _____:

I enjoyed chatting with you during the International Graphics Show. I was impressed with the quality and function of the plotter you displayed.

As I mentioned, I'd like a chance to bid on your ink requirements next year. Would you arrange to have some specs sent to me? I'll have our people review them and then get in touch with your purchasing agent.

I appreciate any help you can provide.

Sincerely,

22-22 Propose seminar for trade show

Dear _____:

Thank you for the opportunity to participate in the Imprinted Sportswear Show seminar program.

While teaching both "Getting into the Embroidery Business" and "The Embroidery Workshop," I realized the need for a third session, "Successfully Selling Embroidery." We are presently teaching great application techniques, offering participants a myriad of vendors from which to buy, and concentrating on the production aspects of the business.

I propose teaching a seminar relating to selling embroidery. Some topics to be addressed might be:

1. Dressing to sell.
2. Body language—what you are really telling your customer and what is your customer telling you.
3. Developing a relationship with a customer.
4. Service—going that extra mile.
5. Helpful selling tools.
6. Different ways to sell embroidery.
7. Potential customers.

I have personally seen the need in the industry to help creative embroiderers develop the successful techniques and personalities for selling their work.

I will attend the Orlando show and would be happy to discuss these topics with you. Please feel free to call at any time.

Sincerely,

Marilyn Kay Reichenberg
Initial Stitch, Inc.
Boulder, Colorado

22-23 Confirm arrangements for client's use of equipment

Dear _____:

We are pleased to accept your request for the use of our Event Tent. Set-up instructions are included in the crate. It is my understanding that you are planning to provide your own transportation and will pick up on ____ and return on ____. Please coordinate these arrangements with ____.

Thank you for the opportunity to serve your needs and if you have any questions or future need of our exhibit materials, please call me at ____.

Also, we would appreciate your alerting us to any damage or missing hardware so we can make the equipment serviceable for the next requestor. Should damage occur during your event, repairs (if required) will be made and cost charged to your account.

As acknowledgement of acceptance of responsibility for these materials, please sign and return a copy of this letter to me by July 18.

Sincerely,

Denise Varra

Tips to sharpen your writing skills

Build rhythm into sentences by arranging elements from shortest to longest, from simplest to complex.
Examples:

- We can supply steak, hamburger and fish fillets.
- They reminded him of reformers and old-style politicians.
- New Orleans arouses thoughts of jazz, Mardigras and Cajun cookin'.
- Her trip covered Rome, Paris and Copenhagen.

Beware of adjectives and adverbs. They can weaken your message.
Examples:

POOR: The marketing plan will *primarily* focus on the products.
GOOD: The marketing plan will focus on the products.
POOR: Our *fabulous new* fall line is available.
GOOD: Our fall line is available. I'm confident you will like it.

Chapter Twenty-Three

Accommodations

Although unexciting, this routine correspondence can make the difference between a smoothly run event and one riddled with confusion and problems. Letters should be clear, containing specific information and instructions.

23-1 Inquire about hotel accommodations

Dear _____:

The Centennial Sales Club will hold its annual meeting in Santa Fe from June 5 to June 10, 19__. We expect 200 people to attend, and we would like to make the _____ our meeting headquarters.

In addition to about 30 rooms, we would require three meeting rooms, capable of holding at least 50 people, and a hospitality suite.

Please let me know whether you can accommodate us at that time. Would you please include a brochure on the hotel along with a listing of your rates?

Thank you,

23-2 Confirm hotel accommodations

Dear _____:

This letter confirms our phone conversation of 3/14/91.

Please reserve 20 rooms for our firm's use at the National Machine Design Convention August 6–10, 19__.

Rate per room will be _____ single, _____ double. Specific room assignments will be confirmed at a later date.

I understand we may cancel rooms without penalty through July 1.

Thank you for your assistance.

Sincerely,

23-3 Confirm hotel accommodations

Dear _____:

Thank you for arranging the hotel accommodations for Illinois Gift and Jewelry Association's annual meeting February 1 and 2. We look forward to enjoying your fine hospitality.

We understand that you have set aside a block of 25 rooms at 5% discount for our members. In addition, you will also make available three conference rooms and a hospitality suite. The suite will be open from 7 a.m. to 10 p.m. daily with complimentary coffee, tea and soft drinks offered during the day. Between 5 p.m. and 7 p.m. a cash bar and bartender will be on hand, and a selection of four hors d'oeuvres will also be available.

We appreciate your help with the meeting. If you have any questions, please call me.

Many thanks,

23-4 Reserve hotel hospitality suite

Dear _____:

The Wisconsin chapter of Salespeople with a Purpose will hold its annual convention at the _____ October 23–25. We have already arranged for a block of rooms, as well as for three meeting rooms.

In addition, we wish to have another room available during the convention as a hospitality room. This room should be easily accessible from the meeting rooms. Coffee and tea should be available between 7 a.m. and 4 p.m. each day.

Between 4 p.m. and 6 p.m. each day, we would like you to furnish a cash bar and bartender.

Please confirm that we will have a hospitality room, and let me know the cost of the coffee and tea, and of providing a bartender.

Thank you,

23-5 Arrange catering for hospitality suite

Dear _____:

Our firm will host a hospitality suite on July 12 during the National Retailers Convention. Would you please provide the following refreshments and bar drinks for 50 guests.

(Specifics re bar drinks and food)

I understand you can provide the above at a cost not to exceed ____.

Please confirm the room number of the hospitality suite as soon as possible, so that we may invite our guests in advance.

Sincerely,

23-6 Confirm catering

A few moments taken to put the catering arrangements in writing can prevent misunderstandings at the event. A letter allows the hotel staff to compare their understanding of the arrangements with yours, while there is still time to settle differences.

Dear _____:

I enjoyed meeting with you yesterday. Your enthusiasm about the menu for our April dinner meeting is contagious. My mouth is already watering!

According to my notes, you will be preparing the following foods for 75 people:

Chicken breasts in pastry shells; pasta in light cream sauce; spinach-raspberry salad; apple cheese tarts; coffee and tea.

Also, your staff will arrive at 6 p.m. to set up the tables; serve the food at 8 p.m.; and handle the after-dinner clean up.

Sound right? Please let me know if you have any questions, and bon appetit!

Sincerely,

23-7 Confirm catering

Dear _____:

This letter confirms our meeting on 3/14/__. We require the following catering arrangements during the National Machine Design Convention August 6–10, 19__.

Tuesday, August 7—7:00–8:30 a.m.
Continental breakfast for 250 in the Upstairs Foyer.
Includes Danish and oat bran muffins, apple and orange juice, coffee, tea, milk.
Price: $____

Thursday, August 9—7:00 p.m.
Buffet dinner for 100 in the Maple Room.
Includes three pasta entrees with meat and cheese sauces, salad, steamed vegetables, rolls, and three types of dessert, coffee, tea, iced tea and milk.
Price: $____

Thank you for your assistance.

Sincerely,

23-8 Arrange for staffing

Dear _____:

We're looking forward to holding our trade show at the Arena, April 6-9. Since we are expecting a capacity crowd, you should plan to have a large staff on hand.

Specifically, we will want people at the doors to take admission tickets, as well as people on the floor to help sales reps find their assigned booths.

Other staff personnel should circulate the floor to help rearrange booth space, locate extra chairs or handle problems with electrical outlets—all the last-minute things that crop up at every trade show.

Also, please see that enough workers are in the food booths to handle the crowd, especially during meal hours. As you will recall, the lines at the food booths during lunch hour last year were depressingly long.

Thanks for handling these matters. With enough staff, I'm confident this year's show will be the smoothest yet.

Regards,

23-9 Thank hotel for outstanding service/accommodations

Dear _____:

Thank you for helping to make the paper products convention a success.

Service at the _____ was outstanding—way above par. The rooms were clean, comfortable and attractive, and the staff was courteous and friendly at all times. In fact, several of our members remarked that the concierge had gone out of his way to make dinner reservations, call taxis and otherwise be helpful—all with a smile.

Whatever you're doing, keep it up! We will certainly be back— and we'll tell our friends.

Regards,

23-10 Thank hotel for outstanding service/accommodations

Dear _____:

I just wanted you to know of the outstanding job your people did in helping to make our diskette drive meeting a success.

Everything we needed was at hand, and the luncheon brought rave reviews from our guests.

With this level of service, you can be sure we'll return for future meetings.

Sincerely,

23-11 Complain about unsatisfactory service/accommodations

Dear _____:

I am disappointed with the buffet dinner arrangements at your hotel during the National Machine Design Convention.

We arranged a pasta buffet for 100 to be held in the Maple Room. Invitations to our guests were so noted. On the evening of the dinner, however, service was switched to the Aspen Room downstairs. Not only did this last-minute change cause confusion for our guests and embarrassment for us, the room was not large enough to comfortably handle a buffet for 100.

Our arrangements with you were made in plenty of time to avoid this situation. I would appreciate your looking into this matter and crediting us for part of the cost.

Sincerely,

Tips to sharpen your writing skills

Keep sentences crisp by cutting unnecessary words and phrases. The following sentences would be better without the italicised words.

- We found her suggestion *to be* innovative and exciting.
- Hanson, *who is* purchasing agent at American, ordered the parts.
- The fabric *that was* included in the order arrived today.
- The argument *that is given* is that customers will respond to lower prices.

Chapter Twenty-Four

Speaking Engagements

You're a celebrity! That's right. Sales reps are often asked to make public appearances. Probably because of the "gift of gab" and ability to capture an audience. In any event, presenting a public lecture or speech to an organization offers an opportunity to build PR for yourself and for your company. Letters are part of the process. They confirm the arrangements (thus eliminating error), and they send a friendly message to the sponsoring organization.

24-1 Inform person you've suggested him/her as guest speaker

Dear _____ :

Hope you'll still speak to me after I tell you I proposed your name as keynote speaker for the Annual Fiesta Fundraiser.

I know how busy your schedule is, but I believe you are the perfect choice for this year's event. The theme is "Making It Happen."

The banquet is scheduled for Friday evening, March 3, 7:00 p.m., at the Downtown Sheraton. We expect an audience of 500. Your appearance will greatly add to the success of this year's program.

John, I will contact you in the next two weeks. Hope your answer will be yes.

Sincerely,

24-2 Invite speaker

Dear _____ :

I really enjoyed the speech you gave to the _____ last June.

It was informative and entertaining at the same time—a happy combination. Would you be available to talk to Rotary, Thursday, April 12, at noon?

I know our members would benefit from your witty insights on today's business climate.

I'll call you the first of the week to get your response.

Sincerely,

24-3 Invite speaker

Dear _____ :

_____ mentioned you are an expert on earthquake prediction. Living near a fault line, members of Santa Clara Lyons Club want to keep informed about the latest technology for determining the likelihood of earthquakes.

Could you speak at a weekly meeting on the Thursday most convenient for you during October? The speech would be about 20 minutes. We would, of course, like you to join us for lunch. Our meetings are held at the Harvest Inn.

I'll check with you in the next few days to confirm a date.

Sincerely,

24-4 Invite press to speaking engagement

Dear _____:

The enclosed press release provides details on the Johnstown Annual Sales Professionals Convention to be held in two weeks.

I call your attention to our featured speaker, Mary Cook, international consultant on human resources and management and author of five business books. Her address on managing the nonsalaried work force will interest many local businesses. Mary will arrive the evening before the session. If you'd like to interview her at that time, please let me know and I'll arrange it.

We appreciate any coverage you can provide for this important event.

Sincerely,

24-5 Accept speaking engagement

Dear _____:

I'd be happy to talk to the Morning Optimists on "Competitive Intelligence." The subject is becoming increasingly popular as even small businesses feel the effects of information leaks.

I'll be at The Grange at 7:15 a.m. Friday, May 20.

Sincerely,

24-6 Accept speaking engagement

Dear_____:

Thanks for asking! I'll be happy to speak to the Rotary Club on Friday, September 28, at noon. My topic will be "Sales: A Changing Game."

I've been in the sales game for twenty-five years. Most of that time I've spent selling electronic and other high-tech materials to international corporations. My job has taken me around the world and given me a new perspective on why American salesmanship must change, if American companies are to remain key competitors on the world's economic playing field.

I look forward to sharing my observations with you and the other Rotarians.

Regards,

24-7 Decline speaking engagement

Dear _____:

Thanks for inviting me to speak at the March Rotary luncheon. I have a business commitment that day and won't be able to accept. I hope you'll keep me in mind for a future date.

Sincerely,

24-8 Decline speaking engagement

Dear _____:

Thanks for your invitation to speak at the September sales meeting. I'm sorry I can't oblige, as I'm booked through September.
Let me know soon if a later date will work.

Sincerely,

24-9 Confirm speaking engagement with speaker

Dear _____:

Thank you for taking part in our 1990 Summer Sunset Series "Sail Away." We are looking forward to "Goin' Railroading" on July 26, ____.
All of the programs will begin at 7:30 p.m., with refreshments served afterward (at approximately 8:30). Please plan to arrive between 6:30 and 7:00, or earlier, depending on your setup

needs. A podium with microphone and a remote-controlled slide projection system are standard equipment. If you will need other audio-visual equipment, including additional microphones, or would like to see the facility, please advise me as soon as possible.

The presentation will take place at:

The Coors Auditorium
(Address)

A map is included and a Guest Relations representative will be at the entrance gate to assist you.

The enclosed brochure will be sent to our mailing list of over 1,000 organizations, businesses, retirement groups and individuals. It also serves as a press release. With last year's release, the *Denver Post, Golden Transcript, Sentinel* and various radio and television stations gave us coverage.

We have reserved six places for you on your presentation night. If you would like more reservations, more brochures, or reservations for other shows, please call me at _____.

We couldn't "Sail Away" without your time and talent, so thank you once again for joining us. It should be a fun voyage for all.

Maridale Powell
Coors Brewing Company
Golden, Colorado

24-10 Confirm speaking engagement with speaker

Dear_____,

I am looking forward to your presentation, "The Competitive Edge in Sales," next Wednesday, September 11, at 7:30 p.m. at the Centennial Building here in Hanover. Enclosed is a map outlining the most direct route to Hanover from the south St. Paul area, plus the brochure on our speaker series.

I will call you before Wednesday, in case you have any last minute questions.

Regards,

24-11 Confirm speaking engagement with speaker

Dear _____:

Thanks for agreeing to speak at this year's Annual Fiesta Fundraiser.

We invite you to bring a guest, with our compliments. The banquet is set for 7:00, Friday evening, March 3, at the Downtown Plaza. Everyone is excited that you will be the keynote speaker.

Sincerely,

24-12 Confirm your own speaking engagement

Dear _____:

I'm looking forward to taking part in celebrating Historic Greeley this summer. I plan to arrive at the auditorium on Tuesday, July 11, at 7 p.m., one hour before my speech. That should give us time to run through the slides, as you suggested, and make sure everything is working.

Many thanks for the invitation. See you on the 11th.

Sincerely,

24-13 Thank speaker

You lined up the speaker. Now it's your job to thank him or her. Let the speaker know how the audience received his or her remarks. It's also a chance to lay the groundwork for another speech in the future.

Dear _____:

Your "Making the Most of the Moment" talk was the hit of the meeting. Our sales staff is still talking about your ideas.

Thanks for participating this year, and please keep a spot on your calendar for us for next May 15. The meeting will be at the Golden Rail Resort. I'll get back in touch.

Sincerely,

24-14 Thank speaker

Dear _____:

Thanks for firing up our sales and marketing team with your dynamic presentation.

I'm convinced the intense excitement you generated will result in increased sales for our company. I certainly hope we will have the pleasure of hearing you speak again in the near future.

Sincerely,

24-15 Thank speaker

Dear _____:

You captivated the audience from the moment you took the floor. Thank you so much for sharing your insights into what qualities the 21st century salesperson must possess to succeed. Your remarks stirred our imagination and reminded us we need to prepare now.

Sincerely,

24-16 Thank speaker

Dear _____:

I personally want to thank you for participating on our National Account Guest Panel at the National Sales Meeting in Tucson.

Improving the communications between our organizations improves our understanding of how we plan to achieve our goals. Throughout the session, it was obvious to me we share several mutual goals, including providing high quality, cost-effective health care to the hospitals we serve.

I believe you represented the interests of _____ very well. We all appreciate your time, effort and candor while participating in our meeting.

Sincerely,

Valleylab, Inc.
Boulder, Colorado

Tips to sharpen your writing skills

Remember, you do not need to say everything twice.
Examples:

- red *in color*
- small *in size*
- *new* innovation
- *unexpected* surprise
- cancel *out*
- *completely* empty
- *most* complete

Chapter Twenty-Five

Business-Social Invitations and Gifts

Deals begun in the office may close at lunch or black-tie dinner. Or social events may be used simply to become better acquainted with clients. Letters should make it clear if a social invitation will include business. Be specific about date, time, place—and clothing, if appropriate.

25-1 Invite to company open house

Dear _____:

We've vacuumed, scrubbed and polished and are, at last, ready to host an open house for all our customers and business friends.

I hope you will be able to join us on Thursday evening, April 3, from 5 to 8 p.m. for a tour of the facilities, special demonstrations and other activities. We'll cap the evening with an outrageous buffet.

Please let us know how many members of your organization will attend.

Sincerely,

25-2 Invite to demonstration

Dear _____:

You have to see for yourself, or you won't believe the improvements designed into our electronic typewriter.

That's why we're hosting a demonstration-breakfast. We hope you will join us at 8:00 Tuesday morning, April 3, at the Summerset Club.

After breakfast, we'll put the Model 15 through its paces. In addition to typing, the machine corrects errors invisibly, erases words or several lines at a time and lets you know when a word is spelled incorrectly. The only thing it doesn't do is applaud at the end of a job.

Please let me know by March 23 if you will be joining us. I know you'll like what you see—and the time and labor savings you'll gain.

Sincerely,

25-3 Invite to company holiday party

Dear _____:

We've decked the halls, trimmed the tree and wrapped a special present for you.

Please join us for our annual holiday party, Tuesday, December 19, 3:00 p.m. at our offices. Santa will be looking forward to seeing you!

Sincerely,

25-4 Invite to auction

The most important part of any invitation? Details. Remember to state the date, time, and place. Include directions, if necessary. Make your invitation as clear as possible.

Dear _____:

Please be our guest at the annual Philharmonic black-tie auction Saturday evening, May 3, 7:00 p.m. We've reserved a table for twelve, and invite you to join us with our compliments.

I know you share our concern for quality musical programs and hope you will take this opportunity to support the Philharmonic. I assure you the selection of auction gifts this year is extraordinary—everything from video cameras to a Caribbean cruise.

Just return the enclosed card by next Friday, and I'll put your ticket in the mail.

Sincerely,

25-5 Invite to lunch

Dear _____:

Free for lunch? Be my guest next Thursday, the 19th, 12:30, at the Petroleum Club.

I'd like to discuss our new equipment that will help make oil exploration profitable again.

Please give me a call and we can work out the details.

Sincerely,

25-6 Invite to breakfast

Dear _____:

Bacon is sizzling. Pancakes are light and fluffy. Even the oat bran is crackling. How about meeting for breakfast at Cinzarra's in Valley Square?

We can discuss your long-range objectives, and I can suggest a purchasing strategy best suited to your goals.

I'll call you to set up a time.

Sincerely,

25-7 Invite to sports event

Dear _____:

The road to the Final Four is the most exciting event in basketball. I have an extra ticket with your name on it to the UNLV game next Wednesday evening. Hope you can make it. Call me by Monday if you are able to go.

Sincerely,

25-8 Invite to theater

Dear _____:

Each summer, the University of Colorado Shakespeare Festival transforms the Mary Rippon outdoor theater into a 16th-century wonderland. One of the productions this year is "King Lear." We have four tickets for the night of July 17. Performance time: 8 p.m.
Would you and your wife like to join us? I know you'll find it a magical event. Please give me a call.

Sincerely,

25-9 Accept social invitation

A nice touch, when you're the recipient of an invitation, is to send a confirmation, especially when the host is a client. Let him or her know you'll be there.

Dear _____:

The patio pool party sounds wonderful. Look for me in the red bikini. Just joking, but I will be there Saturday.
Thanks.

25-10 Decline social invitation

Dear _____:

The invitation to dine Friday with your purchasing team is one I hate to turn down. However, I'm guest speaker at a banquet that evening.

I have two suggestions. Would it be possible to reschedule to another evening? Failing that, my boss, _____, would be glad to fill in for me.

I'll call you when you get back to town to see what we can work out.

Sincerely,

25-11 Thank client for gift

Dear _____:

Thank you for the beautiful poinsettia plant. It added a festive and colorful touch to our home throughout the holidays.

Your thoughtfulness is appreciated. I hope you and your family experienced the joy and peace of the season.

Sincerely,

25-12 Decline gift with thanks

Dear _____:

Thank you for your graciousness in sending me a holiday package.

Because our company has a policy against accepting any gratuities, I must return the gift.

I appreciate your thoughtfulness and wish you all the joy of the season.

Sincerely,

Tips to sharpen your writing skills

Look closely at introductory phrases. They must refer to the subject.

Incorrect:
Using the information, *our policies* could be changed.
Correct:
Using the information, *we* will change our policies.

Incorrect:
Looking at the data, *our sales level* is up.
Correct:
Looking at the data, *we* can see our sales level is up.

Incorrect:
Responding to your telephone call, *the meeting* will be held Monday.
Correct:
Responding to your telephone call, *I* have scheduled the meeting for Monday.

Chapter Twenty-Six

Congratulations and Condolences

Letters marking special occasions, accomplishments and milestones are treasured by all who receive them. Thoughtfulness stands out in today's hectic business climate. Clients know your time is valuable, and they will appreciate your gesture to brighten their day. Come to the point quickly and keep the message brief.

26-1 Appointment to office

Dear _____:

Congratulations on your appointment to the Governor's Task Force on Education in the Inner City.

You have the energy, diplomacy and charisma to make great things happen. We're lucky to have someone of your caliber willing to serve on this important committee.

Sincerely,

26-2 Outstanding efforts of public officials

Dear _____:

We congratulate you and support your efforts to launch a new convention center.

A convention center will give the local economy a terrific boost, and the business community is anxious to help get this project off the drawing board.

As your plans progress, please count on our company to assist in any way we can. Our staff supports the project with enthusiasm.

Sincerely,

26-3 Outstanding work by staff

Colleagues and support personnel like to know you appreciate their efforts. A friendly note helps ensure the next job will also be well done.

Dear _____:

You guys take my breath away. I just received two copies of the "IBM Quality" publication and was absolutely awed by the quality of the product you put out. Here's hoping _____ has shared with you his appreciation for this fine piece of work. I think you've topped even yourself. Please extend my congratulations to all you directed on the project.

Dwayne Cox
IBM Corporation
Austin, Texas

26-4 Outstanding work by staff

John, another good letter that explains everything this company is about.

It's nice to have you on the team.

Keep up the good work!

26-5 Outstanding work by staff

Dear _____:

Please allow me to express my appreciation for the assistance you provided to make the _____ successful.

This was Albuquerque's first "on-line" survey and there were many details to cover and time commitments to meet to insure a smooth, trouble-free process.

Our goals would not have been accomplished had it not been for your support, professional know-how and cooperative attitude. Thank you.

Sincerely,

26-6 Outstanding work by staff

Ladies and Gentlemen:

Just a quick note to say thank you and tell you how proud I am of this area for a job well done. According to the Sales Goals report, we are 94% complete for this fiscal year. Now that the spring selling season is winding down, we can concentrate on strengthening our second plateau position. Let's make sure the model stocks are in order, and check the open-to-sell for possible at-once deliveries. And, maybe our accounts can use closeouts or irregulars.

Regards,

26-7 Outstanding work by business associate

Dear _____:

I thoroughly enjoyed the opportunity to work with you in Oregon and Washington. I gained a lot from the experience and was pleased to have the chance to learn about the Surgical Division of 3M.

Your knowledge of the Sarns 3M product family is very good and your grasp of the oxygenator is super. The rapport you have with the hospitals and staff people, as well as your confidence in the O.R., will serve you well as you progress in the cardiopulmonary business.

As we discussed, the electromechanical portion of the product line is extensive and your continued vigilance, in terms of product identification and application, will solidify your understanding in short order.

Welcome to Sarns 3M. We're glad you chose to continue your career with all of us.

Kip A. Stastny
Sarns 3M Health Care
Ann Arbor, Michigan

26-8 Outstanding work by business associate

Dear _____:

I was delighted to hear that you received a design award for your work on the Model 2733 baby car seat. Everyone is excited about the balance of safety, comfort and style you achieved with this design. Thanks to you, we'll all feel more comfortable with infants aboard.

Sincerely,

26-9 Outstanding work by contractor

Dear _____:

Congratulations and thanks are truly deserved for the excellent design and final outcome of American Seating's New York showroom. All of our guests who attended the grand opening last week commented on the creativity and elegance of design that you and your firm put together for us.

The New York staff are especially pleased with the showroom and the statement it makes about our company. It is truly a dynamic atmosphere in all respects, and we are both pleased and proud of the new facility.

Please share our appreciation with all the members of your organization who played such an important role in making this a success. Honorable mention goes to _____ for all her help and support.

On behalf of all of us at American Seating, my sincere thanks for a job well done.

Frank L. Baudo
American Seating Company
New York, New York

26-10 Outstanding work by contractor

Dear _____:

Please accept my gratitude for your contributions toward the recent printer announcements. Your professionalism, dedication and very hard work helped make the event a success.

Please come to an awards luncheon Monday, March 8, to recognize your successful efforts.

The luncheon will be at the Wainwright Hotel from 11:30 a.m. to 1:00 p.m.

Thanks again for an outstanding job. I look forward to seeing you Monday.

Sincerely,

26-11 Achievement in community

If your client has made a mark in the community, take a few minutes to let him/her know that you appreciate the extra effort. Everybody likes a pat on the back. Handing out congratulations when deserved strengthens the client-salesperson relationship.

Dear _____:

Congratulations on setting up the "Make a Difference Club" fundraiser at _____ High School. I know what perseverance it took to get this food certificate program off the ground. The school can certainly use the extra _____ you raised to enrich many programs hit with budget cuts.

Thank you for your hard work all year long. You have certainly made a difference at ____.

Sincerely,

26-12 Achievement in community

Dear _____:

Congratulations on earning a "Monday Morning Rose" from the Daily Camera.

Your contributions to this community over the past 20 years are nothing short of astonishing. As director of the ____ this year, you have shown outstanding leadership and patience.

A hearty round of applause from those of us who have admired your work for years.

Sincerely,

26-13 Promotion

Dear _____:

Bob, congratulations on your recent promotion to manager of sales and service.

Your diligence and hard work have paid off, and we are pleased that you are now in a position of even wider influence.

Let me know if I can assist you in any way as you take over your new responsibilities.

Sincerely,

26-14 Promotion

Dear _____:

Delighted to see your promotion to senior engineer! I've enjoyed our association and hope we'll have the opportunity to work together again in your new assignment.

Sincerely,

26-15 Promotion

Dear _____ :

Congratulations and best wishes are in order for having been promoted to the position of Area Manager for the New York Metro market. I appreciate the dedication, hard work and loyalty that you have displayed and look forward to your continued contributions as an Area Manager.

American Seating faces many challenges and opportunities, and I'm confident that with your support and others like you, we shall continue to grow and be a successful company.

Sincerely,

Frank L. Baudo
American Seating Company
New York, New York

26-16 Move to new position/job

Dear _____ :

Congratulations on your new job with Colton Fixtures. I'd like a crack at supplying your requirements over there. I guarantee you'll receive the same outstanding products and service that we provided when you were with Atlantic.

Sincerely,

26-17 Move to new position/job

Dear_____ :

I've just heard the good news. Congratulations on becoming Sparks Unlimited's new comptroller. The company's finances are sure to be in good hands.

I've enjoyed working with you over the past five years and look forward to continuing our relationship at Sparks.

Best of luck in your new position!

26-18 Retirement

Dear _____:

Congratulations on your retirement from _____ after 30 years of dedicated service.

I'll miss that cheery hello each morning and the support you gave so freely, but I am happy that you're taking time to kick back.

I glimpsed those travel brochures on your desk the other day. Tahiti. Australia. The Orient. What adventures you have in store. Have a great time. You earned it. Your career with _____ has been legendary.

I wish you and Marge the best.

Sincerely,

26-19 Company anniversary

Dear _____:

Please accept my congratulations on your company's silver anniversary. You have maintained an outstanding reputation for quality products and service for the 25 years you have been in business.

_____ is pleased to have supplied gaskets to Autotron for more than a decade. We look forward to continuing our association in the years to come.

Sincerely,

26-20 Move to new location

Dear _____:

Impressive! That's how I'd describe your new location on Fairfax. Just stepping into the lobby, I could sense the planning and attention to detail that went into the entire facility. It's bright, comfortable and welcoming.

I wish you the best. I know I'll certainly enjoy visiting you there.

Sincerely,

26-21 New account

Dear _____ :

How proud we are of Backert and Sims Advertising for landing the Gulf Shores account. The board members obviously recognized professionalism when they saw it.

The subject should be an exciting one—no lack of sailing opportunities in this state!

Again, congratulations from all of us at National.

Sincerely,

P.S. It's nice to work with #1.

26-22 Graduation

Personal milestones are always a good reason to contact clients. They will appreciate your taking the time from a busy schedule to drop a congratulatory note.

Dear _____ :

I've just learned that you have completed your master's thesis on Marketing in Europe 1992 and have been awarded your Master of Science in Marketing. You are to be congratulated on your energy and perseverance at the conclusion of this extremely worthy goal.

I intend to do some marketing in Europe this fall and will be going to London, Paris and Nice in an effort to establish Human Resource consulting arrangements. I'd welcome any ideas that you might have for me as a result of your research.

Again, congratulations! We thoroughly enjoyed having you work for us part time while you were in college.

Mary Cook
Mary Cook & Associates
Denver, Colorado

26-23 Birthday

Dear _____:

Please accept my wishes to you for a very happy birthday! I hope it will be your best ever. As my gift to you during your birthday month, I would like to offer you a 20% discount on any Mary Kay products you would like to purchase.

Please let me know how you would enjoy using your birthday discount.

Sincerely,

Janet Switzer
Mary Kay Cosmetics
Boulder, Colorado

26-24 Birth of child

Dear _____:

A girl! Congratulations to you and Maria. I know how excited you must be.

I can picture Jennifer now, turning heads at ballet class, setting records for the butterfly at swim meets, running student council. She will bring a great deal of energy into your lives, I'm sure. Hope you can keep up!

Enjoy . . .

26-25 Birth of child

Dear _____:

Congratulations to you and Mark on your new baby boy. Lots of wonderful years lie ahead—fishing and camping trips, basketball and football games, not to mention the first time he drives your new car out on a date.

Take care of yourselves and enjoy every minute with your son!

Sincerely,

26-26 Anniversary

Dear _____:

It's your Silver Anniversary, but your marriage has been pure gold for 25 years.

Please give Rose my sincere congratulations, and best wishes to both of you for the next quarter century.

Sincerely,

26-27 Marriage

Dear _____:

Congratulations and best wishes to you and Lynnette.

May you enjoy a happy and prosperous life together.

26-28 Marriage

Dear _____:

My best wishes to you on your wedding.

May you and Nick enjoy a happy and prosperous life together.

Sincerely,

26-29 Seasonal greetings

Dear _____:

Caring and sharing bring meaning to the Holiday Season. "Spread joy around" is my philosophy in business and daily life.

When counting blessings this year, I realize I must take time to thank YOU for making the year in real estate my best yet. Your referrals, your support, and your positive comments to friends have given me the opportunity to work with many wonderful people in meeting their real estate needs. I appreciate your confidence, and you can count on me to continue to walk the extra mile and give excellent, professional service.

I hope you will give me a call when you have real estate needs. It would be a privilege to return the favor by giving you my best professional service. It really is a busy market, and there are some exciting, unique properties for sale. So, if you have a dream, let me hear about it and help you make it come true!

May the New Year bring you and your loved ones abundant joy!

Glenda Hilty
Moore & Company
Boulder, Colorado

26-30 Seasonal greetings

Dear _____:

The holiday season is a special time for all of us, a time of peace, brotherhood and goodwill. In the spirit of the season, we at Thuro Steam extend our sincere best wishes to good friends such as you.

Your friendship has helped make our year both rewarding and successful. We want to express our deepest appreciation for your loyalty and confidence in us.

With heartfelt gratitude, we wish you and yours a wonderful holiday season and the very best in the coming year.

Sincerely,

Thuro Steam
Denver, Colorado

26-31 Condolences on accident

Don't shy away from condolences They need not be difficult to write. A brief, personal note is all that is necessary to let your client know you are thinking of him/her during a difficult time.

Dear _____:

I was sorry to learn of your car accident. Don't be anxious to get back to your desk. We miss you, but we want you to listen to the doctors and take it easy until you are fully recovered.

Best wishes, and please let me know if you need anything.

Sincerely,

26-32 Condolences on hospitalization

Dear _____:

I was sorry to learn that you are in the hospital. With your vitality and determination, I expect it will be a short stay.
Hope to see you enjoying good health in the very near future.

Sincerely,

26-33 Condolences on death

Dear _____:

Please accept our sincere condolences on the death of your wife/husband. Words cannot express the sorrow we feel. Our thoughts and prayers are with you.
If we can help in any way during this time, please call on us.

Sincerely,

26-34 Condolences on death

Dear _____:

We were shocked and saddened by the tragic events that resulted in the death of your son/daughter.
Please accept our heartfelt condolences and let us know if we may offer any assistance to you during this very difficult period.

Sincerely,

26-35 Thank you for caring

Send thank-you notes to clients or co-workers who extended an act of kindness to you during an illness.

Dear _____:

Your lovely bouquet of fresh flowers brightened my spirits while I was in the hospital.

I'm glad to be back to work. I plan to visit you as soon as I'm at full steam, another three weeks, the doctors tell me.

Until then, thank you for caring.

26-36 Thank you for caring

Dear _____:

Thanks for stopping by the hospital while I was out of commission.

Boredom was really getting to me, but spending an hour with you solved that problem. I chuckled over your stories long after you left.

It's good to be back at the keyboard, and I expect to be "on the road again" by April. Let me return your visit by taking you and Kathy to the Gondolier Terrace. I'll call with a definite date.

Thanks for being a friend.

Advice from the sales experts

Public relations letter writing is the means to an end—the sale. Certainly, many salespeople do make sales without writing this type of letter, but your odds are greater in achieving a successful conclusion if you take the time and expend the energy to write these letters. Just as you lubricate your car to get the best performance, writing PR letters lubricates the sales process to maximize positive results.

When you write a congratulatory letter, a letter of condolence, a letter of appreciation, you are introducing another element into the sales process. You are introducing a personal element—yourself. You are no longer just a conveyor of technical or price information for your product or service. You are now expressing yourself as an individual with a unique personality. You generate good will by taking the time, through letter writing, to acknowledge clients as human beings and friends, rather than buyers or purchasing agents.

Letters of congratulations and appreciation are my favorite categories of public relations letters. You work hard to make the sale. A PR letter is the extra touch that puts the client in a positive frame of mind. The payoff is well worth your time and effort.

Alan Caplan
Former Sales Representative WIOQ FM
Philadelphia, Pennsylvania

Chapter Twenty-Seven

Five Model Sales Proposals

"Hanson, we've gotten wind of a huge project the State plans to bid. Get the bid package and let's write up a proposal."

Sound familiar? Sales reps must often prepare proposals for major contracts. Such proposals can be complex and contain a great deal of technical information. Big bucks are at stake. Jobs are on the line.

Feeling stressed?

Help is at hand.

Here are five successful proposals—proposals that won contracts—that you can use as a guide. They will make the job easier.

These model proposals demonstrate different styles for achieving different goals. For example, if you want to keep the advertising account for the state lottery, be creative. If you want to install a new software system for the state treasury office, pack your proposal with technical details.

These models provide a road map for organizing and presenting material. Let them help you build a strong case that puts your company's best foot forward.

A creative approach lifts a proposal above the crowd. The Karsh & Hagan proposal came in an oversized, bright red plastic container resembling a briefcase—hard for anyone to overlook or misplace. Your cover doesn't have to be elaborate; but fresh, imaginative packaging generates a good impression even before the client looks inside.

It is also an example of a proposal to continue service. It emphasizes expertise, awards received, successful past performance and innovative plans for the future.

27-1 Proposal to continue service

The Colorado Lottery is changing. New management. New commissioners. New directions. New games. And a whole new positive attitude among all those who work at the Lottery and for the Lottery.

As the only advertising agency the Lottery has ever had, we've seen change before.

However, this time it's different. This time it's more exciting than ever before because the current changes are changes for the better. The Lottery is responding to the people of Colorado. The pride is back among Lottery employees. The State is going to realize more income. Legislators, Commissioners, and critics are being heard and are getting positive responses. And players are getting what they want: better games, better tickets, more winnings, more excitement—more fun!

We don't want to miss any of this. We've worked hard for the past seven years to make the Lottery our flagship account. We've given it priority, and we've given it our loyalty.

We've tried to answer every question in the enclosed RFP to the best of our ability with answers that will help you evaluate our qualifications. We hope we've made it clear the Lottery is the biggest event in our corporate life and extremely important to the 35 employees who work on it every day.

We want to be part of the Lottery's future.

The fun is back!

Sincerely,

Pocky Marranzino, Jr.
Karsh & Hagan, Inc.
Englewood, Colorado

[Editor's note: The proposal continued with nine pages of imaginative photographs (5' X 7') and short, punchy phrases. We're including brief descriptions of the photos to help you appreciate the impact of the presentation.]

Photo: Two men in suits wearing Groucho Marx disguises
Text:
Pretend
You Don't Know
These Guys

Photo: Newspaper clips stating: Lottery breaks U.S. record
Text:

Forget, for a Moment,
We've Been Your Ad Agency
for Seven Years

Photo: Many award plaques and certificates
Text:

Put Aside
All the Awards We've
Helped You Win

Photo: Bundles of U.S. paper currency
Text:

And the Sales
Projections We've Helped
You Make

Photo: Colorado Lottery trademark and starting date.
Text:

Imagine We Played
No Part in the Introduction of
the Lottery Scratch Games

Photo: Lotto ball with No. 7 on it
Text:

Or Lotto

Photo: Agency's account team, wearing Lottery Team shirts
Text:

Forget All of
Those Things. And All of Us,
for That Matter.

Photo: Two pairs of Groucho Marx glasses, with eyebrows and noses
Text:

We Don't Want You to Pick
Karsh & Hagan Because We Know the
Lottery Better Than Anyone Else

Photo: The two partners, smiling, without the Grouch Marx disguises
Text:

But Because We Know How to Make
Advertising Better Than Anyone Else. That's What
We Want You to Remember from This Proposal.

[Following the above information, the proposal responded to specific questions. We have deleted the Table of Contents and opening identifying information.]

MEDIA PLANNER/BUYER EXPERIENCE

Planning and buying media for the lottery is too big a job for one individual. To do justice to the budget, an agency must offer a team with the depth and breadth of the Karsh & Hagan media team.

It's not the size of Karsh & Hagan's media department that distinguishes it from the competition, it's the quality of the people. Under the capable direction of VP/Media Director _____, the agency has achieved its goal of 90% or above on every television post-buy analysis. _____ has seven years of experience planning and buying media in Colorado. She has personally overseen all Lottery planning and buying functions for the past three years.

The three additional individuals who have been assigned to the Lottery account have a minimum of two years' experience planning and buying media in Colorado. _____ has been planning media for the Colorado Lottery for the past several months. She will continue. The buyers will be _____ and _____.

SERVICES PROVIDED IN COLORADO

All services required by the Lottery, and provided by Karsh & Hagan, will emanate from our Colorado office.

As a corporate citizen of Colorado, Karsh & Hagan Advertising has a vested interest in fostering the growth of our industry and its support within the state. Our preference is to use Colorado suppliers whenever possible. There are circumstances when, in the judgment of the agency, it might not be in the best interest of the client to eliminate suppliers outside the state. In those cases, of course, it's the agency's obligation to fulfill the needs of a client. However, all things being equal, a Colorado supplier will always get preference.

We conducted a spot check of two time periods during 1988. During those two periods, over 80% of the media purchased and paid for by Karsh & Hagan Advertising was within Colorado. Almost 90% of the dollars directed to production suppliers were within the state.

[In the next section of the proposal, resumes of the staff handling the Lottery account were provided. Although we have eliminated names, we've included the jobs and responsibilities.]

Vice President/Director Research & Account Service

- Participates in the development of all marketing and advertising plans and strategies in cooperation with the Colorado Lottery directors and marketing staff.
- Participates with the Colorado Lottery marketing staff in development of marketing, game and advertising research conducted for the Lottery.
- Supervises and/or assists with the implementation and evaluation of all research as requested by the Colorado Lottery marketing staff.
- Participates in the development of new games and prize structures as requested by the Colorado Lottery.
- Reviews and approves media, advertising, promotional and research plans.
- Maintains up-to-date knowledge of all aspects of lottery industry within and outside Colorado.
- Assists in the selection and approval of all agency personnel assigned to the Colorado Lottery team.

Account Manager

- Directs ongoing advertising strategy development for Scratch and Lotto games in cooperation with the Lottery staff.
- Assists creative department in development of creative plans and materials; assists media department in development of media plans.
- Directs the development and implementation of TV, radio, newspaper and outdoor ads; point-of-purchase materials; and any other collateral pieces supporting the sales effort.
- Participates in the development (and implementation as required) of consumer and sales promotions in cooperation with the Colorado Lottery marketing, sales and public relations staff.
- Coordinates promotions and merchandising materials with Colorado Lottery public relations firm as requested by Colorado Lottery.

- Assists in developing new game and prize structures; and directs agency's involvement in game ticket design in cooperation with Colorado Lottery marketing staff.
- Attends all appropriate Lottery staff meetings.
- Attends all meetings with Colorado Lottery when the agency is presenting plans, strategies and/or executions which the agency has developed for the Lottery.
- Maintains daily liaison with Colorado Lottery marketing staff.
- Generates conference reports of all meetings or phone conversations with Colorado Lottery personnel regarding assignments, project status, budgets, media or any other Colorado Lottery business.
- Directs the maintenance of Colorado Lottery monthly and annual advertising media and promotion budgets.
- Reviews and approves the billing on all projects for the Colorado Lottery and develops monthly billing and budget summaries for submission to Colorado Lottery marketing staff.
- Maintains an up-to-date understanding of Colorado Lottery operation and lottery industry, including attendance at appropriate industry conferences and regular contact with either lottery or agencies of other state lotteries.

CONSUMER RESEARCH

Consumer research is a primary part of the Karsh & Hagan approach to effective advertising. Since Day One, we start work on every account with a research review to identify:

- Existing category research.
- Secondary research sources.
- Proprietary research available from the client.
- Proprietary research available from Karsh & Hagan; our network, Affiliated Advertising Agencies International (AAAI); and American Association of Advertising Agencies, Inc. (AAAA).

The objective and results of this review are to identify the research resources and the specific additional needs for research. This process has led us to design, field or supervise proprietary consumer research in the following areas:

- Category and brand usage and attitude surveys, qualitative and quantitative on a local, regional and national basis.
- Category and brand market mapping, primarily on a regional or national basis.
- Category and brand psychographic mapping, on a local, regional and national basis.
- New product development and evaluation, quantitative and qualitative on a local and regional basis.
- Customer satisfaction surveys for existing and new products, primarily on a local and regional level.
- Product, name and design development research on a qualitative basis. Category and brand awareness studies, pre-post, as well as tracking on a quantitative basis, locally and regionally.
- Advertising concept testing, qualitative and quantitative for radio, television, print and direct response, on a local, regional and national basis.
- Brand advertising positioning testing, both qualitative and quantitative, on a local, regional and national basis.
- Direct response list and media testing on a local, regional and national basis.

Each year over the last five years, we have initiated or supervised an average of _____ major proprietary research projects, totalling over _____, and involving five or more different research suppliers. Of this, approximately four projects per year have been specifically for the Colorado Lottery.

In the last year, we have initiated or supervised _____ major research projects with _____ different research suppliers for _____ current clients and _____ new business presentations. These projects are:

[List of projects.]

In addition to our experience in designing, implementing and supervising proprietary, customized and standardized consumer research, we also provide our clients with the benefits of our access and analysis of major proprietary research services, which include information specific to lotteries:

- _____A national survey with regional breakouts that can be coordinated with media planning.
- _____A major social trend survey which helps identify the current and evolving social attitudes.

- _____A recently developed geo-demographic, single-source research system which coordinates proprietary and standard data, as needed.
- Access to the AAAI and AAAA research libraries.
- Access to the Karsh & Hagan research library.

We are constantly reviewing new techniques and discussing consumer research methodologies with other agencies and/or clients to improve our research resource. Several recent instances pertinent to the Colorado Lottery are:

- A visit to _____ to discuss and review with the agency and the Lottery how they utilize research in game design.
- Our discussions and visits with _____ and _____ regarding their techniques and experience in tracking advertising programs with sales and measuring the advertising input/effectiveness.
- Our membership in the Advertising Research Foundation, which provides us with information on all types of advances and issues in the research field on a regular basis.
- Our use of the AAAA library to help the Colorado Lottery provide references, case histories and document support for presentations to industry and government groups and the Colorado legislature.
- Our current program for reviewing and ultimately recommending a standardized research technique for evaluating various degrees of finished advertising materials. This project has been initiated to address several clients' interest in pre-testing advertising.

In summary, we have always believed in and encouraged our clients to utilize research as a tool in creating more effective advertising and evaluating the effectiveness of advertising. We continually update our capabilities and knowledge in the research field to provide the best possible resource.

CONSUMER PROMOTIONS

First, a point of clarification between consumer promotions and sales promotions. We've defined a consumer promotion as any promotion directed at the end-use consumer, and a sales promotion as any promotion directed to the retailer, agent, etc. who sells to the end-user.

In the last year we developed and implemented _____ consumer promotions for _____ Karsh & Hagan clients including the promotional concepts and projects we've worked on with Colorado Lottery.

Recently, we have seen consumer promotions and sales promotions become more important elements in marketing and advertising plans. Consequently, Karsh & Hagan has been increasing its involvement in the promotional arena.

- We've established a stable of Colorado free-lance promotion consultants who have local, regional and national experience.
- Our membership in a national and local direct marketing organization assures us the continual and timely update of events, regulations, etc. involving consumer promotions in the direct response area.

However, we do not operate a separate sales promotion department, even though the billings and workload might justify it. We believe that promotion strategies and executions (both consumer and sales) should be part of a cohesive and consistent communications plan. This is best achieved by keeping promotions with the same team assigned the advertising.

Last year, exclusive of the _____ consumer promotion projects for Colorado Lottery, we completed _____ consumer promotions in the following areas:

- Two co-op vacation-package promotions for the _____. The first was a joint effort with _____ to package vacations and promote them in specific target markets via print, television and travel agencies. The second was a local cooperative effort with _____ to produce a summer events guide distributed free to Colorado residents to promote in-state vacations.

[Several other specific projects described.]

Over the past year, when taking into account all clients, consumer promotions have accounted for over _____ of our billings, and involved production of over _____ separate items, as well as analysis and implementation of direct marketing programs, mailing lists, etc.

The two largest consumer promotions that Karsh & Hagan has ever undertaken and produced have both been for the Colorado Lottery. The first was for the introduction of the Colorado Lottery and the second was the introduction of Lotto this year. Since the Lottery began, Karsh & Hagan has worked on over _____ consumer promotion projects plus the normal Lottery game point-of-sale materials.

Almost all of these projects for the Colorado Lottery have been developed in conjunction with the Colorado Lottery Sales and Public Relations Departments and coordinated with the Colorado Lottery's public relations agency. Examples of the recent effort for the Colorado Lottery/Lotto introduction can be seen on the following pages.

This joint promotional and advertising effort has just received the *Gaming and Wagering Business* magazine "Lottery Communications Best Marketing Campaign Award." In awarding this honor to the Colorado Lottery, the panel noted the "staggering ____ P.O.S. items . . . including deluxe Lotto play centers."

SALES PROMOTION

Our experience in sales promotions is less extensive than that of consumer promotions primarily because clients tend to handle sales promotions internally. This is the case with most of our clients, including Colorado Lottery.

However, we do believe that sales promotions are an integral part of the selling process, and we encourage our clients to utilize our creative, promotion and production capabilities to help develop and coordinate sales promotions with the consumer promotion and advertising efforts.

[Series of photographs depicting various ad campaigns.]

Our most pertinent quick-turn-around response experiences are the Colorado Lottery. Some specific examples are:

- In May of ____ the new director for the Colorado Lottery requested the agency revise the fiscal year 19__/__ plan to reduce spending by ____. Karsh & Hagan had less than ____ days to completely revise the advertising plan, get approval and implement by July. The entire advertising plan was revised, production and media costs were reduced by over one million dollars, and the program was implemented July 15, ____.

This example of a fast turn-around is also an example of good planning. While we worked very hard to quickly revise the plan to a new set of market conditions and requirements, the result was a new plan that generated the necessary savings and did so while increasing sales almost ____ over the prior year.

- Another example of planned fast turn-around is with the media buying for the Colorado Lottery. We have never placed a Colorado Lottery media plan as planned at the beginning of the year!

This is not unexpected, in fact it is planned for in our media strategy to assure that we receive the necessary and expected efficiencies without penalty when changing scheduling. To do this, Karsh & Hagan has developed a unique negotiation package with the broadcast media in the State of Colorado that guarantees both cost and delivery no matter when the media is run.

The result of this planned fast turn-around is that we can place a media schedule in the market with as little as one week advanced notice and can cancel a schedule with less than a week's notice without incurring penalties or a deterioration of program quality.

- The third and final example of fast turn-around to market conditions relates to what we believe is our dedication to doing the best possible job by doing whatever is needed to get it done right. Examples of this are the efforts to disseminate the correct winning numbers in the traditional game, Million Dollar Sweepstakes #1, and the Lotto jackpot print, radio and television advertising program.

In both cases the agency Lottery team has spent both weekends and late evenings to assure that the appropriate materials have been produced correctly and have been delivered to the media to run on a 24- to 48-hour turn-around schedule. This not only requires a personal dedication and sacrifice but, most importantly, the ability to coordinate production, delivery and media suppliers effectively and without errors.

We do this for the Lottery, and as the following shows, we do this for our other clients as well.

We believe these additional examples of experience in reacting quickly to changing market conditions are even more pertinent to the Colorado Lottery. They show that Karsh & Hagan is able to not only address the Colorado Lottery's fast turn-around needs but simultaneously address any of our clients' fast turn-around needs without sacrificing efficiencies or quality.

[Specific examples of work done for other clients.]

[References provided.]

KEY EMPLOYEE EXPERIENCE

The most relevant experience that key Karsh & Hagan employees have had with a product similar to a lottery product is our experiences with the Colorado Lottery account!

However, we believe equally important has been Karsh & Hagan's commitment to continually upgrade our staffing on the Colorado Lottery account, while maintaining a strong management continuity, to assure an efficient working relationship with the Colorado Lottery staff.

[Specific information on key employees and their experience.]

LOTTERY GAMES EXPERIENCE

At the beginning of this proposal, we asked you to forget Karsh & Hagan has been the advertising agency for the Colorado Lottery since the Lottery's inception in _____. Now, it's important you remember!

Karsh & Hagan was part of the team that introduced the Colorado Lottery and gave it the highest per capita sales ever until California launched its lottery.

Karsh & Hagan was part of the Colorado Lottery team that launched Lotto in January and helped to exceed sales forecast for the startup period.

For both startups, the Colorado Lottery and Karsh & Hagan have received numerous awards recognizing the creative efforts and the marketing efforts behind the record-breaking sales performances.

These results, we believe, come from the experience and blend of people Karsh & Hagan has put together on the Colorado Lottery account. Our key employees average over _____ years' experience on the Colorado Lottery, and each department is headed by someone with _____ or more years' experience on the Colorado Lottery. The _____ key employees have _____ years' total experience on the Colorado Lottery. This experience and the staff continuity we provide will continue to be important contributions to the success of the Colorado Lottery.

In addition to our direct experience on the Colorado Lottery account, Karsh & Hagan has maintained regular contact with sources in lottery states throughout the U.S. We have attended every applicable lottery conference and maintained constant review and information gathering about the lottery industry. For example:

[Describe specific associations.]

The information we gathered is already being put to use to help us and the Colorado Lottery marketing staff to reposition the Scratch game and help solidify Lotto.

The extracurricular efforts reported above were done at the agency's expense and are indicative of the investments we are willing to make to help the Colorado Lottery succeed. They also are examples of how we function as teammates of the Colorado Lottery marketing staff.

OTHER EXPERIENCE

We have indicated the client experience that demonstrates the qualifications of Karsh & Hagan's key employees. In addition, there are two other areas that demonstrate our qualifications to continue to be the advertising agency for the Colorado Lottery.

These areas are: (1) our proven ability to meet the most demanding needs of the Colorado Lottery without sacrificing our work quality for any clients, including the Colorado Lottery; and (2) our commitment to growth, leadership and excellence in this market.

The introduction to the Colorado Lottery's evaluation of Karsh & Hagan's performance over the last year provides a good perspective as to the workload involved (see Exhibit A).

We supported two Scratch games at once, promoted a new Grand Prize Wheel format and introduced Lotto this fiscal year. At the same time, Karsh & Hagan took on the _____ account, increased its advertising involvement with [name new clients].

We did not just "adequately" serve all our clients during this period—we did an "outstanding" job considering the local economic environment! This has been an aggressive year for Karsh & Hagan clients and for Karsh & Hagan's accumulation of creative and marketing awards.

Not the least of those awards has been the recent *Gaming & Wagering* "Marketing Communication of the Year Award," given the Colorado Lottery for its introduction of Lotto. We're proud to have played a major part in this launch, which exceeded the Colorado Lottery sales goals and comparable states' sales levels by over 150%.

Our commitment to growth, leadership and excellence in this market is not only manifested in all our work for the Colorado Lottery, it also represents a real investment in expanding and improving our services, qualifications and expertise in all areas. Examples are:

- In-house typesetting facilities started in 1982 and upgraded with new state-of-the-art equipment in ____.
- Installation of a new, expanded computer system capable of faster data processing, which has allowed us to provide the Colorado Lottery with customized billing and audit reports.
- Off-site electronic backup and data storage.
- In-house focus group facilities for Karsh & Hagan clients.
- $1 Million Errors and Omissions insurance policy.
- Monthly internal and/or external audits to assure ourselves and clients of ongoing fiscal monitoring.
- Membership and participation in major industry associations [names of specific organizations].
- Regular attendance at advertising and marketing seminars for all advertising disciplines; and regular sponsoring of advertising seminars for agency personnel and clients.
- Participation with Colorado colleges for training and teaching advertising disciplines, including summer internship program.

[Information regarding number of employees and other business practices.]

STRATEGIC AND SERVICE CAPABILITIES

The Karsh & Hagan that's been the Lottery's agency for seven years has excellent capabilities for developing effective advertising. The most effective advertising results when

1. The perceptions, attitudes and wants of the consumer are thoroughly understood.
2. The product, its price and distribution are guided by the consumer and are clearly stated.
3. The advertising objectives and strategies are guided by the consumer and are clearly stated.
4. The advertising is created and executed with a commitment to creating an outstanding level of human response.

Understanding the consumer

At the other end of every Lottery communication, there's a human being. If your communication fails to respect that person, or fails to recognize that person's perceptions, or fails to be believed by that person, or fails to be liked by that person, it will fail to create the desired response.

There is no substitute for the kind of concrete understanding that can come from research. From solid, quantitative primary research. From pertinent secondary research. From focus groups. From talking with prospects face to face at the sales counter, on the street, on the phone. What does that person think about your product category? How does it fit into their lives? What feature do they think is most important?

What do they like and what do they dislike about your product? What words and images do they use in discussing your product. What problem does your product solve for them?

Once you know the answers to these questions, the possibility of success is dramatically improved. All of our disciplines are aimed at achieving and advancing that understanding.

The best use of research is in formulating effective strategies for marketing and advertising. Methods used by Karsh & Hagan for this purpose include quantitative surveys, segmentations studies and focus groups. But we also use research to test product features, message communication, and to track advertising effectiveness.

At Karsh & Hagan, primary research is executed through an impartial outside contractor. It is supervised by our director of research/account service. And it is always done with careful input from our clients and account managers, as well as our creative and media teammates. This insures that questions from all parties will be addressed. And the information from the research is actionable for all involved.

Using consumer understanding to guide the marketing mix

If there is something about the product (or the price, or the method of distribution) that the consumer doesn't like, the most effective advertising in the world will not overcome that problem—at least not for long.

Example: For nearly ____ years, lottery players have lived with the negative gratification of losing. Sales in recent years have suffered from the cumulative impact of this problem. While the problem is inherent in the product, the recent improvement in the odds of winning has contributed, we believe, to the recent upturn in sales.

It is also documented that consumers have for some time been opposed to the wheel and the entry process. These factors have also contributed to the decline in sales. In our opinion, the elimination of the wheel and the entry process will also contribute to the growing recovery.

Advertising cannot be completely effective while problems such as these go unaddressed. For these reasons, Karsh & Hagan believes we can be most effective when we act as a marketing partner with our clients. The more we are able to contribute in other areas of marketing, the better we are able to be effective in our advertising efforts.

When we act in the role of marketing partner, our account management team heads up the effort, with active input from the agency principals who supervise the account, and from the creative and media leadership on the account. And we use research to guide our efforts.

Using consumer understanding to guide advertising objectives and strategies

At the planning stage of any given advertising campaign, account management prepares a document called the *Karsh & Hagan SOS* (Situation/Objectives/Strategies). It contains a brief description of the situation in the marketplace: sales trends, competitive environment, consumer perceptions, current positioning. It goes on to clearly establish objectives. And then it outlines strategies including message, support and tone for the advertising.

Once the SOS is completed (and agreed upon by the client and the agency team), the creative leadership prepares another document, the *Karsh & Hagan Creative Workplan*. And the media leadership prepares a *Media Workplan*. These documents have the sole purpose of making sure that the creative and media assignments are stated clearly and in terms relevant to the consumer.

The strategic part of advertising must, after all, provide very precise answers to three questions before it has a chance of being successful.

1. What specific consumer response is desired?
2. What specific message is most likely to cause that response?
3. What media will most effectively reach the consumer?

Commitment to creating an outstanding level of human response

Outstanding response does not happen unless there is a commitment at all levels, including client, account management, creative and media. There follows an explanation of what that commitment means in each of the three agency departments.

Account management commitment

In addition to its involvement in research, marketing and strategic development, our account management team contributes to outstanding results through well defined communication with client, creative and media. The object of that communication is to be sure there is total team commitment. To be sure all aspects of an assignment are understood by creative and media. And to be sure that all aspects of creative and media solutions are communicated to the client.

Creative commitment

Our creative philosophy can be summed up in those two words: "human response." With equal emphasis on each word.

Whether the response you seek is some action, like the purchase of a lottery ticket, or some shift in a *prospect's belief dynamics,* human response is the purpose of advertising.

Human response to advertising is influenced by many factors. We believe the most important factors are these.

1. MEMORABILITY. Studies show that 98% of all advertising goes unnoticed or is forgotten within one day. If your advertising is not among the 2% that registers, you've wasted your money.
Being remembered involves creating irresistible ideas that are relevant to the consumer, and brilliant in their execution, so as to stand out from all other advertising.
2. BELIEVABILITY. If the message is not believed, if the product does not live up to the promise, both response and overall image will suffer. Believability can be enhanced through knowledge of the consumer, through user imagery, through overall tone of advertising. But the promise must ring true.
3. LIKABILITY. People buy from companies they like. When selling propositions are placed in contexts of warmth, fun, humor and humanity, likability of the advertising is enhanced. Hence the advertiser is liked better. Hence the results are better.
4. EMOTIONAL APPEAL. There is one further distinction to the Karsh & Hagan advertising philosophy. On the human side of the equation. Human beings do not make decisions and take actions based solely on logic. Response happens on an

emotional level. And communication must take place on the emotional level.

Media commitment

Advertising that isn't seen or heard by the consumer can't create outstanding levels of response. We practice the following disciplines to ensure media effectiveness.

1. TEAMWORK. We do not work in a vacuum. We work closely throughout the planning process with account management, creative and production, developing comprehensive campaigns.
2. EXPERIENCE. We know that media is not an exact science. Sound judgment is vital. We hire people with strong media backgrounds offering clients the best media skills.
3. RESEARCH. Every media plan at Karsh & Hagan begins with research. We have an extensive media library, which compares with those found only in national agencies. Our customer systems, _____, facilitate both planning and buying by providing quick, concise demographic and psychographic information. _____ is an on-line computer system offering in-depth marketing and media information. With our _____ software program, we are able to analyze the media, build a schedule, measure reach and frequency, generate insertion orders, process billing and complete post-buy analyses simply and accurately.
4. EFFICIENCY. Every buy is negotiated. We are always looking for ways to cut media costs without sacrificing effectiveness. Our annual television negotiation (rather than individual game negotiations) for the Lottery is just one example of substantial media cost savings.
5. RELATIONSHIPS. We value our excellent relationship with our media suppliers. We believe strong professional ties with the media bring more promotional opportunities for our clients, better spot rotation and ad position and, most importantly, an environment for stronger negotiating.
6. CREATIVITY. Each of our clients has different media needs. We do customized media plans with strategies, maximizing media effectiveness for every client.
7. BUYING EXPERIENCE. Whether it's television/cable, daily newspapers, weekly newspapers, special interest newspapers, trade magazines, consumer magazines, agricultural magazines, directories, taxicabs, buses, rotaries, showings or radio buying, we've had experience. Whether it's national, regional,

ADI, TSA, metro or even county-by-county buying, we've had experience.

[Specific examples of client experience.]

8. APPROVAL. All media plans and buys are approved by our clients before implementation.
9. ACCOUNTABILITY. We do post-buy analyses on all broadcast campaigns. And they are consistently on target.
We check commercial rotations. We verify tearsheets. We do not pay media invoices without affidavits. And we negotiate makegoods for all under-deliveries.

Of course, realizing and espousing these ideas is one thing. Delivering them is another. And so there's one other aspect of our capabilities that cannot be overlooked. Our people. Karsh & Hagan is committed to staffing with experienced, talented people who understand the importance of consumer-based strategy and know how to make it work. They can deliver the irresistible ideas and vivid, memorable images. They can deliver brilliant, believable and likable executions. They know how to communicate on an emotional level. They know how to plan and buy for maximum effectiveness. They are the best in the region.

If you don't believe it, look at the Karsh & Hagan you've never seen. Look, not just at the work we've done for the Lottery. Look at the work we do for other clients. And look at the response it's gotten. Look at the industry recognition our work and our people have received.

Strengths and benefits

Forget the strengths you already know—our years of experience and knowledge of the lottery industry. Take a hard look at the agency and judge us on the merits that go beyond the advantages of the incumbent.

Strength: our people. Department by department, Karsh & Hagan outranks its competitors, not just in sheer ability of individuals, but in depth. From account service to creative to media, to traffic and print and broadcast production, the success of each department does not depend on a single star. If something happens to one person, the next stands ready to do equally as well. No other agency in Colorado can match this level of expertise and depth.

Benefit: you are always assured that the work will be done on time, by people who have the ability and understanding to do it well.

Strength: our work. The work of Karsh & Hagan Advertising, measured by its success in the marketplace and by the recognition of our industry, is the best available in the region. The case history for the _____ is a case in point. And so far this year, no other agency has come close to the kind of industry recognition that has been generated by the work of Karsh & Hagan, locally, nationally and internationally.

Benefit: You are assured that the work which represents you in the marketplace will be successful and of high quality.

Strength: our character. No other agency has contributed so much to the Denver community. [Specific details of charitable associations.]

Benefit: If you choose Karsh & Hagan as your advertising agency, you will be able to say to anyone that your agency is the most qualified agency for the job, and the character of your agency is unquestionable.

Strength: management. The spectacular growth of Karsh & Hagan Advertising, and its survival in times of local economic adversity, attest to the strength of its people and its management capabilities.

Benefits: stability and continuity.

Strength: consumer-based strategies and disciplines. As discussed above, a focus on the consumer throughout the disciplines is the hallmark of Karsh & Hagan philosophy.

Benefit: the best assurance there is that your advertising will be effective.

Strength: commitment to outstanding performance and effectiveness. It is this commitment that takes us beyond the normal and accepted bounds of advertising. It is this commitment that enables Karsh & Hagan work to smash the 2% barrier, to be remembered, to beat the odds and produce remarkable results.

Benefit: the Lottery continues to make progress and provide benefits to the State of Colorado.

Here is a list of Karsh & Hagan strengths and benefits in summary form.

K&H Strengths	Colorado Lottery Benefits
1. Knowledge, understanding of lotteries	Experienced team, no retraining, cost savings
2. Staff	Hard-working, proven team
3. Overall service	Dependable, get the job done well
[21 items in chart.]	

Again, we refer you to Exhibit A, our most recent performance evaluation from Colorado Lottery, for a detailed, comprehensive report card of our work, our relationship, team involvement and support of the Lottery mission.

Here's a list of the awards won just for work on the Colorado Lottery. And on the following pages we've included award-winning TV for other clients plus some ads that we believe will be winners next year.

[List of awards.]

SERVICES RENDERED TO LOTTERY

Karsh & Hagan will render all of the services described below. In each of those sections we describe the processes/tools we use to develop our recommendations to clients and indicate if any work will be performed by outside suppliers.

We believe that teamwork and dedication to a cooperative joint effort with our clients is the best tool in creating successful marketing and advertising plans. The cornerstone of teamwork is communications and you will see that most of our specific processes/tools/disciplines are directed toward generating accurate and good communication among all parties.

MARKETING/ADVERTISING PLANNING

Karsh & Hagan will provide assistance to the Colorado Lottery marketing team in developing comprehensive advertising and marketing plans for all games. Karsh & Hagan team members will attend marketing and game-planning meetings with the Colorado Lottery staff. Planning, timing and budgets will be established and incorporated into an overall plan for given games during the fiscal year.

Karsh & Hagan's marketing and advertising planning process utilizes the following steps and disciplines:

- The agency meets with the client on each project to determine the scope of the project, including timing, budgets and the objective for the advertising. We have no rules regarding who should attend this meeting. Anyone who is involved in the project from the agency, the client, or outside suppliers who can provide input to establish parameters and objectives, should be at this meeting.

- A Situation/Objective/Strategy (SOS) analysis is then written by the Karsh & Hagan account services group. This document is forwarded to the appropriate client staff, agency staff and outside suppliers for their review prior to a joint input meeting.

The purpose of the joint input meeting is to review, discuss and finalize agreement to the marketing and advertising objectives and strategies for the specific project and the SOS. This process often takes more than one meeting and can include decisions to utilize additional research or further exploration and gathering of information prior to the confirmation of either the objectives or strategies.

Once the SOS has been approved, it is then translated by the Karsh & Hagan team into the creative and media planning guidelines.

Karsh & Hagan also offers its clients a major marketing planning tool, _____. _____ is a total category and product audit that is jointly conducted by the agency and the client. This audit is most often used by our new clients and by those clients who utilize Karsh & Hagan to assist them in writing their annual marketing plans. Such assistance is another service we are willing to provide the Colorado Lottery.

CREATIVE PLANNING AND EXECUTION

Karsh & Hagan's staff will continue to create and produce advertising materials for print, broadcast and point-of-sale. We will maintain responsibility for all talent payments and royalty fees. And we'll continue to develop budget-saving ideas associated with the creative process.

Karsh & Hagan's creative planning and execution processes are both outgrowths of the marketing and advertising process. For creative planning we have a specific discipline, the Creative Workplan, which is an extension of the approved SOS, clarifying the specific creative projects, targets, brand positioning and media to be used.

The Creative Workplan and the Media Workplan serve as important internal communication documents within the agency to assure coordination between media and creative departments in the development of the specific plans and executions.

For creative execution we have two simple processes. First, talk to each other; communicate with each other. Second, talk to the client; show the client; keep the client involved in the process as the creative is being developed. We believe that creative execution is a creative process, but we also believe that the creative process is everyone's responsibility and that everyone should take a part in helping achieve the best possible results in this area.

Having planned and executed the creative, we now must produce it. Karsh & Hagan uses outside suppliers for its production beyond mechanical art. Our process, to assure the best quality at the best cost, is to bid a minimum of three outside suppliers for each job. Recognizing the sensitivities of a Colorado State account, we also bid only Colorado suppliers unless costs or services require otherwise.

MEDIA PLANNING AND PLACEMENT

Karsh & Hagan will help develop an overall media budget for the Colorado Lottery. We will plan, place and evaluate all media for the Colorado Lottery. This will include post-buy analyses of all broadcast placed and a recap of all media budgets.

We will negotiate all appropriate media to the best of our ability, always seeking ways to maximize the Colorado Lottery investment. Contractual arrangements and fulfillment of media contracts for purchase of time and space, with verification prior to payment, will continue as a standard service from our media department.

Karsh & Hagan's media planning and placement process begins at the initiation of the project. The media department begins work specifically on the projects planned with approval of the SOS and translation of that SOS into the Media Workplan. The media planning is then broken down into three stages: planning, buying and post-buy. The following describes each of these stages and the processes involved.

[Details of three stages.]

To assist the media department in developing the most efficient and effective media plans, we use a large selection of media planning and placement tools. The following lists the immediately available media and planning placement tools to which we subscribe.

[List of tools.]

And finally, a very important discipline we practice is "remaining informed."

We do this by remaining in constant communication with our media representatives. We do this because the world of media buying is changing dramatically; new types of media become available constantly and negotiation is possible in areas previously considered untouchable. Merchandising extensions have become the rule rather than the exception.

At Karsh & Hagan we believe staying on top of this ever-changing media world begins with strong relationships with our media salespeople. We encourage this and expect this from all our media staff.

MARKETING AND ADVERTISING RESEARCH PLANNING, CONSULTATION, AND MANAGEMENT

The Karsh & Hagan management and account service team will continue to be involved in planning, budgeting, implementing and interpreting research for the Colorado Lottery. Research will continue to help us structure sound advertising and marketing planning and provide us with evaluation tools to assess the marketing and advertising effectiveness.

In terms of research planning and consultation management, we have three processes which help identify needs that Karsh & Hagan can then help the client to address. The processes are _____, the marketing and advertising audit, which includes a review of existing research resources; the SOS, which will identify any situation and strategic issues that need further clarification; and the media planning process, which also identifies missing information.

Research also plays an important role in evaluating the marketing and advertising effort. We believe that game design, new product development, and advertising communication are key areas where research can help evaluate the effectiveness and eliminate mistakes. Rather than lock ourselves and our clients into standardized processes, we prefer to evaluate the need for research, the objectives to be measured, and then recommend the best research methodology to achieve those ends. As indicated, Karsh & Hagan regularly plans and supervises research projects which evaluate the effectiveness of advertising communications and products.

Almost all research projects initiated by Karsh & Hagan and its clients are fielded by outside suppliers and supervised by both Karsh & Hagan and client research groups. As with creative production, we try to utilize Colorado-based research suppliers. This has led to a strong and cooperative association with _____, a primary supplier for quantitative and qualitative research for the Colorado Lottery since 1984. However, this firm has not been the exclusive supplier for the Colorado Lottery nor for Karsh & Hagan.

We continually review research services and suppliers to find the most up- to-date research resource. [Description of specific system.]

We believe this technique is a major breakthrough in pre-testing research methodology and are currently considering recommending some form of the technique to our clients for pre-testing needs.

SALES PROMOTION PLANNING AND EXECUTION

Karsh & Hagan will continue to create and produce point-of-sale collateral items and direct mail for the Colorado Lottery. We will continue to emphasize game graphics and continuity for better image-related reinforcement.

When requested, we will provide creative designs and direction for ticket and game graphics. All materials created by us will be copyrighted. All sales promotional materials will directly relate to overall game planning.

The Karsh & Hagan process is straightforward: maintain continuity by utilizing the same account and creative teams that work on the Colorado Lottery to work on any sales or consumer promotion extensions, and utilize assistance of internal or external suppliers.

We have described Karsh & Hagan's capabilities in the consumer and sales promotion areas. In some cases described, we have used outside consultants. However, in all cases, we have maintained continuity by keeping the same creative and account management team on the sales/consumer promotion project.

PUBLIC RELATIONS PLANNING AND EXECUTION IN COOPERATION WITH THE LOTTERY'S PUBLIC RELATIONS CONSULTANT

The agency will continue to assist the Colorado Lottery public relations staff and its consultant. We will coordinate activities so that advertising and public relations are headed in the same direction.

The coordination of the advertising and public relations activities is the responsibility of the Karsh & Hagan account service group in conjunction with the Colorado Lottery staff. Since the Colorado Lottery has a separate public relations consultant, Karsh & Hagan's involvement has been to coordinate production of materials, supply camera-ready art, generate concepts, and at times coordinate prospective co-promotion partners. All of these activities have been handled internally by Karsh & Hagan's staff, and we expect that to continue.

SERVICES NOT INCLUDED ABOVE

Karsh & Hagan will continue to provide accurate and timely billing, customized monthly budget recaps and sound accounting management and recordkeeping for all Colorado Lottery purchases and payables. We agree that employees, and members of employees' immediate family, shall not play any Colorado Lottery game.

Karsh & Hagan maintains a sophisticated job-tracking and billing system, which provides the Colorado Lottery with immediate access to our fiscal records. Our computerized system provides efficient and effective management of projects and their billing. The annual audits conducted by the Colorado Lottery have confirmed both the efficiency and the care in which Karsh & Hagan has managed their fiscal responsibilities to the Colorado Lottery and the State.

Karsh & Hagan has always offered any of its management personnel to assist the Colorado Lottery in negotiations or discussions regarding media relations, legislative relations, etc. The most recent example of this undefined service is Karsh & Hagan's participation in the negotiations for a consortium to broadcast the Lotto drawing shows. This resulted in over _____ savings for the Colorado Lottery, as well as an upgrade in the station consortium coverage.

PROCESSES TO POSITION LOTTERY

Over the last seven years we have developed a healthy respect and sensitivity for the importance of satisfying all of the Lottery's constituents. Important constituents include _____.

We recognize the importance of maintaining a positive Lottery image.

We do everything possible to avoid providing ammunition to our detractors. In the past we have used up-front research to detect any "red flags" relating to advertising concepts. We provide equal opportunities for all people and businesses we work with on behalf of the Lottery. We achieve relatively even statewide media coverage. We avoid language which ties the Lottery to gambling.

We always try to represent the Lottery as having an upbeat, fun personality. We post odds prominently on the advertising. We maintain a balance between over-promising and a player's ability to win. Above all, we know that we must always exhibit good taste and operate in a "squeaky-clean" environment.

In positioning Lottery products in the future, we think that the fundamental process that will lead to success combines research and good solid communications.

The Research Process

1. Conduct a research audit.

Let's review what we know, what we don't know, and what we want to find out. This audit would be segmented by key publics—players, retailers, the Commission, the Legislature, etc. In the process, we can isolate problems and explore opportunities. Our mission is to isolate likes and dislikes and misunderstandings about the Lottery and fix them, if possible.

2. Conduct strength/weakness analysis.

We will (with the Lottery staff) examine the relative strengths and weaknesses of the Scratch and Lotto products. This will give us a base to consider changes in the Lottery's product mix.

3. Examine the Lottery's promotional mix.

Together, we will arrive at an efficient and effective level of promoting each Lottery product, eliminating any waste and maximizing dollars. This will take time and some testing.

4. Cost control/feedback.

We must make a concerted effort to control costs. We can help reduce the Lottery's _____ overall operating budget to the _____ level. We must monitor projects closely to realize greater efficiency. We will cooperate with the Colorado Lottery and the Department of Revenue in their proposed new cost-accounting system.

5. Pre-testing.

By pretesting games and advertising communications, we can help avoid mistakes and reduce risks. We also can test the promotional mix changes suggested above as well as media alternatives to efficiently maximize our expenditures.

The Communications Process

1. Staff, Commission, agency communications.

It is extremely important to facilitate a better understanding of the Lottery's marketing goals and efforts—specifically the role of advertising and public relations within the marketing mix.

We propose a staff/Commission/agency retreat where we discuss pertinent issues. In this process we clarify objectives and strategies and clear up misunderstandings. Also, this process will provide Commission members the knowledge/information they need to answer detractors. We are a team, and we should all be playing from the same sheet music.

2. Communication with legislators/State government.

We believe that a quarterly briefing (even a newsletter or roundtable discussion) for the legislature is essential. Again, there is misinformation, particularly about proceeds allotment, advertising and prize structures, that needs to be clearly communicated to this key constituency.

The Lottery should make its case on a more consistent basis in a proactive manner rather than reactively fighting fires.

3. Communications with retailers.

We propose a series of formal interviews with key retailers. Let's find out why retailers are happy and why they aren't. Let's help them even more to sell our tickets. Let's outline the problems and opportunities. Retailers are a key public that we must keep happy to achieve increased profits. More communication and understanding on the retail level can help avoid criticism, apathy and a non-winning attitude. A similar process with the Lottery sales staff is a good idea.

4. Two-way communication with players.

Communication is a two-way process. We must make sure we analyze feedback on the Lottery's game designs, products, advertising concepts and prize levels with players and prospective players.

Some of the product/positioning issues we believe we need to explore in the future are listed below.

[Specific recommendations for Lottery and Lotto improvements.]

5. Word-of-mouth communication.

We know through our Lottery experience that successful lotteries thrive on a *winning experience*. Lotteries are momentum-intensive. The more winners there are, the more sales there are. Thus, winner awareness is a key to running a long-term successful lottery. And word-of-mouth winner awareness is the foundation of success.

Winner awareness is much more than publicizing winners in local media. Winner awareness is the public's (and player's) knowledge, experience and feeling that they can—and do—win!

Winner awareness is as important to the retailer who sells the Lottery product as it is to the legislator who approves the Lottery budget.

In fact, the winning feeling precipitated by winning experiences will silence those who scrutinize the Lottery most.

Different publics will, for instance, criticize advertising because it is so visible. And advertising is a matter of taste. Some people like some ads and some don't! Advertising will always be criticized. However, in a positive sales environment, the lottery will be criticized less on all fronts because it is providing the state with more proceeds.

The net effect of "winning" can be summed up by slightly altering the Lottery's first theme line. Instead of *When Colorado Plays, Colorado Wins,* we should consider *When Colorado Wins, Colorado Wins!*

Even operating costs and advertising investments can be reduced through the creation of winner awareness and a winning experience.

It is Karsh & Hagan's goal to help the Colorado Lottery create a winning experience. And the way we do that is to start with the product, because advertising follows marketing.

These are examples of the research and communications process we would recommend to reposition the Scratch game, to re-establish Lotto, and to avoid public criticism. Success and a winning experience go hand-in-hand. The more we create an atmosphere of winning, the less scrutiny and criticism we will experience from our detractors.

A product mix with more winners will build more player acceptance. This results in more product and winner awareness. This, in turn, creates momentum and enthusiasm on the player, staff and retailer levels. This will have a positive affect on advertising, public relations and promotions.

The end result will be increased profits and an improved public perception of the Colorado Lottery as a significant revenue source for the State.

MINORITY VENDORS

Karsh & Hagan believes in providing equal opportunity for minority-owned businesses. This year, we have met with several minority-owned businesses to discuss opportunities for the Colorado Lottery and _____.

The measures K&H would take to assure equal opportunity include a continuing process of meeting with minority media and vendors.

Step One: meet the principals in the business

Step Two: assess capabilities

Step Three: encourage bids

Step Four: award bids and feedback to the Colorado Lottery in writing on number of bids submitted and won by minority-owned businesses.

Whenever we can be assured of acceptable quality, acceptable delivery and competitive pricing, a job will be awarded to a minority vendor. Our experience is there are excellent minority vendors in our community. We welcome the opportunity to do business with them.

As noted, we believe in doing business with Colorado Sheltered Workshops for the physically and mentally handicapped. We have ongoing relationships with several of these projects, which include all manner of handwork. Recently we learned of a workshop at Ft. Logan and plan to include them in future bidding.

Each year the Karsh & Hagan media department compiles the *Guide to Minority Media in Colorado.* This comprehensive directory includes evaluations of every available minority and special-interest broadcast and print media.

Together with the Lottery, we have selected the following Black- and Hispanic-owned radio stations, newspapers and magazines for inclusion on all Lottery/Lotto media schedules:

[List of media.]

ADVERTISING BUDGET

Karsh & Hagan understands that the Lottery must use well-planned and thoughtful marketing strategies in conjunction with prudent management of all advertising and promotion costs to enhance efficiencies and generate maximum proceeds to the State.

As a matter of course, we communicate with a number of lottery ad agencies and lottery staffs in other states. We keep up with the latest products and promotional techniques. This knowledge and experience, along with the contacts we've made over the years, helps us and the Lottery staff avoid *re-inventing the wheel* during the design and execution of games.

We use research extensively. The tracking study gives us a handle on problems, opportunities, attitudes and awareness of game play. We use qualitative research to help identify *red flags* and isolate motivations. Game concepts are pre-tested to ensure that we are clearly and persuasively communicating with our prospects.

The Karsh & Hagan account group uses strategy disciplines to outline direction on specific assignments and next steps.

Estimates are completed and approved prior to starting a project. Frequently, Karsh & Hagan negotiates prices up front based on experience of similar jobs. No less than three printing bids are required on each printing job. Television production is bid on a similar basis.

Budget recaps for each job are reported on a weekly basis. And weekly status reports focus on meeting deadlines.

Because the Lottery has been spending over ____ a year in media, the media planning, buying and analysis functions are extremely important.

Because broadcast media is a commodity item, rates are negotiated up front. Annual up-front television negotiations have saved the Lottery approximately 25%.

Karsh & Hagan pioneered a unique service to the Lottery. We ask the TV media to guarantee target rating points. After each game, Karsh & Hagan conducts a post-buy analysis. If target rating points are not delivered, Karsh & Hagan negotiates spots/rates to ensure channels make up the difference.

Advertising invoices are not paid until Karsh & Hagan is satisfied as to placement and performance.

Here are specific examples of ways Karsh & Hagan has saved the Lottery money during 1988 and 1989.

[Details of savings.]

CONFORMITY WITH SCOPE OF WORK

Without exception, Karsh & Hagan currently performs all of the services detailed in ____ for Colorado Lottery. And we are prepared to continue such effort under the conditions of this RFP.

More specifically, we have presented our agency, our qualifications, our experience with the Lottery and other related advertising accounts, our total capabilities, and our desire to remain on the Colorado Lottery team.

With our experience, our expertise, our professional staff, and our enthusiasm for the Lottery account, we believe that no other agency can match us in performing the scope of work required.

The fun is back! And we want to be part of it!

27-2 Proposal to assume defined tasks

You're proposing to take over a specific job. Show that your company has the necessary expertise and experience—and more. Point out why your company's capabilities are unique. What makes you stand out from the rest? Then, move into the financial details: costs, expenses, and how you will be recompensed. Follow that with more specific details of how you can benefit the client. (You can rearrange this information, placing the financial details at the end.) Close by reaffirming your company's desire to work with the client and meet the client's needs.

Dear _____:

Thank you for your consideration of Pinkerton* Investigative Services to provide the State of Colorado's Women, Infants and Children (WIC) program with a thorough, professional, and cost-effective compliance purchasing service.

Pinkerton takes pride in providing a "Demonstrably Superior" service which is comprehensive and responsive. We appreciate the opportunity to be the investigative resource in this fact-finding effort, as defined in the following narrative description.

NARRATIVE DESCRIPTION

A. Pinkerton Investigative Services has more investigation experience and tradition than any other private company in existence today. We believe that dependability is the difference that speaks out when defining our management and organizational qualities. Our extensive background and reporting skills are a must in all investigative efforts. In addition, our Compliance Purchasing (shopping testing services) is a defined service that provides clients with quality information on employee performance, ethics-honesty (cash/merchandise transactions, sales records information, discrimination information, etc.), and proper and adequate representation of products and programs. The Denver Pinkerton's office provides Compliance Purchasing programs for various clients throughout Colorado and surrounding areas.

B. This office, immediately upon receipt of the Invitation and Bid, initiated liaison with various Pinkerton offices (Chicago/Hillside, Albuquerque/Santa Fe, and Clayton/St. Louis) to further develop insight and direction in order to establish a successful investigative liaison program with WIC of Colorado. Although this office has not recently been involved in public entitlement programs, we believe the above defined "Draw from Proven Success and Experience Approach" is a much needed resource and incentive, as well as a teamwork asset.

C. Compensation:

1. Rates: _____ per individual compliance buy (test). If a series of tests are scheduled: _____ per individual compliance buy. If tests are to be conducted in isolated regions, a flat rate of _____ per hour would apply. All above rates include test time and report time.

2. Expenses: _____ per mile for auto expense/mileage. Parking fees: actual amount reimbursed by client. Phone calls made solely at client request: actual amount reimbursed by client.

3. Court Appearance/Testimony: _____ per hour for court appearance/testimony plus all related travel expenses originating and concluding at the Pinkerton Denver office.

4. Lodging: Any overnight lodging at the approval of the client will be charged to the client at cost. (Every effort will be made to secure reasonably priced lodging.)

5. If investigators are out of town the entire day, breakfast and dinner will be charged to the client; if investigators are out of town during the breakfast or dinner period only, this meal will be charged to the client. (A maximum of _____ per meal will be charged.)

A combined (completely itemized) invoice of services will be forwarded to the client on a regular basis (weekly, bi-weekly, or monthly) at the preference of the client.

D. Our Senior District Investigative Office in Denver directs the efforts of operative investigators in Colorado Springs, Pueblo, Greeley, Cheyenne, Gillette, as well as Metro Denver and surrounding areas. This vast network, combined with several WIC program offices, will be a very important mutual resource.

Pinkerton was founded in 1850 by Allan Pinkerton. It is the oldest and largest private security company in the world. With our development of investigative services and expertise, our members (employees and clients alike) can take pride in timely, professional results. This is reflected in the variety and size of assignments the company handles for several thousand clients throughout a network of more than 150 offices in the United States, Canada, and the United Kingdom.

1. Training—Effective investigative training involves strict implementation, management supervision, and follow-up. While many investigative agencies may propose a comprehensive training program, at Pinkerton's that program is a reality.

Pinkerton has developed a complete and organized training program.Pinkerton's complete training program for operative investigators is detailed (but not limited) to Introduction, Preparation of Case Journals and Reports, Company Policy, Internal/Undercover Surveys, Background Investigations, Surveillance, Insurance Investigations, Store Detective Procedures, and Compliance Purchasing.

Few companies have come close to the imaginative advances in practical training made by Pinkerton. We welcome the opportunity to express the teamwork attitude and approach towards the WIC specific training outlined on page 8 of the Request for Proposal. We are proud of our training accomplishments and we invite your organization to visit and use our facilities and materials in conjunction with your program.

2. Contract Project Director—[Name, address, and telephone.] [Insert brief biography.]

_____ maintains daily supervision and management of all investigative processes (cases, client contacts, training, administration and quality assurance) to insure productive results in a timely and professional manner. He recruits and selects operative investigators, trained and specialized in various investigative roles.

3. Senior District Manager—[name.] [Insert brief bio.]

_____ manages the Denver Office and also has responsibility for Security Officer Service and Investigations at the Colorado Springs, Pueblo, Salt Lake City, Gillette, and Billings offices.

E. Pinkerton is willing to follow the requirements and tasks as outlined in the RFP, Bid _____.

F. We have submitted a comprehensive proposal in order to assist you in making a decision. The proposal discusses the many areas of expertise that add up to Pinkerton's being the best return on the investment in compliance purchasing made by the Colorado WIC program. We look forward to demonstrating our ability to serve you.

After you have reviewed our proposal, we would be happy to answer any question or provide additional information.

Very truly yours,

Bradley Van Hazel
Pinkerton
Denver, Colorado
*Pinkerton is a registered trademark of Pinkerton.

27-3 Proposal to provide facilities and services

For proposals about facilities and services (such as for day care, academic, correctional, senior citizen), convince your clients you are the company for the job—you can provide the physical, social and emotional support required. This proposal's comprehensive Table of Contents is a road map of information that should be included in similar proposals. In short, you want to

- Anticipate and answer all the client's questions.
- Describe the facilities.
- Explain how your company is organized.
- Tell about your staff's training and experience.
- Point out the professional guidance you will use.
- Outline the programs you will provide.
- Explain safety and security measures.

The tone of your proposal is important. It must reflect the caring, respectful regard that you have for individuals entrusted to your care.
In this next case, the transmittal letter underscores the urgency created by the need to complete a real estate transaction for the facilities by a certain date.

Dear ____:

Please accept the enclosed submittal, including one original and ten copies, and the original Invitation and Bid sheet, as Morgan County Prerelease Center, Inc.'s proposal to provide Specialized Community Corrections Program services to the Department of Public Safety, Division of Criminal Justice, as delineated in RFP-BF-XXXXX.

I have enclosed one full-size copy of the facility plans and specifications, as the letter-size copies contained in the original and copies are difficult to read.

As stated in the Invitation and Bid, the *proposed* bid selection date is ____. If at all possible, I would greatly appreciate notice by ____, as the Commercial Real Estate Contract entered into with the owners of the facility requires that the remainder of the down payment be remitted by ____, or lose the earnest money of ____, as well as the opportunity to purchase.

I am prepared to respond to any inquires concerning the contents of the proposal or to provide additional information, if necessary. To this end, I may be contacted at the above address and telephone number.

On behalf of Morgan County Prerelease Center, Inc., I thank you for your consideration.

Very truly yours,

Rick E. Mohnssen
Morgan County Prerelease Center, Inc.
Denver, Colorado

TABLE OF CONTENTS

E. FIRE CODES

F. REGULAR FACILITY SAFETY INSPECTIONS

G. INSECT AND RODENT CONTROL

H. FACILITY AND GROUNDS SEARCHES

I. PERSONAL SEARCHES

CHAPTER V—PROGRAMS

A. COMMUNITY REFERRAL

B. OFFENDER INITIAL INTAKE AND ORIENTATION

C. INITIAL ASSESSMENT AND INDIVIDUALIZED
   TREATMENT PLAN

D. INDIVIDUAL COUNSELING

E. INDUSTRIAL THERAPY

F. EDUCATIONAL AND INSTRUCTIONAL CLASSES

G. INDUSTRIAL THERAPY

H. RECREATIONAL THERAPY

I. EMPLOYMENT AND VOCATIONAL PREPARATION
   ASSISTANCE

J. SELF-HELP GROUPS

K. SUBSTANCE ABUSE EDUCATION

L. CONFRONTATION–SENSITIVITY AND CRIMINAL THINK
   GROUPS

M. FACILITY RESIDENT MEETINGS

N. OFFENDER TRANSPORTATION

O. FINANCIAL ASSISTANCE

P. CLIENT RULES AND POLICIES

Q. CLIENT LEVELS SYSTEM

R. PROGRAM STRUCTURE AND SCHEDULES

CHAPTER VI—SERVICES

A. FOOD SERVICE

B. MEDICAL CONSULTATION

C. MEDICAL EMERGENCY

D. OFFENDER CASE RECORD

E. PHOTOGRAPH AND FINGER-PRINTING EQUIPMENT

F. OFFENDER SIGN IN/OUT

G. URINE MONITORING

H. BREATHALYZER

I. MEDICATION/ANTABUSE MONITORING

J. MONTHLY REPORT

K. ANNUAL INTERNAL PROGRAM AUDIT

L. ELECTRONIC FILE MANAGEMENT AND COMMUNICATION

M. FACSIMILE TRANSMISSIONS

N. SHORT-TERM DETENTION

CHAPTER VII—RELEASE PREPARATION

CHAPTER VIII—ESCAPES

A. SECURITY CHECKS AND OFFENDER MONITORING

B. PROCEDURE IN THE EVENT OF ESCAPE

EXHIBITS:

Exhibit A Organizational Chart
Exhibit B Articles of Incorporation and Bylaws
Exhibit C Proposed Agency Documents
Exhibit D Anticipated Budget
Exhibit E Letter from ____
Exhibit F Morgan County Community Corrections Board
           Client Selection Criteria
Exhibit G Letters of Reference
Exhibit H Position Descriptions
Exhibit I Resumes of Key Personnel
Exhibit J Facility Plans and Specifications
Exhibit K Photographs of Facility and Groups and Map
           of Surrounding Area
Exhibit L Commercial Contract to Buy and Sell Real Estate
Exhibit M Map of the ____ Area

Exhibit N Certificate of Occupancy
Exhibit O Emergency Procedures
Exhibit P Information Concerning the ____
Exhibit Q Confrontation–Sensitivity Concept
Exhibit R Example Client Rules and Policies
Exhibit S Client Levels System
Exhibit T Programming Schedule
Exhibit U Monthly Report Form
Exhibit V Letter from ____ Concerning Short-Term Detention
           Services

Proposal to Provide
Specialized Community Corrections Program Services
to the State of ____
Department of Public Safety
Division of Criminal Justice

INTRODUCTION

Morgan County Prerelease Center, Inc. (a Colorado Corporation), proposes to provide contract Specialized Community Corrections Program services to the State of ____ Department of Public Safety, Division of Criminal Justice, as delineated in RFP-BF-XXXXX. The anticipated start-up date shall be the later part of June ____ or 45 days subsequent to contract award.

Morgan County Prerelease Center, Inc. proposes a facility located in ____, which was previously used by the ____ to provide similar services. The proposed facility location is excellent for several important reasons. The facility does not infringe upon a residential neighborhood, yet it is on a major highway within 90 minutes of the ____ metropolitan area. This location will have minimal impact on existing uses, one of which is a secure juvenile detention facility, and others are mostly industrial. The outside of the facility is fenced, and the structure itself can be easily modified to address the security requirements outlined in RFP-BF-XXXXX.

The principal owner and project developer, ____, intends to employ his extensive community corrections experience to offer a unique proposal for the establishment of a specialized community corrections program in _____._____ is a well-established and successful community corrections contractor, providing similar services in both Colorado and Wyoming. _____'s qualifications are further outlined in this proposal.

The proposed offender services and associated program structure shall offer each assigned offender an opportunity to develop a behavior pattern which is more consistent with that of a responsible and productive member of society. The services shall be provided within a group-oriented, short-term treatment modality that will employ a progressive, incentive-oriented behavior methodology and utilize various strategic therapeutic interventions and techniques to effect positive change. The short-term treatment modality shall be based on an average three-month length of stay. The program structure shall be designed to address issues specific to both Track I and Track II offenders.

This proposal will cover the scope of services that Morgan County Prerelease Center, Inc. intends to provide and, to a large extent, the manner in which it intends to provide them. This proposal is divided into eight chapters. The Table of Contents outlines the location of each chapter and the items covered within that chapter. The enclosed Exhibits, A through V, are intended to supplement information provided in the chapters, and are located at the end of this proposal. In the event there is a service category not addressed or sufficiently covered in the contents of this proposal, the principals are prepared to further elaborate on any category of service or to discuss the provision of additional services.

Certain exhibits contain documents intended to demonstrate this offeror's ability to complete similar work as Morgan County Prerelease Center, Inc., and should not be considered as actual or complete documents. These documents are replicas of existing documents that were created for other programs administered by _____ and should be modified to conform to Morgan County Prerelease Center, Inc. requirements, subsequent to contract award.

The offerors hope the contents of this proposal are sufficient for the reviewers to evaluate the offeror's ability to provide the requested services. To this end, the offerors are prepared to provide further explanation of all facets of this proposal.

CHAPTER 1: ADMINISTRATION

A. ORGANIZATIONAL COMPOSITION

1. Positions

Executive Director
Director
Secretary
Secretary
Case Manager Supervisor
Case Manager
Case Manager
Case Manager
Client Manager Supervisor
Client Manager/Transportation Coordinator
Client Manager
Client Manager
Client Manager
Client Manager
Client Manager
Client Manager
Client Manager—Part Time
Client Manager—Part Time
Food Service Supervisor Cook
Cook—Part Time

[Material deleted.]

B. PROGRAM MISSION, OBJECTIVE, AND EXPECTED RESULT

The Agency mission shall be to provide quality community corrections services to offenders referred through the Department of Corrections, the Colorado Board of Parole, or community corrections, with the goal of markedly benefiting both the offender and the community while ensuring public safety. The objective shall be to assist offenders in preparing for an orderly transition to independent living or to a community corrections placement within a short-term treatment modality, emphasizing the use of community resources in the offender's area of residence to further facilitate and support the transition process. The expected results shall be that offenders placed in the care, custody and control of the Agency will benefit by their placement to the extent that when they re-enter the community, they will be better prepared to conduct themselves as productive, law-abiding citizens.

[Material deleted.]

D. POLICIES AND PROCEDURES MANUAL

The Agency Policies and Procedures Manual shall contain information concerning the Agency administration, including: organization and management; fiscal management; personnel; records and reports; safety and emergency procedures; medical care and health services; quality assurance; facility; facility sanitation and food services; residential services; and security and client management. The manual shall be available for staff review and reference, and to appropriate authorities upon request. Throughout the year the manual shall be annotated in pen to indicate minor changes, modifications and revisions as they occur, and it shall be reviewed and updated annually. Initially, the Agency shall rely on a modified replica of the _____ Manual, which has been created according to American Correction Association Standards. A Policy and Procedures Manual specific to Morgan County Prerelease Center, Inc., that conforms to the requirements of the Department of Public Safety, Division of Criminal Justice, Community Corrections Standards shall be created and completed within nine months of contract award.

E. PROPOSED AGENCY DOCUMENTS

Examples of various documents that Morgan County Prerelease Center, Inc. intends to use are enclosed as *Exhibit C*. As previously stated, certain documents shall require further modification prior to implementation.

F. FISCAL MANAGEMENT

1. Fiscal Responsibility

[Material deleted.]

2. Record Keeping/Fiscal Audits

The Agency fiscal year shall be the calendar year. A double- entry accounting system shall be used. All accounting policies, procedures and record-keeping systems shall be in accordance with generally accepted accounting principles. Fiscal audits shall be conducted at the request of the Board of Directors or in accordance with contractual obligations.

3. Anticipated Income Sources

   a. Morgan County Community Corrections Board
   b. Department of Public Safety, Division of Criminal Justice

4. Anticipated Budget

Morgan County Prerelease Center, Inc.'s anticipated monthly budget is enclosed as *Exhibit D.*

5. Financial Statement

As Morgan County Prerelease Center, Inc. was created for the sole purpose of providing the specialized community corrections services to the Department of Public Safety, Division of Criminal Justice, there is no "concise audited financial statement" available, as required in ____. In lieu of this requirement, a letter from ____ is enclosed as *Exhibit E,* which substantiates that the principals, ____, have a line of credit through ____ that allows for a portion of the line to be used for affiliated entities and, further, that ____ will seriously consider providing a ____ loan to Morgan County Prerelease Center, Inc. for start-up purposes, should Morgan County Prerelease Center, Inc. be the successful bidder.

G. INSURANCE

Morgan County Prerelease Center, Inc. shall maintain adequate comprehensive general and professional liability insurance coverage, which shall include employer's non-owned automobile liability coverage, and property and content damage insurance coverage in amounts that comply with Colorado statutory requirements for community corrections services providers. The insurance coverage shall be arranged through ____, immediately subsequent to contract award. Copies of certificates of insurance shall be forwarded to the appropriate authorities upon request.

H. COMMUNITY LIAISON STRATEGY

Morgan County Prerelease Center, Inc. management staff shall establish and maintain liaisons with the [list of agencies] and other governmental entities that exercise official control in the Morgan County area. Further, Agency staff shall establish and maintain liaisons with local colleges and vocational schools, local mental health and counseling services, religious organizations, and other community organizations, which may be used as resources.

I. MORGAN COUNTY COMMUNITY CORRECTIONS BOARD

The Agency Executive Director, Director and other administrative personnel shall interact with the Morgan County Community Corrections

Board in the manner established by Colorado statute and as directed by the Community Corrections Board to ensure prompt and responsible attention to their concerns. The Morgan County Community Corrections Board Client Selection Criteria is enclosed as *Exhibit F.* Morgan County Prerelease Center, Inc.,'s offender acceptance criteria shall be consistent with that established by the Morgan County Community Corrections Board.

[Material deleted.]

CHAPTER II: PERSONNEL

[Material deleted.]

3. Staffing Pattern

Management and administrative personnel shall be on duty Monday through Friday during regular business hours.

The Case Manager Supervisor and Case Managers shall be on duty Monday through Friday from 8:00 a.m. to 8:00 p.m. Case Manager work hours shall be structured to allow the Case Managers to be available for service delivery for the majority of the offenders' waking hours.

Initially, at least one Client Manager shall be on duty to provide facility coverage 24 hours a day, each day of the year. When necessary, an additional Client Manager shall be added and then at least two Client Managers shall be on duty to provide facility coverage, 24 hours a day, each day of the year.

The Food Service Supervisor or a Cook shall be on duty Monday through Friday from 10:00 a.m. to 6:00 p.m. A part-time Cook shall be available on Saturday, Sunday and Holidays from 10:00 a.m. to 6:00 p.m.

[Material deleted.]

CHAPTER III: FACILITY

A. DESCRIPTION

The proposed facility, located at _____, has been vacant since the closure of the _____, a community corrections program operator that used the building for similar services to those requested in RFP-BF-XXXXX. The facility is _____ square feet, less than four years old, and was designed to accommodate as many as _____ residents. Within the facility there is a recreational and lounge area, a private office area with several offices, a kitchen and dining area, storage space, laundry facilities, sleeping quarters, and bathing and toilet facilities. The sleeping quarters are designed for occupancy by four individuals and have adequate storage space. The facility can be available for occupancy by the latter part of June ____. A copy of the facility plans and specifications are enclosed as *Exhibit J.* Photographs of the facility and grounds and a map of the surrounding area are enclosed as *Exhibit K.* ____, the present owners of the facility, have agreed to sell the building to ____. [Material deleted.]

B. ZONING

The facility is located in an area where this type of institution is allowed by a Special Exception Use Permit. Morgan County Prerelease Center, Inc.'s Executive Director was advised by representatives of ____ that the appropriate juncture to apply for such a permit would be subsequent to contract award. As such, ____ will apply for the necessary Special Exception Use Permit if awarded the contract. [Material deleted.]

C. BUILDING CODES

Prior to occupancy, the facility shall comply with all applicable building codes. The facility has previously been inspected by the local building authority to certify and substantiate compliance with local building codes and a Certificate of Occupancy was awarded. If current deficiencies exist, they shall be corrected or an approved plan for correction shall be submitted to the local building authority prior to facility utilization. A copy of the Certificate of Occupancy is enclosed as *Exhibit N.*

D. SANITATION AND HEALTH CODES

Prior to occupancy the facility shall comply with all applicable sanitation and health codes. The facility shall be inspected by the local sanitation and health authority to certify and substantiate compliance. Any noted deficiencies shall be corrected or an approved plan for correction shall be submitted to the local sanitation and health authority prior to facility utilization. A copy of the Certificate of Inspection or an approved plan for deficiency corrections shall be forwarded to the appropriate authorities upon request.

E. FIRE CODES

Prior to occupancy the facility shall comply with all applicable fire codes. The facility shall be inspected by the local fire authority to certify and substantiate compliance. Any noted deficiencies shall be corrected or an approved plan for correction shall be submitted to the local fire authority prior to facility utilization. A copy of the Certificate of Inspection or an approved plan for deficiency corrections shall be forwarded to the appropriate authorities upon request.

F. PHYSICAL CONDITION OF THE FACILITY

The physical condition of the facility is excellent and no substantial renovation, repair or maintenance is necessary at this time. The facility will require minor modifications and equipment installation in the kitchen area prior to utilization.

G. PARKING

The parking ratio will comply with zoning regulations for the type of zone in which the facility is located. No less than 1:3 ratio shall be provided. There shall be more than adequate parking available to accommodate staff and visitors.

H. OUTSIDE RECREATIONAL AREA

The Agency shall endeavor to accommodate numerous outside recreational activities, including basketball, volleyball, baseball, horseshoes, gardening and croquet.

I. FACILITY SERVICES

The Agency shall provide residents with laundry facilities and supplies, linens, pillows, beds, bedding, towels, and personal hygiene items.

J. SECURITY PROVISIONS

[Material deleted.]

K. PRIVATE HEARING ROOM

In accordance with requirements delineated in RFP-BF-XXXXX, Morgan County Prerelease Center, Inc. shall provide, within the facility, a private hearing room that can accommodate as many as ten individuals.

CHAPTER IV: SAFETY AND SANITATION

A. EMERGENCY PROCEDURES

A copy of the Morgan County Prerelease Center, Inc., Emergency Procedures is enclosed as *Exhibit O.*

B. EMERGENCY EVACUATION PLAN

A facility Emergency Evacuation Plan shall be created, immediately subsequent to contract award, and provided to the appropriate authorities upon request.

C. FACILITY SECURITY CHECKS

[Material deleted.]

D. FIRE AND EMERGENCY EVACUATION DRILLS

Monthly fire and emergency evacuation drills shall be conducted in accordance with the Department of Public Safety, Division of Criminal Justice, Community Corrections Standards and local fire authorities. Agency staff will ensure that the offender population is familiar with the proper procedures in the event of an emergency. All emergency evaluation drills shall be documented on forms designed for this purpose and in the facility operational log book. Any unusual events detected during the drills shall be noted and the proper administrative authorities shall be notified. The completed forms shall be stored in a secure and locked file, and become part of the Morgan County Prerelease Center, Inc.'s operational records.

E. FIRE CODES

As stated in Chapter III, Morgan County Prerelease Center, Inc., shall comply with all local fire codes. The facility shall be inspected by the appropriate authority on an annual basis to ensure continued compliance. All inspections shall be documented in the facility operational log book, and any records concerning the inspections shall become part of the Agency's permanent operational records.

F. REGULAR FACILITY SAFETY INSPECTIONS

Morgan County Prerelease Center, Inc. shall contract with local vendors to inspect the facility fire extinguishers, smoke alarms and stove hood systems on a regular basis, to insure that all equipment is in optimal operating condition. The Director shall thoroughly inspect the facility fire extinguishers, smoke alarms and stove hood fire extinguishing systems, as well as facility grounds, on a weekly basis. Any malfunctions shall be corrected in a timely manner and completion of these inspections and necessary repairs shall be documented in the facility operational log book. Client Manager staff shall check the facility and grounds during routine facility security checks to assure that no potentially dangerous or unsafe conditions exist. If such conditions are discovered during Client Manager checks, they shall immediately be brought to the attention of the Director.

G. INSECT AND RODENT CONTROL

Morgan County Prerelease Center, Inc. shall contract with a local exterminating company to inspect the facility and grounds on a routine basis to ensure that both are free of insect and rodent infestations. Evidence of these routine inspections shall be kept on file and shall become part of Morgan County Prerelease Center, Inc.'s permanent operational records.

[Material deleted.]

CHAPTER V: PROGRAMS

A. COMMUNITY REFERRAL

Morgan County Prerelease Center, Inc. shall maintain liaisons with numerous community agencies throughout the State to augment Agency services and to provide for continuity of care. Morgan County Prerelease Center, Inc. shall use a referral documentation system that shall allow the offender's Case Manager to monitor and document the services provided by the community agency and to assure that such services are provided consistent with the offender's Individualized Treatment Plan, if provided locally. If services are to be provided to the offender subsequent to discharge, the Agency shall ensure that the referral information is forwarded to the offender's Parole Officer or community corrections placement facility.

B. OFFENDER INITIAL INTAKE AND ORIENTATION

The assigned Case Manager shall be responsible for assuring that the initial intake and orientation process is completed for each offender. The initial intake and orientations shall be conducted as soon after the offender's arrival as possible and, to the extent possible, in a private setting. The intake process shall include, but may not be limited to the following: a review of the referring agency documents and identification of immediate needs, such as medical treatment or mental health evaluation (as determined by mental status exam); executing documents that require the offender's review and signature; addressing the offender's questions concerning the Client Rules and Policies; discussing the Individualized Treatment Planning process; completing the initial assessment documents; photographing and fingerprinting the offender; assigning the offender a room and linen; orienting the offender to the facility; explanation of the program structure and schedule of activities; discussing the Orientation Phase requirements. At this juncture the offender shall be provided with the Client Self-Evaluation and Proposed Release Plan documents and instructed to complete these documents within seven days. These self-report instruments shall be used by the offender's Case Manager in the treatment planning process.

C. INITIAL ASSESSMENT AND INDIVIDUALIZED TREATMENT PLAN

The assigned Case Manager shall be responsible for completing an Individual Treatment Plan (ITP), in conjunction with the offender and other members of the treatment team, within ten days after the offender's arrival. In preparation, the assigned Case Manager shall conduct an assessment of the offender's background and history. The assessment shall include a review of the offender's criminal history, social history, substance abuse pattern, educational and work experience, physical and mental health, and any other pertinent areas relevant to the offender's criminal behavior and current predicament. As part of ITP assessment process, the assigned Case Manager shall use the Case Management Classification system, the Addiction Severity Index and a yet-to-be-determined literacy assessment tool. The ITP shall then be developed using a problem-oriented approach and shall address the identified problem areas, including their resolution, within specified time frames.

Areas of concern may include the offender's initial orientation and adjustment period, vocational, educational and academic pursuits, leisure time activities, employment, reunification with family or significant others, mental health, conduct, substance abuse, medical concerns, discharge plan, or other problem areas identified by the offender, the Case Manager, other members of the treatment team, or the referring agency. Identified problems shall be prioritized based upon their possible influence on continued criminal behavior and the Agency's ability to address them effectively within the specified time frame. Changes, revisions or modifications in the original ITP shall be outlined in monthly ITP Updates. Each offender shall be required to sign the original ITP or the ITP Update to indicate willingness to comply.

The ITP or ITP Update shall serve as a contract between the offender and Morgan County Prerelease Center, Inc. regarding the offender's treatment course. An offender's violation of a condition, as set forth in his ITP or ITP Update, may result in the imposition of disciplinary sanctions or other appropriate corrective action.

D. INDIVIDUAL COUNSELING

Each offender shall receive individual counseling provided by the assigned Case Manager, in accordance with established need, as set forth in the offender's ITP or ITP Updates. The individual counseling sessions shall be a minimum of thirty minutes in length. The focus of individual counseling shall be the resolution of identified problems, as indicated in the offender's ITP or ITP Updates. The assigned Case Manager shall primarily employ treatment techniques that are popularly referred to as the "here and now reality-based therapies." The bases for these therapies were developed by ____. The Agency shall utilize their publications as training tools and guides for the Case Management staff. The principal publications that shall be used are ____. Each offender's participation in an individual counseling session shall be documented in the offender's case file, using the problem-oriented Subjective-Objective-Assessment-Plan (SOAP) documentation method.

F. EDUCATIONAL AND INSTRUCTIONAL CLASSES

Each offender shall receive educational and instructional classes, provided by Morgan County Prerelease Center, Inc. Case Management staff, and other members of the treatment team. These educational and instructional classes shall be modularized and based on a ninety-day time frame. The Agency shall utilize two models developed by ____. These educational packages, ____, are designed specifically for stigmatized populations and for persons experiencing life problems. Information concerning the educational models offered by ____ is enclosed as *Exhibit P*. In addition, educational and instructional classes shall focus on issues such as obtaining a driver's license, arranging for insurance, renting an apartment, cooking, managing personal finances, opening a bank account, obtaining a social security card, establishing credit, locating community services, problem and conflict resolution, maintaining personal health, AIDS, GED, etc. Each offender's participation in an educational or instructional class shall be documented in the offender's case file using an outcome-oriented documentation method.

G. INDUSTRIAL THERAPY

Each offender shall be required to participate in regular industrial therapy at the direction of Morgan County Prerelease Center, Inc. Client Management staff. Industrial therapy shall be structured and encompass regular chores, as well as maintenance of the facility and grounds, laundry duties, gardening, yard upkeep, kitchen work, community service projects, etc. Offenders shall receive credit for Industrial Therapy at the Agency commissary. The amount of credit provided to each offender shall be dependent upon the offender's level status, from $15 to $30 per month. The provision of credit to offenders shall not be considered a wage or an exchange of value for work, but as a therapeutic tool that shall allow offenders to have a means to purchase sundry or other personal items, such as soda, candy, shampoo, toothpaste, etc.

H. RECREATIONAL THERAPY

Each offender shall be required to participate in regular recreational therapy at the direction of Case Management staff. Recreational therapy shall be structured for group activities, although certain activities may be designed for the individual offender. These activities may include volleyball, basketball, softball, horseshoes, structured exercise, structured relaxation, table tennis, group games, videos, etc. Also, each day physically able offenders shall be required to participate in exercise activities. This daily activity shall include stretching, anaerobic exercises, mild, low-impact aerobic exercises, and a cool-down period. These activities shall be conducted outside to the extent possible.

I. EMPLOYMENT AND VOCATIONAL PREPARATION ASSISTANCE

The Case Manager, or other members of the treatment team, shall provide regular employment and vocational preparation assistance to each offender. The objective of employment and vocational assistance shall be to orient offenders to the local job market of the community that the offender intends to transition to, whether the transition is to a community corrections program or to parole, and to offer offenders an opportunity to develop or increase their skills in retaining and maintaining competitive employment. Areas of concentration may include: determining vocational aptitude and interest, targeting the appropriate positions, completing an application for employment, preparing a resume, the interview process, appropriate dress and manner, relationship with management and co-workers, and discussing criminal history with prospective employers. More specialized training may be provided to offenders with developmental disabilities.

Each employment assistance counseling session shall be documented in the offender's case file, using the outcome-oriented documentation method. Morgan County Prerelease Center, Inc. intends to use the ____, developed by the ____. This instrument shall be obtained as soon as possible and provided to the appropriate authorities upon request.

J. SELF-HELP GROUPS

Morgan County Prerelease Center, Inc. shall coordinate and structure regular self-help groups for the offender population, which include Alcoholics Anonymous and Narcotics Anonymous. These groups shall be provided in the evening hours and shall be voluntary unless an offender commits to attendance vis-a-vis their Individualized Treatment Plan. Each offender's attendance at a self-help group shall be noted in the offender's case file.

K. SUBSTANCE ABUSE EDUCATION

Morgan County Prerelease Center, Inc. shall provide specified offenders with Level II Substance Abuse Education classes. These classes shall be provided by a Colorado Division of Alcohol and Drug Abuse certified counselor in accordance with ADAD standards. Each offender's participation in a group counseling session shall be documented in the offender's case file in the problem-oriented, SOAP, documentation method.

L. CONFRONTATION–SENSITIVITY AND CRIMINAL THINK GROUPS

Morgan County Prerelease Center, Inc. shall provide regular Confrontation–Sensitivity and Criminal Think Groups to each assigned offender. These specialized groups shall be facilitated by Case Management staff and shall be the primary method used to positively effect and control the offender's behavior while the offender is a participant in the program and, hopefully, thereafter. The Confrontation–Sensitivity axis shall be based on principles of direct communication and feedback, referred to as the _____, as originally developed by _____. This methodology has been successfully used to effect positive change and control behavior in therapeutic community setting since the 1960s. A Confrontation-Sensitivity concept is enclosed as *Exhibit Q.* The Criminal Think axis shall be based on principles developed by _____ and documented in the book, _____. Together, these two methodologies will provide a powerful vehicle to help shape offender behavior and resolve current as well as long-term problems. It is also an excellent vehicle to allow participants to deal with immediate problems and issues, such as frustration, anger or anxiety provoked by daily life in a correctional setting, relationships with other offenders or Agency staff, etc.

M. FACILITY RESIDENT MEETINGS

Morgan County Prerelease Center, Inc. shall conduct regular weekly meetings of the entire offender population and key Client Management and Case Management staff to assure that the channels of communication are maintained between staff and residents, to discuss any prevailing issues, or to advise residents of rule or policy changes. An agenda shall be prepared prior to each meeting and outcome-oriented notes shall be kept and later word processed for distribution to staff and residents. Copies of the notes shall be available to residents and posted in common areas for review. These notes shall be kept on file and shall become part of Morgan County Prerelease Center, Inc.'s permanent operational records.

N. OFFENDER TRANSPORTATION

Morgan County Prerelease Center, Inc. shall provide transportation for offenders from the institution of confinement to their community corrections or parole placement, or to or from any other mutually agreed-upon location. The Agency's Client Manager/Transportation Coordinator shall be the principal person responsible for coordinating offender transportation and shall be required to possess a valid Colorado driver's license of a class that allows the operator to transport persons for commercial purposes. The Agency shall utilize a multi-passenger van for transporting offenders. Occasionally, other Agency staff may transport offenders to and from appointments or other destinations and shall also be required to possess a valid Colorado driver's license and have appropriate vehicle insurance. This offender transportation shall be provided at the prevailing State rate and charges for this service shall be included with the monthly billing for the specialized community corrections services.

O. FINANCIAL ASSISTANCE

Morgan County Prerelease Center, Inc.'s Director shall administer a Financial Assistance Program for offenders who are indigent and in need. All financial assistance shall be dependent upon the availability of funds. No interest shall be charged in connection with this assistance, and it shall be provided on the basis of individual need. The Agency shall also provide funds to offenders so they may purchase sundry or other personal items. These funds shall be provided to offenders in connection with their participation in the Agency Industrial Therapy, explained in Chapter V.

P. CLIENT RULES AND POLICIES

Offenders must agree to abide by Morgan County Prerelease Center, Inc.'s Client Rules and Policies prior to their final acceptance in the program. The Client Rules and Regulations shall be forwarded to prospective offenders prior to their placement. A copy of Morgan County Prerelease Center, Inc.'s Client Rules and Policies shall be prepared immediately subsequent to contract award and forwarded to the appropriate authorities upon request. When created, the Client Rules and Policies will resemble those of the other community corrections programs operated by _____, except for necessary modifications specific to the Morgan County Prerelease Center, Inc. operation. An example of Client Rules and Policies is enclosed as *Exhibit R.*

Q. CLIENT LEVELS SYSTEM

Morgan County Prerelease Center, Inc. shall utilize a Client Levels System to provide offenders with incentive to progress within the program structure. A copy of the Client Levels System is enclosed as *Exhibit S.*

R. PROGRAM STRUCTURE AND SCHEDULE

Morgan County Prerelease Center, Inc. shall provide a highly structured therapeutic environment within the group-oriented short-term treatment modality. Each offender shall be provided with a programming schedule specific to their individual program Track. At the time the offender's ITP is completed, or as ITP Updates are completed, the assigned Case Manager shall determine, in conjunction with other members of the treatment team, the treatment options that will best address the offender's identified problems. To the extent possible, the program will be structured so that Track I and Track II treatment options are exclusive to offenders from that particular Track. An example of a Programming Schedule is enclosed as *Exhibit T.*

CHAPTER VI: SERVICES

A. FOOD SERVICE

Morgan County Prerelease Center, Inc. shall provide each offender with three nutritious meals per day. The Food Service Supervisor, in conjunction with the Dietician or Medical Consultant, shall ensure that meals are nutritionally balanced and tasteful. Menus shall be determined on a monthly basis, and these menus shall be posted for offender review and comment. Special diets may be developed for offenders with legitimate medical reasons or religious beliefs. All food stuffs shall be provided by Morgan County Prerelease Center, Inc. and shall be purchased at commercial wholesale or retail outlets. Offenders shall be responsible for preparing their own breakfasts. The Cooks shall prepare lunch and evening meals, Monday through Saturday, as well as brunch on Sundays or holidays. Morgan County Prerelease Center, Inc. menus and the food service facilities shall comply with the Department of Public Safety, Division of Criminal Justice, Community Corrections Standards for all local health codes. A copy of the Sanitation and Health Department Environmental Health Inspection Report shall be provided to the appropriate authorities upon request.

B. MEDICAL CONSULTATION

Morgan County Prerelease Center, Inc. shall employ a Medical Consultant, on a contractual basis, to provide consultation services to staff. The Case Manager shall interview an individual offender upon arrival to assess any medical treatment needs and confer with the Medical Consultant, as necessary. The Medical Consultant shall be available on an on-call basis to handle emergency situations. Morgan County Prerelease Center. Inc. shall also maintain a liaison with local hospitals and clinics to assure prompt response to offender medical emergencies or problems.

C. MEDICAL EMERGENCY

Morgan County Prerelease Center, Inc. staff shall be certified in basic first aid and CPR within six months of their employment. Medical emergencies shall be immediately reported to the Director to ensure that the incident is managed according to Agency policy and referring agency requirements. The Director shall properly document the incident and notify the appropriate referring agency. Morgan County Prerelease Center, Inc. shall maintain and have available a properly supplied emergency first-aid kit. [Material deleted.]

D. OFFENDER CASE RECORD

Morgan County Prerelease Center, Inc. shall maintain an individual case file for each offender. The offender's case file shall be kept in a secure and locked location with limited access to appropriate Agency staff.

All information contained within the file shall be assumed to be confidential and not subject to public disclosure without the signed consent of the offender or the approval of the appropriate referring agency. The offender's case file shall contain such information as the offender's photograph and fingerprints, Individualized Treatment Plan and ITP Updates, urine monitoring record, medication monitoring record, documentation of participation in individual and group counseling, sign in/out record, intake documents, financial records, Pre-Sentence Investigation Report, Executive Assignment Order or other placement order, institutional confinement records, and all other records relative to the offender's placement at Morgan County Prerelease Center, Inc.

E. PHOTOGRAPH AND FINGERPRINTING EQUIPMENT

Morgan County Prerelease Center, Inc. shall maintain and utilize Polaroid cameras and finger-printing equipment to photograph and fingerprint each offender as part of the initial intake and orientation process. The offenders' photographs and fingerprints shall be maintained in their individual case files.

F. OFFENDER SIGN IN/OUT

Morgan County Prerelease Center, Inc. shall maintain a sign in/out record for each offender. Offenders shall be required to document, on their sign in/out records, the date, time of departure, destination address, purpose for departure, and expected return time each time they depart the facility. The approved Morgan County Prerelease Center, Inc. staff member escort shall then review the entry to assure that the entry is correct and authorize the offender's departure by signature on the sign in/out record. Upon return, the offender must document the time of return on the sign in/out record. The Morgan County Prerelease Center, Inc. staff member escort shall verify the accuracy of the entry and indicate such by signature on the sign in/out record. Offenders shall not be allowed to depart the facility groups without an approved escort, such as a Client or Case Manager or Parole Officer.

G. URINE MONITORING

Each offender shall be required to provide random urine specimens, as directed by Morgan County Prerelease Center, Inc. staff. The specimens shall be clinically tested, at an approved laboratory, to detect the presence of alcohol or drugs in the offender's system. The frequency of specimen provision and the types of tests conducted shall conform with _____ and shall be based on the individual offender's history and severity of drug and alcohol use and the offender's ability to maintain abstinence, subsequent to placement in the Morgan County Prerelease Center, Inc. urine monitoring program. A minimum of three urine specimens per month shall be collected and tested for two controlled substances. The result of each clinical test shall be documented in the individual offender's case file, on a form designed for this purpose. Appropriate action shall be taken in the event the offender has provided a positive urine specimen, as reported by the approved laboratory.

H. BREATHALYZER

Morgan County Prerelease Center, Inc. shall conduct periodic and unscheduled breath analysis of the offender population to control and detect the use of alcohol. Breath analysis shall also be conducted at any time there is suspicion that an offender has recently consumed alcohol. The Director shall be responsible to ensure that each offender is subjected to breath analysis at least four times per month. Results of each breath analysis shall be documented in the facility operational log book and the offender's case file and, if necessary, the appropriate referring agency authorities shall be notified.

I. MEDICATION/ANTABUSE MONITORING

Morgan County Prerelease Center, Inc., shall monitor an offender's ingestion or topical use of all medication, prescription or otherwise, to ensure that all medications are used in an appropriate manner consistent with a physician's order or manufacturer's suggestions. Use of nonprescription medication by an offender must be approved, in writing, by the Director. The Director may authorize an offender to self-medicate, if the circumstances so warrant. Such authorization shall be documented in the facility operations log book and in the offender's case file. A record of each offender's use of medication shall be maintained in the individual offender's file, on a form designed for this purpose.

J. MONTHLY REPORT

Morgan County Prerelease Center, Inc. shall generate a Monthly Report that will include information required by various referring agencies, as well as other program-related information. The Monthly Report shall be designed to meet the reporting requirements of each referring agency, in a single document, and to serve as a management tool. The report shall contain such information as agency staff recruited and terminated, staff anniversaries and birthdays to occur in the next month, anticipated program changes to occur in the next month, improvement projects completed, the completion date of various routine program audits, the completion date of various program monitoring and other related activities, agency training conducted or other training completed, community relations activities, occupancy type and rate information, client arrival and termination summary and other relevant information. The Monthly Report will normally be published and distributed by the 15th of the month following the reporting period. A copy of the proposed Monthly Report form is enclosed as *Exhibit U*.

K. ANNUAL INTERNAL PROGRAM AUDIT

Morgan County Prerelease Center, Inc. shall conduct an annual internal audit of the Agency's administration, facilities, programs and services to help improve and ensure the Agency's operation and integrity. Morgan County Prerelease Center, Inc. shall provide a copy of the audit to the Morgan County Community Corrections Board or other appropriate authorities upon request.

I. ELECTRONIC FILE MANAGEMENT AND COMMUNICATION

All records and reports shall be maintained within the facility computer system, and regular tape backups shall be conducted to ensure that the records and reports may be reproduced in case the original document is lost, stolen or destroyed. Only designated Agency staff shall have access to the computer system and files. The computer system shall consist of [type of equipment].

Morgan County Prerelease Center, Inc. shall utilize this equipment to maintain a client data base that will assist in fulfilling the requirement referenced in RFP-BF-XXXXX, Section X, which states: "Develop a data collection process to document the level of services and programming within the facility for use in evaluating program activities and success of participants in later community or parole placement." The Agency shall collect demographic information on each offender, including the offender's name, aliases, permanent residence, referral source, Department of Corrections identification number, Social Security Number, FBI number, if applicable, current charge, assigned Case Manager, arrival date, program termination date, program termination status, parole eligibility date, sentence discharge date, if known, Parole Board hearing date, individualized treatment plan elements, individualized treatment plan compliance, program participation elements, release plan elements, etc.

The electronic analysis of this information, as it relates to eventual offender outcome cannot be addressed at this time, as the data base components shall require significant development and customization, specific to this operation. The Agency shall collect this and additional information on each offender and set about data base development as soon as is practical, subsequent to commencement of operation.

M. FACSIMILE TRANSMISSIONS

Morgan County Prerelease Center, Inc. shall use a ____ facsimile machine compatible with the protocol of the majority of facsimile machines in operation today, including the machine used by ____.

N. SHORT-TERM DETENTION

Morgan County Prerelease Center, Inc. shall utilize the Sheriff for the purpose of providing short-term detention of offenders. A copy of a letter forward to ____ from ____ indicating his willingness to provide the short-term detention services is enclosed as *Exhibit V*. This letter is included with the permission of ____. Please refer to her letter located in *Exhibit G*, Letters of Reference.

CHAPTER VII: RELEASE PREPARATION

As indicated in Chapter V, Programs, the offender's assigned Case Manager shall be responsible for preparing an ITP within a specific period, subsequent to the offender's arrival and admission. A major component of the ITP shall be release preparation and the development of a discharge plan. The main focus and purpose of an offender's treatment at Morgan County Prerelease Center, Inc. shall be the facilitation of successful transition or return to community placement or parole. As such, the offender's assigned Case Manager shall be expected to assure that the individual's release preparation and discharge plan is completed, in a timely manner, in conjunction with the appropriate referring agency representative and consistent with established requirements.

The program elements shall focus on one of two Tracks identified in RFP-BF-XXXXX, either community placement preparation or relapse prevention for regressed community offender and technical parole violators. A Track I offender's ITP would include an orientation to the intended community placement site and a consultation with Morgan County Prerelease Center. Inc. Case Manager staff and the Case Management staff of the community placement facility to discuss the offender's treatment course and other pertinent issues to assure continuity of care. A Track II offender's ITP would include an orientation or re-orientation to the parole conditions and a consultation between the Morgan County Prerelease Center, Inc. Case Manager and the intended Parole Office to discuss the offender's treatment course, anticipated transitional problems or other pertinent issues, as well as continuity of care.

CHAPTER VIII: ESCAPES

A. SECURITY CHECKS AND OFFENDER MONITORING

Morgan County Prerelease Center, Inc. Client Managers and administrative staff shall monitor the behavior and whereabouts of offenders on a scheduled and random basis, by conducting security checks and by visibly monitoring offender activities. The objective of this monitoring is to help ensure the offender's adherence to program rules and policies and to assure optimal community protection. This scheduled and random monitoring will enable staff to detect an offender's violation of program rules and policies and, as well, to be alerted to the possibility of escape. As offenders in this specialized community corrections program will not ordinarily be allowed community access, these monitoring activities will focus exclusively on the facility and grounds. Of course, if an offender is off grounds for an approved purpose with a staff escort, the offender's behavior and whereabouts will be monitored by the escort.

B. PROCEDURE IN THE EVENT OF ESCAPE

Offender escapes shall be handled as emergency situations and the on-call management level administrative authority shall be notified immediately, who, shall provide instructions to attending Client Manager with respect to notification of the appropriate referring agency representatives, local police or sheriff, or other responsible governmental agencies, and advise as to the collection and secure storage of the offender's personal property.

27-4 Technical products proposal

Technical proposals need not be difficult. The key is organization and clear language. Remember, these proposals are often read by presidents or CEOs who may not have technical backgrounds. Say it simply. If you must use technical descriptions, keep the sentences short.
Begin with an overview of the proposed system and explain how it will apply to the client's tasks. Then, discuss all the elements important to the project: installation, hardware/software, implementation, training, support, expertise of key employees. Place lists of equipment, software, pricing and such in tables or charts apart from the text.
While your client must know details, he/she doesn't want to be bored or overwhelmed. We have selected the following sections from a lengthy, technical proposal to help you sidestep such dangers.

Dear _____ :

ADS Associates, Inc., is pleased to propose Public Treasury RE-SOURCE with modifications in response to the State's request for Investment System Software. The family of RESOURCE Treasury Information Management Systems has been purchased by over _____ organizations since the first RESOURCE installations in 19__. It is the most widely used microcomputer treasury workstation software production in the world.

Current State Treasury RESOURCE clients are the states of [list of states].

RESOURCE is a modular system, and the State could choose to install selected functions and features initially and add other capabilities later. Also, optional special product features not referenced in the footnotes, such as System Audit Log-In Trail and Market Sector Reports, can be deleted or deferred from the price quotes. In all cases, additions would be incorporated to insure continuation of a fully integrated treasury operation.

ADS Associates is prepared to cooperate in all aspects of customizing, in addition to that which is proposed herein; traditionally, the firm has done extensive customizing for its clients, before and after initial installation.

In addition to the proposed RESOURCE functionality, there could be additional value. For example, RESOURCE has built-in growth capabilities for expanding the system to include RESOURCE Cash and Banking, and Debt Management Systems. Further, these additional systems integrate with each other so that data flows automatically from one to the other.

We are confident that the State of Colorado will find Public Treasury RESOURCE to be a cost-effective treasury management tool. Also, a business relationship with ADS Associates provides an assurance that your treasury system purchase will serve you exceptionally well now and in the future—because we specialize in treasury applications.

Installing a widely used software product insures on-going support, including enhancements and customization, which will be to the long-term benefit of the State.

ADS Associates concentrates on understanding the needs of treasury managers and specializes in investment, debt, and cash management applications. Other ADS software products are installed for "financing desk" systems, "matched book" systems, interest rate futures handling, and cash and futures market spread analysis. Client references attest to the professionalism of ADS' systems design and implementation.

This Proposal remains firm until July 27, _____. Delivery can begin in 90 to 120 days from the date of contract, assuming normal cooperation from State personnel, including their availability for timely training and installation activities. A phased installation could be undertaken as early as 60 days from contract for the standard system features, with multiple installation visits required for the full implementation.

The hardware recommendations are generic in the sense that a specific manufacturer's equipment is not mandated. The brands, quantities and capacities above the minimums shown herein are the State's choices. However, ADS would procure the hardware if you prefer.

Please review this Proposal carefully, as it represents our understanding of your needs and, therefore, the product we intend to deliver to you.

Please direct to me or Mr. Harvey R. Holman any questions about this Proposal.

Sincerely,

Peter W. Melitz
ADS Associates, Inc.
Calabasas, California

[Excerpts from this proposal show how technical information can be provided clearly and concisely. The entire Table of Contents is included to illustrate the various elements contained in the document.]

TABLE OF CONTENTS

INTRODUCTION

Public Treasury RESOURCE is a comprehensive system consisting of multiple functional modules. The modular functionality provides management, account, and reporting tools for investment, as well as debt management and cash and banking management.

Application and system utilities modules provide pooled investment accounting, cash flow forecasting, general ledger interfacing, and ad hoc reporting. The system's communications capabilities permit teleprocessing with all public data communication networks and all known bank balance reporting and electronic funds transfer systems.

Public Treasury RESOURCE is a fully integrated, stand-alone, interactive system that is easy to use and cost effective. In addition, Public Treasury RESOURCE design modularity provides the flexibility necessary for satisfying a broad range of user requirements and for accommodating the changeable and unique needs of users.

Public Treasury RESOURCE is a public sector version of Corporate RESOURCE, which has been available commercially since 19__. There are over ____ installations of RESOURCE with public and private sector organizations. Public sector clients include [list of clients].

ADS Associates, Inc., specializes in financial and banking application software for microcomputers and minicomputers. ADS is an affiliate of ____.

SYSTEM OVERVIEW

Public Treasury RESOURCE, a Microcomputer Treasury Management System, provides modern, versatile tools to assist in information management, reporting and record keeping. RESOURCE matches ____ and compatible microcomputer equipment with the latest computer software technology to provide more features than are available in any other system of its type.

DESIGN

Much of a software system's inherent value results from its basic system design. RESOURCE software is designed by people who combine years of hands-on operating experience with state-of-the-art software development techniques and creative programming talents. With this background, they understand both the functions that a treasury management system must perform and the importance of system expandability. Essential RESOURCE design characteristics follow.

RESOURCE is comprehensive—a complete treasury information management system—the system's numerous modules, which include Investment and Debt Management, Cash and Banking Management, Cash Flow Forecasting, and General Ledger Interface, are fully integrated, and the flow of data between them is entirely automatic.

RESOURCE provides flexibility for enhancements and customization—the System's modular design makes possible flexible packaging to suit each customer's current and future needs. A user-defined reporting module enables customers to design their own reports, extract their data from any RESOURCE database, and output the result to a printer, file or spreadsheet.

Customization is generally a relatively minor programming task. Should a customer desire capabilities beyond those met by a standard RESOURCE module, the software easily incorporates custom features. The Systems Division of ADS Associates performs customizations on schedule, smoothly and at low cost.

RESOURCE is easy to use—ADS recognizes that ease of use is essential for satisfying financial executives; therefore, all operation and interaction between the system and the user is prompted from menu-driven video screens. Errors are diagnosed immediately, with an explanatory message displayed on the screen. Use of RESOURCE software requires no special computer background or skills, or understanding of "computereze." RESOURCE "speaks" in familiar business language.

The following Treasury functions are automated and provide a fully integrated flow of meaningful management information:

- **Investment/Debt Portfolios**—Extensive position and transaction accounting and reporting, on a cash and/or accrual basis, for all fixed-income investment and debt items and for equities securities, are provided.

- **User-Defined Reporting**—An easy-to-use report writer enables the user to create unique reports using any data elements stored in RESOURCE databases. The capability of interfacing any RESOURCE database information to _____ or _____ is also available.

- **Cash Flow Forecasting**—The facility for making projections of future cash flows, using receipts and disbursements history and known critical events that will impact future cash flows, is integrated with Investment and Debt Accounting.

- **Pooled Interest Apportionment**—A system for recording receipts and disbursements and maintaining a fund balance for each participating agency is provided as a stand-alone feature for pooled investment fund accounting and interest apportionment.

- **Swap Analysis**—A screen display is provided for entering bid and offer quotes and generating an analysis of swap and trade opportunities quickly.

- **Investment Risk Monitoring**—A management tool is included for analysis and control of risk associated with investing in various security types and with various issuers.

- **Collateral Tracking**—Multiple pieces of repo/reverse repo collateral can be market priced, monitored for margin requirements, easily substituted, and reported in consolidated position inventories.

- **General Ledger Interface**—The Interface extracts general ledger account number information from the applicable RESOURCE databases, automatically prepares general ledger entries, and prints a posting list or presents a database in ASCII format for electronic transmission to a mainframe system.

- **Autodial and Balance Reporting**—Using ADS AUTOCOM* software, the microcomputer can dial all the user's reporting banks and/or reporting services for balance and transaction activity; AUTOCOM handles all types of data transmission. A special data-entry screen is provided for entering transaction activity not transmitted via an electronic reporting system. The information received is reformatted for consolidated reporting.

- **Daily Cash Worksheet**—An automated worksheet provides both screen display and hard copy and calculates the user's total cash availability by consolidating all RESOURCE data. Adjustments are made easily via "windows" into the worksheet.

- **Cash Ledger**—The Cash Ledger is a record of all automated cashbook transactions and is a subsidiary ledger to the user's general ledger. The automated assignment of G/L codes and entries is an extra cost option.

- **Book Reconciliation**—Two sets of activity and balances can be maintained on any cash account; side-by-side presentation facilitates comparison of bank balances to internal book balances for daily reconcilement.

- **Electronic Funds Transfer**—The EFT module provides a capability to warehouse and transmit repetitive wires, ACH transactions, DTC's and freeform wires.

*AUTOCOM is a trademark of ADS Associates, Inc.

- **Cash Projection**—Projections utilize RESOURCE's integrated cash, investment, and debt databases to establish a net cash position for a user-selected future time frame.
- **Target Balance Management**—Daily bank account balances are automatically monitored and compared to target balances established for each account; recommended adjustments are calculated and may be displayed on the Daily Cash Worksheet screen.
- **Bank Relationship Management**—Detailed bank account information, such as names and phone numbers of bank representatives, authorized account signatories, and the purpose of each account, is stored for easy retrieval.
- **Signatory Management**—Bank Relationship Management can be expanded to provide detailed parameter files of authorized and required signatories and to automatically generate the addition and deletion letters necessary to effect appropriate changes.
- **Account Analysis**—An automated cost control program is available for analyzing and comparing ongoing bank service charges.

FEATURES

- **Menu Driven**—RESOURCE functions and reports are all accessible via menus or sub-menus. Functions are selected by moving the highlight bar or entering the designated two- or three-character code. Once the user becomes familiar with commonly-used function codes, these can be entered from any menu to immediately select the desired function or report.
- **Utility Functions**—RESOURCE includes a number of programs which facilitate ease of maintenance and system monitoring. All utility functions are accessible via menus, saving the user from having to exit the system and manually enter long and complicated DOS (Disk Operating System) utility commands.
  Utility functions include data backup and restore, periodic purge of inactive data, retrieval of database statistics, file reorganization, and file integrity and structure checks.
- **Error Detection**—RESOURCE performs validation and integrity checks upon data as it is entered. The user is signaled with an audible tone when an entry error is detected. The user can either correct the error immediately or mark the prob-

lem, continue data entry, and correct the error later. The system prohibits adding data to the database until after all data entry errors have been corrected.

- **Data Entry Audit**—RESOURCE prints an audit report of all data items upon completion of data entry but prior to posting new items to the database. This report encourages the user to check for discrepancies prior to posting. The user can easily correct any errors discovered and, subsequently, produce another audit report.

  The system assigns a unique sequence number to each transaction. This number is used when recalling a transaction, thus providing a convenient means for correcting the database should an error be detected after posting.

- **Error Correction**—RESOURCE is a transaction-oriented system, which greatly facilitates correcting errors: Erroneous historical records can be recalled and corrected from the transaction date-entry menu even though subsequent dependent transactions have occurred and have been entered into the database. For example, an incorrect security price entered at time of purchase is discovered after a subsequent partial sale(s) or additional purchase(s); therefore, prior yield statistics and amortization calculations may have been in error. Nevertheless, the system will recalculate and correct all successive calculations, producing an audit report that shows the deleted transaction and the changed transactions for all subsequently affected portfolio activity. Manual intervention in this process is not necessary, except to rerun historical reports that may have to be revised.

- **Batch Processing**—RESOURCE menu functions, individual and multiple, can be placed in a job control file, which can then be initiated on demand or at a pre-specified time, Monday through Friday, or seven days a week. An unlimited number of job control files are supported, and up to 20 jobs can be in the automatic execution queue at any time. The user can create, cancel and view the status of batch job control files from the RESOURCE menu.

- **AUTOCOM and Scanner**—RESOURCE includes the ADS automated communications package, AUTOCOM. AUTOCOM enables the user to communicate in an unattended mode with any computer system that supports asynchronous dial-up terminal access. AUTOCOM is used to poll bank balance reporting services on a daily basis without user intervention, using the RESOURCE Batch Processing facility.

Scanner is the system's universal parsing program. Scanner can accept *any* text or report file and scan it for useful information as specified by the user. Scanner converts the data captured from balance reporting systems into a standard internal transaction format for further use throughout RESOURCE.

- **TTY-Dumb Terminal Emulator**—RESOURCE allows the microcomputer to emulate a standard ASCII dumb terminal connected to any remote system. Operation is asynchronous mode at transmission speeds from 110 to 2400 baud (10 to 240 characters per second). The feature enables the user to instruct a modem to dial appropriate telephone numbers and to communicate in an interactive mode with a host computer system. TTY can be used to transmit data to a mainframe and to receive reports back to the microcomputer.

- **Additional Terminal Emulations**—RESOURCE emulates _____ remote batch terminals such as _____, operating with bisynchronous modems at transmission speeds up to 2400 baud. It also offers communications to in-house mainframe equipment using the _____ on-line terminal communication protocol, providing full or partial feature support, depending upon the configuration of the user's in-house communication facilities.

- **Networking**—The standard RESOURCE system operates effectively as a single-user system on a variety of microcomputer Local Area Networks (LANs). A multi-user database access option provides a secure, controlled environment for multiple, simultaneous updates and accesses of information on the system's databases.

- **Product Development Tools**—RESOURCE enhancements and customization are performed using a set of proprietary "ADS Tools." The tools include a comprehensive database management system with complete utility and editing functions, a security administration system, a batch processing system, a menu handler, a data-entry control mechanism, complete communications facilities, a data parser, and a report creation system. These tools are integrated to maximize efficiency in accessing the database and modifying the system.
MADAM, ADS <u>M</u>icrocomputer <u>A</u>pplication <u>D</u>atabase Man- ager, is one of the ADS tools. It is data-dictionary driven and stores information in an easily accessible and modifiable form. MADAM is available to the more technical user to review and

alter the system's file structure should the storage of new client data elements become necessary.

SECURITY

RESOURCE Access Control program enables the client's system manager to restrict or permit user access to any application function through the assignment of user passwords to fifteen (or more) individuals. A master password is established during installation, which enables the system manager at the client site to change the master password, create user passwords, and determine user access controls. Users enter passwords during the sign-on process. The menus displayed will contain only those functions sanctioned for that user.

HARDWARE

RESOURCE operates on ___ and compatible microcomputers. Following are the minimum requirements for hardware components:

[List and description of requirements.]

OTHER SOFTWARE

The proper functioning of RESOURCE requires that ____ or ____ or higher operating system be installed. Also, ____ is required for use with RESOURCE spreadsheet generation feature and G/L interface.

LOCAL AREA NETWORK CONFIGURATION SUPPORT

The following LAN hardware and software are supported in RESOURCE:

[List of hardware and software.]

When RESOURCE is running on a LAN, up to ten RESOURCE users may concurrently access the system's databases for data entry, inquiry, and report retrieval. Special software controls user activity to insure the security and integrity of the databases. RESOURCE is currently operating or has been successfully tested on ____. RESOURCE is designed for compatibility with any LAN supporting the DOS version 3.1 network calls. For information on compatibility of a specific network configuration, please contact ADS Customer Services.

STRUCTURED QUERY LANGUAGE

ADS has just introduced a link with ____'s relational database management software as an optional feature of the RESOURCE product. The query tools within ____ provide sophisticated analytic capabilities at the user request level. The portability of _____ allows the user to decide whether the tools are best applied within the micro-, mini- or mainframe environment. _____ provides the user with a comprehensive set of fourth-generation language and tools.

OTHER SUPPORT

ADS provides on-site training during installation and continuing support services after installation. Over _____ users have installed cost-effective ADS solutions to their treasury data management problems.

[Proposal continues with Application Software Description, System Requirements and other pertinent information.]

27-5 Joint, technical proposal

In this technical proposal, two companies have become business partners to handle a complex project. Now the task is to convince the client
that two heads are better than one.

The proposal contains two parts covering the tasks each company
will handle. Since the parts are similar, even though they address different issues, we included excerpts from the first part only. Note that
the cover letter summarizes key points developed in the proposal. This
directs the client's attention to the most important information.

Dear_____:

Thank you for the opportunity to present our proposal for the
Department of Water Resources Ground Water Information and Permitting System (Bid Number_____). Realizing that this project requires
expertise in the areas of Colorado ground water management practices, custom software applications development, and Geographic Information Systems, Digital Design Group, Inc. and Environmental
Systems Research Institute, Inc. (ESRI) have united our efforts and
are pleased to present this proposal for your consideration.

We see the requirements of the GRIPS as essentially a two-part
system: one, a large, multiuser, tabular database management and
permitting system, the other, a Geographic Information System (GIS)
for mapping and spatial analysis. The permitting system will utilize
the existing Department of Natural Resources' _____ computer system
and _____ workstations linked via DNR's Local Area Network. The
GIS will be based on _____ workstations linked to the _____ via TCP/IP
for the purpose of transferring key spatial and tabular data between
the two system components. In this design, tabular data will be handled within a hardware and database environment that maximizes
transaction efficiency. GIS tasks, which involve CPU intensive operations of spatial overlay and polygon processing, will be performed
within a hardware environment designed specifically for graphics
applications and using a database model best suited for geographic
data.

Digital Design Group and ESRI have already begun a coordinated
effort on this project to couple these two distinct, yet interrelated,
systems. Each firm is expert in the respective fields of custom software
design and development and the implementation of turnkey GISs
and supporting services, and both firms have long histories of successful working relationships with the State of Colorado. Together,

our companies represent a credible and knowledgeable team that will provide an efficient GRIPS system to meet the stated intent and goals of the Division of Water Resources.

Very truly yours,

Benjamin L. Binder
Digital Design Group, Inc.
Denver, Colorado

TABLE OF CONTENTS

This proposal is composed of two parts. The first part, prepared by Digital Design Group, Inc., describes those components of GRIPS related to Permit Processing and maintenance of the Ground Water Database. The second part, prepared by Environmental Systems Research Institute, describes the Geographic Information System components of GRIPS.

Part I

SECTION I—Introduction

SECTION II—GRIPS System Description

SECTION III—Software Description

SECTION IV—Hardware Description

SECTION V—Implementation Plan

SECTION VI—Training

SECTION VII—Vendor Information

SECTION VIII—Cost Proposal (Bound Separately)

[Note how the body of the proposal is organized:

- Demonstration of familiarity with the tasks the client must perform and with the client's existing systems.
- Discussion of how to handle the job.
- Detailed description of hardware and software.
- Outline of company's experience.]

SECTION I: INTRODUCTION

VENDOR

Digital Design Group, Inc., provides a full range of data processing consulting services. The work we perform for our clients encompasses the evaluation of their data processing requirements, assistance in selecting appropriate hardware and software, software customization, and the design, development, and implementation of new systems. We draw upon our many years of experience with a variety of data processing systems to help our clients develop systems that are responsive to their needs, reliable, and easy to use.

We enjoy taking on challenging assignments that require a multidisciplinary approach to solve unique problems. We employ time-tested budgeting and project management techniques to establish and manage project budgets and schedules, but we are not top heavy with administrative overhead. All members of Digital Design Group are data processing professionals with years of experience designing, developing, and implementing data processing systems.

Services

- REQUIREMENTS EVALUATION
- FUNCTIONAL SPECIFICATIONS
- PROJECT SCHEDULING AND MANAGEMENT
- SYSTEMS ANALYSIS
- HARDWARE SELECTION
- DATA BASE DESIGN
- PROGRAMMING
- DOCUMENTATION
- TRAINING

Digital Design Group, Inc., has developed a number of large, on-line, multi-user systems similar in scope to the DNR Ground Water Information and Permitting System. We genuinely enjoy designing and developing complex data processing systems and are proud of the excellent working relationships that we have developed with agencies such as:

[List of clients.]

Our proposal utilizes the existing Department of Natural Resources _____ minicomputer as the hardware platform for maintaining the large on-line database of applications, permits, wells, drillers, contractors, contractor violations, court decrees, permit fees, subdivision water supply plans, ground water levels, water quality, and correspondence. This system will be programmed to automatically process and print permits for applications that meet criteria established by DNR. Applications that require evaluation by Water Resource Engineers will be automatically routed to the appropriate evaluator.

The system will include modules to produce management reports on the number of applications received and permits processed and contain a basic revenue accounting package to prepare reports of permit fees received. A combination Evaluation and Comment/Correspondence Log/Tickler File will quickly inform DWR staff of all activities affecting an application and alert staff of items that require attention. Compliance modules will list expired permits, permits missing completion reports, and variances between permit and as-built data.

The system database will be designed to permit the use of the _____ Report Writer. This powerful report generator can be utilized to prepare numerous ad hoc reports required to make informed management decisions. This facility, together with existing _____ utilities, will allow the transfer of data from the central database to _____ for further manipulation by _____ spreadsheets, database managers, and word processing packages.

Realizing that evaluating applications for ground water permits requires the examination and processing of spatial relationships among proposed well locations, surrounding wells, municipal boundaries, ground water basins, ground water management districts, Denver Basin aquifer boundaries, subdivision water supply plan boundaries and other geographic entities, Digital Design Group has joined forces with Environmental Systems Research Institute, a recognized leader in the field of Geographic Information Systems.

The GIS will run on _____ workstations. The GIS will store geographic coordinates for all applications, permits and wells; a section, township and range grid; and the boundaries of:

- Designated Ground Water Basins;
- Ground Water Management Districts;
- Municipalities;
- Water and Sanitation Districts;
- Subdivision Water Supply Plans;
- Division Boundaries;
- Water District boundaries;
- Circles of Appropriation of Pre-SB 213 Wells;
- Boundaries of Parcels Allocated to Post SB 213 Wells;
- Areas With Known Water Quality Problems;
- and other geographic overlays.

The GIS will permit DWR staff to prepare maps containing a mix of any of the above features at a wide range of scales for any portion of the State. The GIS will contain programs to determine boundaries that surround a proposed well location and those wells that are located within a given distance of a proposed location. This information will be passed to the ____ for further processing.

We believe this solution combines the best features of the existing ____computer with the unique capabilities of the engineering workstation for processing geographic data.

SECTION 2: GRIPS SYSTEM DESCRIPTION

THE PROBLEM

Water is *the* most valuable natural resource in the West. The State Engineer is charged with the responsibility of administering and enforcing Colorado surface and ground water laws. In this capacity, the Office of the State Engineer processes all applications for ground water permits and serves as a repository for all information related to the permitting process. This information is used by Division of Water Resources personnel, other governmental agencies, and the public. The administration of ground water laws is complex, and before a permit is granted, Division staff must review entities as diverse as water and sanitation district boundaries, subdivision water supply plans, pre-1973 subdivisions, adjacent wells, aquifers, the boundaries of the Denver Basin, and areas of tributary versus non-tributary ground water. There is currently no comprehensive ground water database, and DWR staff is hampered by the inability to readily gather the information necessary to process a permit.

We have found it useful to describe the problem at hand as one of developing a reliable and easy-to-use system that will assist in the performance of the following eight functions:

- Maintenance of a comprehensive integrated Ground Water Database;
- Processing and routing of applications for water well permits;
- Monitoring of compliance with permit conditions;
- Regulation of licensed drillers and pump installers;
- Monitoring of ground water levels;
- Accounting for application fees and other payments;
- Providing other governmental agencies and the public with access to ground water data;
- Mapping.

SECTION III: SOFTWARE

[Technical details of software.]

SECTION IV: HARDWARE

HARDWARE PLATFORMS

One of our objectives in formulating this proposal is to utilize, where feasible, existing Division of Water Resources and Department of Natural Resources hardware and systems software. This will minimize

- front-end acquisition costs for items such as CPU, operating system, database software, utilities, communication network, workstations, tape drives, and other existing devices that can be utilized by GRIPS;
- ongoing maintenance costs for hardware and systems software;
- systems administration personnel costs related to training, upgrades to operating system and utilities, and maintenance of on-site and off-site backups.

We therefore propose utilizing the Department of Natural Resources existing _____ minicomputer as the platform for the GRIPS tabular database. We believe that this hardware is appropriate and well suited for the maintenance of the Ground Water Database.

The _____ offers an existing high-speed communication link with terminals located within the Office of the State Engineer and does not present the telecommunication bottleneck inherent to the _____ mainframe alternative. The _____ is a commercial grade multiuser system that offers the level of reliability and security necessary for critical operations such as processing applications for well permits and maintaining the Ground Water Database. The _____ also supports optical image processing. While we are not proposing the scanning, digital storage, and retrieval of ground water related correspondence at this time, it is wise to keep these options open.

Realizing the benefits of the current generation of engineering workstations for the CPU intensive applications, Environmental Systems Research Institute has proposed the use of _____ workstations as the platform for all GRIPS Geographic Information System data and functions.

The _____ has been installed at the Department of Natural Resources and utilized by the Division of Water Resources for several years. For this reason, we have not included a description of the _____ in our proposal.

The _____ workstation, associated disk drives, interfaces, and GIS hardware including digitizer and plotter are described in ESRI's section of this proposal.

We have taken the time to estimate file sizes both to determine required disk capacity and to shake out any problems with respect to record length or file size.

[List of data files and estimated VS disk storage requirements.]

Because there are 19 local printers connected to the _____, we are operating under the assumption that sufficient local printers exist to serve GRIPS users and have not included costs for additional printers in this proposal.

COMMUNICATION LINKS

[Description of physical network and manufacturers' information.]

WORKSTATIONS

ESRI, in the section of this proposal addressing GIS hardware components, has described the _____ workstations that will be used for displaying and manipulating the GIS components of the GRIPS database. The existing DWR _____ configured with 640KB main memory, 384KB extended memory, 40MB/28ms hard disk, monographics monitor, 101-key keyboard, _____ local communications adapter, serial port, parallel port, and full-size expansion chassis exceed our requirements for the standard GRIPS workstation.

HARDWARE WARRANTY AND MAINTENANCE

The hardware components required by this proposal fall into three categories:

[List three categories.]

We have included the cost for the purchase of additional _____ DASD, _____ controller, and interface in our cost proposal but recommend purchasing these devices directly from _____ or alternative sources under existing state purchasing awards. Warranty and service for these products will be provided by _____ or selected alternative sources.

ESRI will be the vendor for all proposed GRIPS GIS hardware components. Warranties and service for GRIPS GIS hardware components are described in ESRI's section of this proposal.

[Section V time table deleted.]

SECTION VI: TRAINING

The development of GRIPS will take place over a period of approximately ____ years. Training will take place as each program module is designed, developed, tested, and placed into production. Training will therefore be phased throughout the development of the system and not take place during one short time interval.

During the final design and development of the system, many decisions must be made with respect to database design, program features, data-entry screens, report layouts, program algorithms, and program logic. The Division of Water Resources staff will be encouraged to participate in the design of each data file and program. We have found that involving users in the design of a system is beneficial for several reasons. First, users, because of their detailed understanding of the functional requirements of the system, can make significant contributions to the design of a system. Second, it is an excellent way to introduce individuals to the system. When users are involved in the system design, they better understand the structure of the system and the functions that each program performs.

Before each program module is coded, DWR staff will be presented with a detailed set of program specifications explaining the purpose of the program, its internal logic and functions, and the program options available. The written program specifications will provide DWR personnel another opportunity to discuss and comment upon the design and features of each program. We expect key members of DWR staff to understand the basic functions of most programs before the programs are coded.

After a program is coded and thoroughly tested by our staff, we will train designated DWR users and technical support personnel on the operation of the program. We will also be available to provide assistance to the users as each program goes into production. With respect to Division Offices, we have budgeted time and travel expenses for two full-day visits to each office.

Digital Design Group will also present an executive level summary of the system to the DWR management and attend meetings and give presentations on selected topics as requested.

Documentation

Documentation will include a user's manual with detailed instructions for each program, screen layouts, and sample reports; a data elements dictionary giving definitions, data formats, and valid codes; DMS control file listings describing record layouts and primary and alternate keys to each file; a system summary giving an overview of GRIPS and the salient features of each program; internally documented source listings; procedure listings; and an on-line data base which includes the file name, library, and short description of all programs and files used by the system.

SECTION VII: VENDOR INFORMATION

KNOWLEDGE OF WATER WELL PERMITTING AND COLORADO WATER PRACTICES

In 19__, Digital Design Group developed a small system for the _____ to maintain a database of all water wells permitted and/or drilled on the three million acres of school trust land. Realizing the complexity of ground water permitting procedures, and unable to find a reference text summarizing statues, rules, regulations and practices of ground water administration in the state, Digital Design Group commissioned the water resource engineering firm _____ to prepare such a report. The table of contents of that report is included at the end of this section.

Digital Design Group's project manger for the GRIPS project, _____, is a Colorado registered professional engineer and land surveyor with the technical knowledge of legal descriptions, geology, and computations required to design GRIPS. _____ has attended ground water workshops and seminars sponsored by the Colorado Water Resources Research Institute, the Colorado Water Congress, and the Colorado Ground Water Association.

Digital Design Group worked with Division of Water Resources staff to develop the preliminary functional requirements for GRIPS. During the process of compiling the preliminary requirements, several hundred hours were spent:

- Interviewing members of the ground water section;
- Compiling results of questionnaires completed by DWR staff;
- Studying Colorado Ground Water Statues, Division of Water Resource Ground Water Rules, State Engineer Policies, Ground Water Management District Rules and Regulations, State Board of Examiners of Well Construction and Pump Installation Contractors Rules and Regulations, and other related documents;
- Attending design meetings with senior level staff.

While we do not profess complete knowledge of ground water issues, we are well aware of the complexities of the permitting process that must be addressed by GRIPS.

EXPERIENCE IN THE DEVELOPMENT OF SIMILAR SYSTEMS

EXPERIENCE IN DEVELOPING SYSTEMS FOR THE STATE OF COLORADO

Digital Design Group, Inc. has successfully developed a number of large systems for: [List other clients.]

Like ground water permitting, oil and gas lease management, royalty accounting, well permitting, and production accounting are not simple. Several other states have spent _____, and the US Department of Interior upwards of _____, developing oil and gas systems that have fallen short of their intended goals. The system developed by Digital Design Group, on a very limited budget, was granted an Exemplary Systems in Government Award by the Urban and Regional Information Systems Association. The system was subsequently selected for use as an oil and gas production accounting system by the _____.

PROJECT: State Lands Inventory, Oil & Gas Lease Management and Royalty Accounting
CLIENT: [Name.]

State Lands Inventory

The State Lands Inventory database maintains information on all mineral and surface rights owned by the State of _____ including: legal descriptions, acres, percent ownership, minerals owned, counties in which the rights are located, trust funds to which the rights belong, and certificates of purchase that encumber the lands. As in the other _____ subsystems, encoding of legal descriptions was standardized to accommodate future geographic and automated mapping applications. There are currently _____ parcels in the State Lands Inventory database covering _____ acres of mineral rights and _____ acres of surface rights.

In addition to standard reports that list State Lands Inventory data in many different formats and according to different selection criteria, the system also includes a program to automatically compare all _____ wells in the _____ Well file with the _____ parcels in the State Lands Inventory and prepare a report of all wells located in sections in which the state has oil and gas royalty interests.

Oil and Gas Lease Management

Approximately _____ acres of lands owned by the state of _____ are currently leased for oil and gas exploration and development. These _____ acres are covered by _____ separate lease agreements. Revenues from oil and gas leases include bonus payments, annual rentals, royalties, shut-in royalties, late fees, and interest payments.

The Oil and Gas Lease Management subsystem maintains a database of information about each state oil and gas lease. This information is used in processing rental payments, bonuses, interest charges, and late fees, and to prepare reports generated by the Lease Management subsystem.

Users can rapidly display all data on a given lease, all leases in a specified location or all leases for a specified lessee. The user can also print reports of either all leases or leases that satisfy specified selection criteria. Additional hardcopy reports include the Lease Cross-index Report; Extension Candidate Report; Termination Candidate Report; Alert Letters and Report; and the Unearned Rentals Report which apportions each rental payment into an earned amount and a remaining liability for purposes of accrual accounting.

Royalty Accounting

Of the _____ active state oil and gas leases, _____ have been successfully developed and contain producing wells. The Royalty Accounting Subsystem was developed to assist the State Board of Land Commissioners in ensuring that:

- The state receives oil and gas royalties on all production to which it is legally entitled;
- The royalty rates, unit prices, and other factors used in calculating royalties are in conformance with the provisions of the oil and gas leases;
- All interest charges and penalties for late payments are properly invoiced and collected;
- All rentals, royalties, and related payments are accurately accounted for, posted to the proper accounts, and deposited in a timely manner.

Each month, the SLB receives a royalty payment for each product sold from each division order lease in which the state has a mineral interest. New oil and gas royalty report forms were designed to be completed by the royalty payors and accompany all remittances. Interactive royalty data entry programs:

- Prompt the user for all input data and perform extensive interactive on-line edit checks for all detectable errors.
- Store information reported on oil and gas royalty remittance documents in the royalty report database.
- Determine the proper Trust Fund and General Ledger Account numbers and write a record to the cash receipts journal for each payment.
- Use the month and year of production, date received, and payment amount to determine if late fees and interest charges are due. If so, calculate the penalties and write appropriate records to the accounts receivable data file. (Separate programs exist for invoicing and generating aged receivable reports for items in the accounts receivable file.)

Once royalty payments for a month have been entered into the system, the following programs are run to detect delinquent payments and payments that are suspiciously low and therefore candidates for audits. These programs take advantage of ____ ability to access and automatically cross-check information that is entered and maintained by separate agencies. In addition to generating reports, several programs automatically prepare letters addressed to the responsible parties.

- List of reporting errors and letters to reporters
- Aged delinquent report and letters
- SLB royalty volumes vs. OGCC production volumes variance report
- SLB sales proceeds vs. conservation levy proceeds variance report
- SLB royalty payments vs. conservation levy exemptions various report
- SLB royalty unit prices vs. field average unit price variance report
- Oil price bulletin variance report
- Moving average variance report

PROJECT: Oil & gas well permitting production accounting, conservation levy, underground injection control
CLIENT: [Name.]

Well Permitting

The well permitting subsystem maintains a database of information on all active oil and gas wells in the state of ____ including wells drilled on state, federal, Indian, and private lands. The system stores information reported to the OGCC in the Application for Permit to Drill, Well Completion Report and Log, Sundry Notices, and the Producer's Certificate of Clearance and Authorization to Transport Oil or Gas from a Well. The well database includes up-to-date information on each well's API (American Petroleum Institute) number, location, county, oil field, operator, driller, permitted formation, lease, ownership, depth, producing formations, well logs, casing, liner, tubing, and production rates, and approximately 50 additional data elements.

The well permitting subsystem allows the user to display all data for a specific well by entering the well's API number, or to rapidly list all wells for a specified section, township, operator, or lease.

Hardcopy reports include a list of all or selected wells; a list of expired permits and delinquent reports; a drilling summary that tabulates drilling activity by county, operator, and oil field; and an operator verification report that lists all leases for a specified operator together with all wells on each lease.

Production Accounting

The _____ maintains records on the monthly oil and gas production from each producing lease in the state including production from state, federal, Indian, and private lands. Approximately _____ production reports are received each month. In addition to the leases that are currently producing, the system also maintains historical cumulative production data on wells that have been plugged and abandoned.

Monthly production data processed and stored by the system includes:

- Beginning of month inventory
- Barrels of oil produced
- Barrels of oil sold
- Adjustments
- End of month inventory
- Oil gravity
- Oil transporter
- Gas produced
- Gas flared
- Gas sold
- Gas BTU
- Barrels of water produced
- Water disposal facility

To maintain integrity of the data stored in the database, programs extensively edit all entries. The user can view selected data for a lease for an entire 12-month period or zoom in on the detailed data for a particular month. Delinquent production reports are automatically detected and the delinquent report program generates letters to operators listing production reports that have not been received. Reports that have been received but contain reporting errors are also listed in these letters.

Using data stored in the Monthly Production data file, the system automatically produces monthly and annual production reports sorted by county, field, formation, operator, and lease. These reports list monthly and cumulative production and sales volumes with subtotals at the reservoir, field, and county levels. Commencing in January of _____, all operator monthly reports of oil and gas production and sales have been entered into the system. The system currently contains _____monthly reports in the on-line production database.

Conservation Levy

Conservation levy payments are remitted quarterly for each producing oil and gas lease. The conservation levy subsystem was developed to ensure that conservation levy payments were remitted for all marketed production not otherwise exempt from the levy. The conservation levy subsystem also creates a database of sales proceeds and unit prices used to generate unit price statistics to assist in audits of royalties and state severance taxes.

In addition to reports that summarize conservation levy collections, the conservation levy subsystem includes a set of variance reports that compare conservation levy payments with lease and production data and list delinquent and under-reported conservation levy payments.

Water Disposal

Oil and gas operations often result in the production of significant quantities of water along with the oil and gas. The water is often contaminated with salt and other impurities and must be disposed of by approved methods. There are currently _____ approved evaporation pits and _____ water injection wells in _____.

The water disposal subsystem assists the Oil and Gas Conservation Commission in regulating the disposal and reinjection of water produced in association with oil and gas operations. Information on permits, injection wells, and retaining pits may be rapidly accessed by facility number, operator, field, or location. One set of programs assists OGCC staff in completing EPA Underground Injection Control Federal Reporting System forms. These programs generate statistics on the permitting and inspection of all underground injection wells in the state.

The Enhanced Recovery and Disposal Well Injection Volume Report lists and summarizes injected volumes. Another report lists all monthly injection reports that have not been remitted and are delinquent. The Onsite, Central, and Commercial Pit Disposal Volume Reports use information collected by the production accounting subsystem to generate statistics on pit disposal volumes. Another report compares the volumes disposed of at each pit with the size and evaporation rates of the permitted pits. This report lists all leases that show a discrepancy between the volume of water that must be disposed of and the capacity of the approved pits.

PROJECT: Oil and Gas Production Accounting
CLIENT: [Name.]

The _____ Oil and Gas Conservation Commission regulates oil and gas exploration and development in the state of _____. In ___, that agency performed a search for an oil and gas production accounting system that would satisfy their needs. Their staff reviewed the system we developed for _____ and decided that it came very close to meeting their requirements. They subsequently negotiated an agreement with the state of _____ to utilize the software and contracted Digital Design Group to modify _____'s system to fully satisfy their requirements. As a part of that contract, we also developed a detailed implementation plan that included work items for programming, testing, training, loading master files, printing new reporting forms, informing industry of new reporting requirements, and performing a pilot test of the full system.

This system is currently used to track the production and disposition of hydrocarbon products and associated saltwater from all oil and gas wells in the state of _____.

PROJECT: Surface Lease Management System
CLIENT: [Name.]

Digital Design Group worked with the _____ State Board of Land Commissioners (SLB) to design, develop, and implement a surface lease information management system to assist that agency in managing the three million acres of surface rights owned by the state. The State Board of Land Commissioners administers these lands for the benefit of eight separate trusts. Management functions performed by the SLB include:

- Leasing of surface rights for agricultural, grazing, commercial, and other purposes.
- Overseeing the progress of development leases.
- Reviewing and granting rights-of-way.
- Issuing and processing certificates of purchase.
- Granting patents.
- Protecting the state's interests in all water wells located on state lands and all ground water and surface water rights that benefit state lands.
- Approving and denying permission to construct improvements on leased land.
- Accounting for all financial transactions related to the above activities.

   The surface lease information management system (SLIMS) maintains a database of and assists in the management of the following activities:

   agricultural and grazing leases rights-of-way
   commercial and development leases
   water wells and water stock certificates
   improvements
   certificates-of-purchase

   Each functional area comprises a separate subsystem containing its own data entry, on-line inquiry, and report programs. In order to facilitate the preparation of consolidated financial reports and simplify reconciliation with the state's central accounting system, all subsystems share common accounting and financial reporting modules.

   All programs in the system are linked together with a set of easily understood menu screens. The system denies users access to programs that individual users are not specifically authorized to run. A special executive inquiry menu was developed for individuals authorized to view data in the _____ database but prohibited from running data entry, report, and special processing programs.

   The surface lease system that we designed is a straightforward data management system. Its power and capabilities stem from the ability to edit, store, and rapidly access information on all documents and financial transactions related to the activities listed above. The system was fully integrated with the oil and gas lease management and royalty accounting systems previously mentioned in this proposal. This integration permits the preparation of consolidated financial reports that summarize income from both oil and gas and surface leases. The integration of surface and minerals systems also permits the preparation of reports listing all of the following data on land parcels selected by the user:

   surface ownership
   mineral ownership
   surface leases
   oil and gas leases
   oil wells
   water wells
   water rights
   rights-of-way
   certificates-of-purchase
   improvements

   The surface lease system consists of an additional _____ programs and _____ procedures, or job streams, to execute those programs. In total, the State Land Board system consists of ____ programs executed by ____ separate procedures.

The development of the surface lease information management system was completed in April, ____. It is now used by the State Board of Land Commissioners to account for all surface rights and leases.

In addition to oil and gas leases and surface leases, the SLB also issues special use permits, sand and gravel permits, geothermal leases, coal leases, and other miscellaneous solid mineral leases. We recently completed modules for automating these remaining permits and miscellaneous leases. While these leases account for only a small percentage of total SLB revenues, it was a nuisance to maintain a separate set of manual files to account for them.

The solid minerals project completed our development work for State Board of Land Commissioners. They are now fully automated and have comprehensive and up-to-date records on ownership, leases, royalties, and all other revenues.

PROJECT: State Lands Information Management System
CLIENT: [Name.]

The State Lands Information Management System is utilized by the State Land Department to manage ____ acres of mineral rights and ____ acres of surface rights owned by the state. This system is based upon the design of the ____ and ____ systems that Digital Design Group developed for the State of ____. After years of struggling with an obsolete automated system, ____ reviewed systems used by other western states and selected ____'s system as the model for the design of a new system. While the functions performed by ____'s system are similar to those performed by ____'s, due to differences in lease terms, state accounting systems, policies with respect to lease assignments, practices of the department, and interfaces with ____ oil and gas databases, most programs were completely rewritten. One of the unique aspects of the ____ system is the interface with the state's central data processing mapping system. This will allow the land department to automatically plot maps of state ownership, leases, and unleased properties.

The ____ system was developed on a ____ system utilizing the ____ data management system and ____ as the primary programming language.

PROJECT: Limited Leftover Big Game Licensing System
CLIENT: [Name.]

This on-line system was used by the Division of Wildlife to issue big game licenses remaining after the primary lottery. The system provided a bank of phone operators the ability to interactively enter hunter and credit card data and immediately issue licenses. Licenses were reconciled with funds received, and credit cards printed. Daily transactions were transferred to the General Government Computer Center _____ mainframe, where master databases of all hunters and licenses were updated and licenses printed.

STAFF RESUMES

[Provide detailed resumes of staff that will work on project. Resumes highlight the education and experience that qualifies person for the project.]

Tips on writing successful proposals

Clients want to be assured not only of a "fair" deal, but a great deal. You must convince them that your credentials and solutions can't be beat. Use details to persuade clients of your knowledge, professionalism, commitment to excellence.

Here's how to draft a proposal:

- Make a random outline of every topic you wish to include.
- Make an organized outline. The most important topic should come first. If the tasks are undefined, what you can do for the client is most important (such as in Proposals 27-1, 27-2, 27-3). If the tasks are defined, your company's expertise is most important (such as in Proposals 27-4 or 27-5).
- Arrange other topics in descending order of importance.
- Write from your outline.

When you have finished writing the proposal, write a one-page summary. State what you are proposing and *why it will benefit the prospective client.* Point out the most important features in your proposal. Place the summary at the beginning of the proposal or make it part of the cover letter.

Place tables, charts, lists apart from the text or in the appendix.

Create a table of contents for lengthy proposals. They allow clients to zero in quickly on particular sections. End your proposal by calling attention once again to the benefits to the client. Emphasize your willingness to work with the client to handle situations and solve problems.

When clients finish reading your proposals, they should be convinced that yours is a market-driven company with the talent and expertise necessary to provide the best solutions for their needs.

Bonus: 100 power words and phrases

The following power words and phrases were selected from letters and proposals in this book. Look for places in your writing that will come to life with a sharp phrase or snappy verb.

company's bean counters
computer jock
savvy
key solutions
highlight the advantages
sharp looking
virtuoso
playing from the same sheet music
sharpening my pencil
taking over as quarterback in the middle of the game is tough
we can pilot and fully exploit the challenges
smash the barrier
tackle
seasoned pros
I haven't sailed into the sunset—just changed mastheads
war stories
small and rugged
clock is ticking
color me excited
number-crunching
fired up
moving vans are loaded and rolling
coffee pot is on
market-driven
knock your socks off
silky smooth
Hooray! No price increase
under the umbrella of
explore the issues
global marketplace
I will ski a run for you in Colorado
raised the bar
irresistible ideas and vivid, memorable images

creative solution
folks
keep me posted
fashion adventure
run it through the art department
fresh powder, blue skies, loads of sunshine
we'll make it easy
toying with the idea
wintertime blues
deal you'll want to connect on
Whoops! We turned on the machines and forgot to turn them off
cherished client
eligible for a discount
Lamborghini
reap dividends
bold designs
phone with your verdict
sun-swept plains
ablaze
distinctive and stylish uniform
not the least costly, but the most cost effective in the long run
can I count on you?
classic, not faddish
mutual energies
elite clique
silent messenger
earn your confidence
positive about our partnership
your satisfaction is important to us
you have run past my tolerance
sympathize with your cash flow problems
here's the deal
stopped me in my tracks
blame the error on alien interference
fresh direction
we salute your efforts
we support the goals
what's going on?

let me get this straight
heavy hitter
bogged down in clerical work
winning the battle
printing has come a long way since Gutenberg
vanguard technologies
clincher
witty insights
outrageous
decked the halls, trimmed the tree and wrapped a special present
you guys take my breath away
absolutely awed by the quality
topped even yourself
not top-heavy with overhead
fun is back
flagship
at our company that program is a reality
sound familiar?
we've seen change before
we take pride
convince a client two heads are better than one
focus groups
human response
merits that go beyond the advantages of the incumbent
hard look
solid now, solid in the future
talk to the client, show the client
we asked you to forget, now it's important you remember